THE
END OF
LOVE

THE
END OF
LOVE

RACISM, SEXISM,
and the DEATH
of ROMANCE

SABRINA STRINGS

BEACON PRESS ▪ BOSTON

BEACON PRESS
Boston, Massachusetts
www.beacon.org

Beacon Press books
are published under the auspices of
the Unitarian Universalist Association of Congregations.

27 26 25 24   8 7 6 5 4 3 2 1

This book is printed on acid-free paper that meets the uncoated paper
ANSI/NISO specifications for permanence as revised in 1992.

Text design and composition by Kim Arney

Many names and identifying characteristics of
people mentioned in this book have been changed.

Library of Congress Cataloging-in-Publication Data is available for this title.
ISBN: 978-0-8070-0862-1; e-book: 978-0-8070-0863-8;
audiobook: 978-0-8070-3507-8

To all my sistas seeking romantic love:
Know that *you are love.*

CONTENTS

INTRODUCTION

I wasn't sure I wanted to continue dating men, but that was only the first problem. I had recently returned from a year living in France, which had changed my mind about the utility of aspiring to be heterosexual. There, in quick succession, I had almost gotten engaged to a man who proposed in order to keep me after he'd cheated; dated a six-foot-seven athletic North African—one of the finest men I'd ever laid eyes on—who revealed only after he was in my feels that he was living with his pregnant girlfriend; and fallen in love with a married man who rooked me by using the classic "I'm planning to divorce her" gag. After being pummeled with this level of romantic disrespect—in a country where I had far better dating prospects than I have ever enjoyed in the United States—I started to rethink the wisdom of the scripted "one man and one woman."

In the end it was my friend Richard who convinced me otherwise. Richard, a Black man, had been telling me for weeks that his friend and roommate, Cody, who is white, liked me and wondered if I wouldn't chat to him? According to Richard, we had a lot in common: we both liked the outdoors, were vegetarians, and were sociologists.

I went along with it. It was early 2010. I was a graduate student at UC San Diego, which meant I had little money, little time, and little in the way of distractions. At that time, I had started wearing my thick shoulder-length hair natural, and, to my surprise, men loved it. Cody was no different. Our first date was more like an interview. My tactics were Gestapo-lite: *What do you want with me again?* He tried his best to plead his case: He was not looking to just get down with the brown. He was actually looking for a girlfriend. He seemed genuine.

The early days of the relationship were golden. Turns out we had more in common than either of us anticipated. We never fought and were always laughing about something or other. After six weeks, I felt like I trusted him enough to call him and say, in a breathy voice, "Hey."

"Hey, you," he replied quizzically.

"Wanna come over? Right now."

"Oh? Like now?!" he replied excitedly.

"Yeah. Now."

When he arrived, I greeted him wearing only a T-shirt and panties. After we'd done what I'd invited him to do, he sprang from the bed, singing, "I'm having the best day!" We went out to dinner, both pleased with our growing intimacy.

But we were both holding back. My betrayal fatigue led me to keep him at arm's length. He was a divorcée who, after a nightmarish divorce, was emotionally unavailable but said he wanted to work on that. Before we'd had sex, he kept asking me when he'd be able to tell people I was his girlfriend. I was like, "Let's not put a label on it." Afterward, we both agreed to be exclusive.

Sex being out of the bag, Cody started to reveal more of who he was and what he was looking for. One day, while we were idling in his car, he asked me something that had clearly been on his mind since the start of the relationship.

"How much do you weigh?"

The question caught me off guard. "Why does it matter?" I rejoined.

"Do you weigh 110 pounds?" he pressed.

"What? No," I returned.

"114?"

I didn't reply. He frowned, finding my silence worrisome.

"118?"

Silence.

"124, 128? What. . . "

"Stop guessing!" I finally said. "It's somewhere in those many numbers. But what difference does it make?" I asked.[1]

He didn't reply. He lowered his gaze, disappointed.

A few weeks later he invited me to dinner with his brother, his brother's wife, and their kids. He gave me a primer: "People in my family are racist," he said. "You'll never meet my parents. All they do is sit in their recliners and watch Fox News."

"Ugh! Sounds scary," I replied.[2]

"Yeah. But my brother will be better." He seemed to be trying to convince himself.

The dinner with his brother's family went as expected. I don't know if he told them I was Black, but his kin were certainly surprised to see me when I showed up. Several members of his family are independently wealthy. Being at dinner with a flush white family as a whole entire Black woman, I could sense that they were skeptical of my intentions.

The restaurant was located near the water, so we took a walk on the beach afterward. Big hair no like water. Outside in the humidity, I could feel my hair making unauthorized moves. I suppose Cody found it unseemly, because for the first time in our relationship, he looked at my hair, mortified, like it was trying to embarrass him in front of his elegant sibling.

Sensing that my appearance was out of place in his life marked the beginning of the end. The fatal blows were to be struck soon thereafter. He'd been asking me to hang out with his friends, 98.3 percent of whom were white. I knew that hanging out with them would feel like a microaggression. So I kept putting it off. Once, I'd agreed to show up but didn't, which was a shitty thing to do. I tried to apologize, but I'm sure I didn't explain that I was afraid his white friends—many of whom I knew—would say something racist. Because I had known more than one of them to do just that.

After that, whenever either of us reached out, we couldn't be sure to get a return call or text. I knew I was far from innocent, but it also felt like he was trying to prove something to me by refusing to call or text or show up for anything anymore.

Then it happened. On February 15, 2010, the majority-white UCSD fraternity Pi Kappa Alpha held a blackface party they called the "Compton Cookout." The invite read as follows:

> February marks a very important month in American society. No, I'm not talking about Valentine's Day or President's Day. I'm talking about Black History Month. As a time to celebrate in hopes of showing respect, the Regents Community cordially invites you to it's very first Compton Cookout.[3]

That a mostly white fraternity would create an (intended annual) blackface party as a slapstick commemoration of Black History Month was disturbing enough. But those who were paying attention noted that almost all of the degrading imagery used to promote the party was heaped upon the bodies of Black women. In a detailed explanation of how to dress "Compton," the white students did not have anything specifically denigrating to say about Black men, writing,

> For guys: I expect all males to be rockin Jersey's, stuntin' up in ya White T (XXXL smallest size acceptable), anything FUBU, Ecko, Rockawear, High/low top Jordans or Dunks, Chains, Jorts, stunner shades, 59 50 hats, Tats, etc.

Black women, however, were referred to as high-drama, loud, low-class "ghetto chicks":

> For girls: For those of you who are unfamiliar with ghetto chicks— Ghetto chicks usually have gold teeth, start fights and drama, and wear cheap clothes—they consider Baby Phat to be high class and expensive couture. They also have short, nappy hair, and usually wear cheap weave, usually in bad colors, such as purple or bright red. They look and act similar to Shenaynay, and speak very loudly, while rolling their neck, and waving their finger in your face.

I was shocked and outraged. But I had another concern, which was that less than two weeks prior, I had been elected Vice President of

Diversity Affairs for the Graduate Student Association. The uproar over these minstrel depictions sparked an overnight social movement on campus. As a Black woman and the ranking diversity officer for graduate students, I knew I had to get involved.

I brought my concerns to Cody over dinner at my apartment.

"I feel like I should do something, but I'm not sure what," I said, worried.

"Why do you have to do anything?" Cody asked, lifting his eyes from his tilapia and holding my gaze.

"I am the VP of Diversity Affairs for the GSA. I have to make a statement. I have to be present at these events." I replied, my voice wavering.

Seeing my emotionality, Cody took my hands in his. "You're not expected to do anything about this. This will blow over. Isn't your job supposed to be more like working with admin to get more resources for Black students?"

"That's why I took the job. But I cannot ignore this," I said.

"I don't see what you can do. And I don't think this is your job," he said, then turned his attention back to his dinner.

I was on my own.

Protesters came out by the thousands.[4] They occupied the campus in response to this baldly racist event for days. I showed up to as many of the protests as I could, delivering speeches in solidarity with the BSU and on behalf of the graduate students. I regularly ran into grad students and faculty from my department of all races and ethnicities. I ran into everyone except my partner.

Until one day he showed up. I was lingering in the back of a demonstration chatting with one of my committee members when I saw him ambling across the quad. He was headed straight toward me.

"You came!" I exclaimed. I was so happy to see him.

"Well, no. I'm on my way home. I have a conference presentation I gotta work on," he said, as he faced me reluctantly.

"But you can do that anytime. Can't you stay? This is important to me," I pleaded.

"Sorry, I really have to finish this. Are we still on for dinner tomorrow night?" he asked.

"Yeah," I said meekly and watched him walk away.

That next night at dinner, we were going to have it out. I was going to confront him on his white privilege. It was white male privilege that led him to ignore an uprising against antiblackness, an uprising resulting from an event in which his own girlfriend is both derided and, as a local politician, implicated in its redress.

I began with *We need to talk.* This made him anxious. When I stated my case, he was relieved. He had feared I was going to break up with him. He kept telling me how much he liked me—as he did regularly throughout our relationship.

In explaining my position, I used the metaphor of a white man on a people mover wondering why other people aren't going as fast as he is. He did not like this. He said, "I just don't want to be critiqued all the time."

"I don't want to critique you *all* the time," I replied. "But this is important. I felt like you weren't there for me. Because you weren't. Racist things were going on, and you didn't support me. I'm a Black woman, and your girlfriend."

He sat silently with this before replying, "I feel like you don't support me. You don't show up to spend time with my friends. They all think I'm only pretending to be dating you! You don't pay attention to what's going on with me. I got a haircut, and you didn't even notice!"

I studied him then. Couldn't tell about the haircut. There was an asymmetry in the magnitude of offense. Still, we both apologized. We agreed to do better. I asked if he wanted to do something. He thought that meant sex and got excited about that part of the make up. I explained that I meant did he want to go out? He was not enthusiastic about this prospect. He decided to go home instead.

A few days later, Cody called me explaining that he wanted to talk. I agreed, thinking that this was an opportunity for us to get back on the right footing. He arrived wearing a solemn expression. He asked if we couldn't sit down on my couch for this conversation? I nodded, gesturing for him to take a seat.

"I can't do the things you've asked of me," he began. "It's just that you and I might be too different. I can't change that much. This is who I am," he concluded.

I sat silently. Not because I was crushed. I wasn't. I sat quietly because his ruse could not have been more transparent. He was trying to
George Costanza me.

You know that episode of *Seinfeld* in which George is dating a
woman he considers out of his league and because of that he realizes he
has no control over her, no "hand" as he calls it? Then in his insecurity,
rather than enjoying his time with a beautiful and accomplished woman,
he feels the need to take her down a peg to make himself feel better. He
concocts a ploy to get hand over this woman by breaking up with her.
It's terribly petty and misogynistic, and there I was in the middle of it.
I looked Cody in the eyes while he made his phony case. When it was
over, I simply said, "OK."

I stood up to walk him to my door. Once there, he leaned in for an
awkward and prolonged kiss on the cheek. Eventually he pulled back,
expecting to see my face filled with emotion. Instead, he was met with
indifference. This startled him. I opened the door for him to file out
without further delay. A look of shock and dismay crossed his face as I
shut the door on him.

A few days later, Richard invited me to play tennis on one of the
shabby courts peppering our decrepit apartment complex. The sun shone
particularly bright that day. I delighted in its soft warmth. I twirled and
waved my arms in celebration of life's felicity. On the other side of the
net, Richard explained that Cody wasn't doing quite as well. He was
sulking and had admitted to Richard that he thought he'd made a mistake.

"How do you feel?" Richard asked.

"I feel free."

I never got back with Cody, even though he (and Richard) continued to try to put us back together multiple times over the next several
years. The only way forward with a man like Cody was apparently to
pretend the racism and sexism I experienced in the relationship weren't
really there.

And, as an apt addendum to this story, it was not until I sat down
to research and write this book that I found out that the Compton
Cookout—and its defamatory representation of Black women—was the
brainchild of Jigaboo Jones, a rapper, comedian, and Black man.[5]

THE STATE OF AMERICAN ROMANCE

My relationship with Cody was unique only in the details. The way his feelings for me progressed from lighthearted affection to concerns about my appearance, suspicions around my (financial) intentions, and attempts at emotional manipulation will read for countless women like the horror story that is their own romantic lives. I am only one of the millions of Gen X-to-Gen Z women who have endured a seemingly endless parade of miserable relationships with men.

It seems we are all trying to navigate a newly mystified mating game. The old rules of courtship have been shorn. But a more modern set of ideas has not yet taken their place. Rather, the uncertainty left by the upending of the old way has left a gaping maw that women have stared into without answers. Numerous men, for their part, have tried to fill the void with a more pronounced misogyny, leaving women everywhere to grapple for solutions to a host of male behaviors many call "toxic." Instead of trying to spackle over the collective breakdown in male-female relationships, more women should embrace the undeniable truth: what we are witnessing is the end of romantic love.

Evidence of this end of love, of the dying off of romantic relationships, is all around us. In 2020, the Pew Research Center released a report revealing that nearly 50 percent of US adults claim that dating has gotten harder in recent years. The study found that the majority of women and men who were single and searching in 2019 were dissatisfied with their dating history *and* their future prospects. That same study revealed that nearly two-thirds of single and mingling women polled had been harassed or assaulted on a date or in another context by a person they were dating.[6]

Since dating for women seeking men appears to have a multitude of new hurdles and forms of sexual manipulation and exploitation, it should come as no surprise that marriage rates in the US have hit an all-time low. According to a report cited in the *Wall Street Journal*, US marriage rates fell sharply in 2018, settling at the lowest level since record keeping began in 1867. When asked what could possibly explain this historic dip, the report's author, Sally Curtin, opined that there was "no clear reason" for the recent sharp decline seen largely among millennials.[7] However, other sources point the finger at the ease of finding partners via online dating—and disposing of them just as easily via text.[8]

If relationship prospects are grim for women seeking men writ large, the situation for Black women is just shy of dire. Already by the 1960s, studies suggested that Black women had become the least likely group of women to find the kind lasting partnerships that would result in marriage.[9] Fast forward to 2018, and 32 percent of Black women between the ages of twenty-five and fifty-four were married, compared to 62 percent of white women.[10] Even when just considering casual dating, Black women's experiences, as related on social media, have proven harrowing enough that those simply hearing about them want to tap out.[11]

With straight attachments in shambles, the number of new books dispensing wisdom about romantic relationships is so prodigious they are practically falling off the shelves. There are, to name a noteworthy few, books detailing the rules of modern dating,[12] books offering advice on how to get married,[13] and books detailing strategies for coping with the hardship of marriage.[14]

It should come as no surprise that the target audience for most of these books are women. But it might surprise you that many of them were written or cowritten by men. Indeed, several advice books, such as Bruce Bryan's *Never Chase Men Again*, Steve Harvey's *Act Like a Lady, Think Like a Man*, and Greg Behrendt and Liz Tuccillo's infamous *He's Just Not That Into You: The No Excuses Truth to Understanding Guys*, present us with men offering women advice on how to procure altar-bound affections.

And yet, not enough people are asking the obvious questions: How did things get like this? What happened to romance?

As recently as sixty years ago, feminists were agitating for the right to delay marriage or not marry at all. Now, scores of women are scrambling at the opposite end of the spectrum, many desperately seeking partnerships, long-term relationships, or marriage commitments from men that are not in the offing. How did women, historically the gatekeepers of sexual partnerships, find themselves behind the eight ball? How did so many of us become utterly lost and confused by this relatively recent relational decay, worried that we might not be able to secure the kinds of relationships that women just a few short generations ago took for granted? And why, oh why, has the romantic rot hit Black women harder than women of other races?

This book endeavors to address these questions. In this book, I show that the dissolution of straight relationships has not happened by chance but by design. I argue that a formation of male media moguls has worked to erode romance as a direct backlash to the twentieth-century feminist and civil rights movements. They have managed to do this by hiding their intent in plain sight. Through a series of messages communicated among themselves (and to us!) via the mass media, prominent men across racial and ethnic groups in the US have worked to kill romance by asserting that it should be limited to special cases involving the "right" types of women.

In its place, they effectively erected a new world sexual order. The new order depends on *withholding love* as a means of manipulating us and maintaining the upper hand over us. Said differently, many men in positions of power have worked doggedly to undermine heterosexual romance in a direct effort to usurp what little power women used to have in matters of affection. They have done so as a way of reinforcing the racial and gendered status hierarchy that was rattled during the movement era.

THE ROMANTIC IDEAL

Americans tend to treat romantic affairs as if they are a natural part of being human. But the truth is, romance had a beginning. The "Romantic Ideal" on which our Western model of courtship is based originated in Europe during the twelfth century. The term "romance" is a reinvention of "romanz," the French vernacular in which many of the stories detailing what would ultimately be regarded as the rites of coupledom were written. "Romance," then, originally described a style of literary expression.

The foundational romantic tales tell of the unassailable love of a chivalrous knight for the lady who has captured his heart. One of the most enduring, *Lancelot; or the Knight of the Cart*, was written by the French poet Chrétien de Troyes in the late twelfth century. Lancelot was a valorous knight, serving at the behest of the legendary King Arthur, who was himself the subject of several stories contained in iconic medieval romances known as "the matter of Britain."[15]

In Troyes's account, Guinevere, King Arthur's wife, is abducted by the malevolent knight Meleagant. The king sends his best knights in pursuit of his beloved, and the queen, too, sends a missive to her preferred knight, Lancelot. Lancelot has been nursing a secret infatuation with Guinevere, and she has started to succumb to his charms. Hearing the news of her capture, Lancelot tears off in the direction of his love, facing tremendous odds to free her from captivity.[16]

He descends on Meleagant's castle riding, ashamedly, in the back of a cart. (In his haste to reach his destination, he has ridden his horse so hard that it died from the strain.) Appearing in a cart, instead of on a stallion befitting a man of his station, is not an act he savors. Upon arrival, he is met by an indignant Guinevere, who, learning that he hesitated to take the cart, wonders why he should have put his pride over her safety. The tiff sparks a rift between the lovers. Their reconciliation is only achieved after Lancelot, having been imprisoned and then challenged to a duel by Meleagant, wields his mighty sword to mete out a final vengeance.[17] In the end, despite all of Lancelot's many travails, he and Guinevere do not end up happily ever after. Because she is still the queen, she returns to Arthur, the love between herself and Lancelot having been doomed from the start.

This may not be the romantic ending we'd expect. But more important for our purposes than the ending is the tale's narrative structure. Early romantic stories such as this laid out the blueprint for how men and women should behave when courting. The men were to be gallant, self-effacing, and valorous. They were often knights, meant to be loyal servants to the king and the realm, willing to fully commit to the love and protection of those they held dear. When they fell in love, it was to be to one woman whose love they were willing to pursue for the remainder of their days, and whose honor they'd be willing to defend with their lives. Women for their part were supposed to be gentle and unassuming. If they wanted to be deserving of a courtly love, they needed to be of spotless character—save the extramarital affair—meaning kind, honest, and virtuous. And the women had two additional requirements not foisted on men: they needed to come from one of the cultivated classes and to be considered unmatched beauties.

A critical ingredient in early romantic tales was that the knights pursued women of a higher status than themselves. The idea that a knight—a servant—would be reaching for the hand of a lady who was not infrequently the partner of his lord or king, added crucial dramatic tension. The knight had to violate his vow of service to prove the depth of his love, a move that was at once devotional and dishonorable. Such men were not to lower themselves for women who were socially beneath them.

The Romantic Ideal, then, at its origins depended on a man in love effecting the behavior of principled knights toward a woman who is his superior, a lady. The twelfth-century writer Andreas Capellanus, in his iconic—if irreverent—take on romance in *The Art of Courtly Love*, draws out the role of class in romantic pairings. Capellanus devotes nearly seventy-five pages to a skewering portrait of how men from the middle classes through the highest nobility ought to speak to women from this same array of backgrounds. The verdict is simple: men must try harder and expect less when pursuing a woman who is a social superior. And this is treated as a most worthwhile pursuit; it does not make sense, it would seem, for a man to entertain a woman who is not at least his social equal.

Capellanus allots a mere page to the romantic possibilities of people without titles, the serf underclass. First, he claims, romance is the purview of the cultured. It "rarely happens," he writes, "that we find farmers serving in Love's court," even though peasant men may, too, fall for "a Venus, as nature's urging teaches them to do."[18] Therefore, "it is not expedient," he declaims, that peasant men "should be instructed in the theory of love."[19]

If lower-class men, in Capellanus's cheeky rendering of the rules of courtship, lack the cultivation necessary for romantic love, serf women are undeserving of it. If a man happens to fall in love with such a woman, Capellanus encourages the man to deceive the woman, to woo her sufficiently to open her nose to the possibility of a sexual encounter, and then to drop her without explanation at the first available opportunity.

He entreats men to "puff [such women] up with lots of praise, and then, when you find a convenient place, do not hesitate to take what you seek and to embrace them by force."[20] This forcible "embrace" is a polite euphemism for what we would now call assault.

Capellanus's writing on this topic reflects the reality of the time: that women who were low on the social hierarchy were seen as undeserving of courtly behavior and a man needn't observe the rules of romance for one. But, if a man did happen to accidentally fall in love with a lower-class woman, he would "know, in brief compass, what to do." That being to use her body and then discard her. He gives similar advice to cut and run if a woman is a whore or seems a little too fond of gifts and money.[21]

Lastly, it was imperative for the well-heeled man looking for romance that his intended be a real looker. Queen Guinevere's elite social standing and sweet nature are matched only by her captivating beauty, and this trifecta makes her an ideal candidate for a man's undying love. And while descriptions of her looks have varied over the years and through various translations, many have described her as "blond. . . very fair of skin and delicate of body," an appearance which signals helplessness and the need "to be protected by her man."[22] Others have insisted she had silky black hair and deep blue eyes.[23] Which is to say that although there has been some disagreement about her hair color, the woman representing one of the earliest and most enduring characters deemed worthy of an epic romance was a wealthy noble, with long (usually) blond hair, a willowy figure, startling blue eyes, and skin as white as snow.[24]

We can easily recognize these features today as those representing the apex of whiteness, even though race did not exist at the time of Troyes's writing. Nevertheless, to the extent that some of these representations occurred before the seventeenth century dawn of race science, they have what historians have called a "proto-racist" bent.[25] Indeed, scholars have shown that the preference for light skin, hair, and eyes existed prior to the advent of racism,[26] and that these characteristics were co-opted by it and enlisted for the purpose of installing a global pigmentocracy.

For a further twist, historians have shown that the ideas about the heady nature of love articulated by Troyes and other early romantic authors were most likely inherited from Muslim Spain.[27] But there are critical distinctions between the Moorish representation of a woman worthy of sexual love and devotion and that articulated by Christian Europeans. First, the Moors write about loving women across class lines, from the noble to the slave. Moorish men writing about love during the eleventh century—a century prior to the romances—convey a willingness to abandon themselves to love and lower themselves to please a partner despite her social rank, a sentiment that is largely absent from the romances.[28] Which is to say that for the Moors love was ennobling, but for romantic Christian writers, courtly love was the province of nobles.

Second, there were a number of high-ranking Christian women who either personally penned romantic fables or advised men on what they wanted to read. Eleanor of Aquitaine, who held titles as Queen of France and later as Queen of England, is one example. Mother of the famed Richard the Lionheart, the queen was considered among the most powerful women of twelfth-century Europe, and scholars argue that it was she who had introduced the Moors' tragic love stories to the north.[29] Moreover, her daughter, Countess Marie, is credited with nothing short of providing Chrétien de Troyes the inspiration for writing *The Knight of the Cart*.[30] In addition to the influence of the queen and countess, there were a number of high-born women who wrote their own romantic tales. Not a few of these excoriated men for their phoniness, writing about chivalrous ideals that they apparently had no intention of living up to.[31]

I've unspooled this brief romantic history so that women might understand something important about romantic love: since its inception, it was meant to be the purview of European elites. The stories were written or commissioned by the gilt-edged, for the enjoyment of aristocrats and nobles, and especially for the women of these classes. The love they foretold intentionally excluded the lower sorts, and especially the lower sorts of women. Men were advised not to fall for a woman unless she was moneyed and cultivated, unblemished of character, and pale of skin—features, among others, that marked her as a high-class Christian European. If a man did choose to get involved with a woman who was not well-to-do or cultured, who was a slave or whose skin was not milky white, she could be used for consensual sex or nonconsensual assault but should never be treated as a serious romantic partner.

The Romantic Ideal then, has been since its flowering fraught with a core contradiction: On the one hand, the love is supposed to be intense and unwavering. Both parties should be willing to sacrifice, but the man in particular should be willing to do anything for his love. On the other hand, feelings for a lover are predicated on that lover meeting certain *conditions*. Which is to say the ideal is described as a passionately eternal and yet still a conditional love.

Further, romantic love was not originally intended to lead to a long-term commitment in the form of marriage. When the idea of romance took hold in medieval Europe, the stories that captivated audiences told of love and loss. As with *The Knight of the Cart*, an untold number of romantic tales written—and commonly sung by lyric poets known as troubadours—seduced audiences with their depth of emotion and moved them with their tragic conclusions.[32]

But between the twelfth and eighteenth centuries, the common understanding of the relationship between courtly love and marriage transformed. For if in the twelfth century, romantic tales told of passionate love affairs between gallant knights and married noblewomen that were doomed from the start, by the eighteenth century, romantic courtship had slowly evolved into a major basis for long-term partnerships.

The shift began with the Industrial Revolution. Marriage had long been primarily an economic arrangement. In Europe during the Middle Ages, it was common for large families to arrange marriages. Often, the bride's family paid the husband a dowry.[33] But with the Industrial Revolution, the nuclear family, rather than the extended family, came to be seen as the primary economic unit. There was an increasing presumption that men would choose their own partners. When choosing their intended, men commonly relied on the courtship rites structured by the much-vaunted centuries-old Romantic Ideal.

According to researchers at the National Women's History Museum, in the eighteenth century, "expectations increased that marriage would be built on a foundation of love," meaning courtly love as "[c]ourtship became a distinctive phase of partner selection, and familiar rituals evolved." Central to these rituals was the expectation that men would take "the lead in partner selection, choosing which women to pursue while women waited to be selected." There was also now a greater expectation that men should be providers. Critically, for our purposes, questions of status (i.e., class standing and networks), character, and appearance that had been present in arranged marriages were collectively retained when romance went to the altar: "Women's eligibility for marriage became increasingly tied to their appearance and social ability, though wealth and familial connections remained important factors to prospective partners."[34]

The Romantic Ideal, no longer just the stuff of swoon-worthy tragedies, became by the eighteenth century one of the driving imperatives for courtship and, ultimately, marriage among Western Europeans. And with it, a woman's looks, social status, and wealth were all validated as important factors for men hoping to secure the love of a lifetime.

WHITE ROMANTIC PRIVILEGE

This being our Western Romantic legacy, we should not be surprised that many of these original prejudices are still with us. Today, a woman's romantic value is still based on her social status, appearance, and wealth. And yet, the eighteenth century gave the Western world another important innovation that was intended to aid men in the assessment of these attributes.

This new technology would do away with the vagaries of men's notions of what features and behaviors signify which women are "beautiful" and "ladylike" enough to be worthy of a romance—the inconsistent and unguided applications of which are lampooned in the classic novel *Don Quixote*. This new tool would function as a romantic sorting hat, advising men on the types of women beautiful and honorable enough to qualify for a forever love *before* they had to get to know them. I am speaking, of course, about race.

Race was invented as a value-laden, color-coded human dragnet during the late seventeenth century. It was intended to confer privileges on a (white) few. These unearned advantages would manifest in an assortment of venues. But usually when we talk about whiteness as privilege, we are describing the preferential treatment white persons enjoy in the public sphere (e.g., while pursuing education and careers, or merely walking around the neighborhood).[35] We have not yet fully appreciated the role racism and white privilege play in loving partnerships.

The under-examination of race in romance is strange, given the legacy of the concept. The first-ever race scientist, Frenchman François Bernier, devoted a considerable portion of his "scientific" career to detailing the physical charms (or lack thereof) of women across the globe. Which is to say that delineating what made women in various regions of the world un/desirable was integral to the earliest forms of race science.

The seedlings of Bernier's ideas on race appeared in his 1671 work, *Travels in the Mogul Empire*. The book was written, fittingly enough, during the reign of the Sun King, the notorious philanderer Louis XIV. In the text, Bernier sings the praises of the women he sees during his journey. He is particularly taken with the women of Kashmir, whose faces are, in his view, handsome enough to rival women in any part of Europe.[36] This comparison establishes European women as Bernier's implied standard for beauty. Yet as his travels through the empire unfold, he becomes convinced that the women from divers parts of Asia could hold their own. The women of Lahor, he intones, are "the finest brunettes in all the Indies, and justly renowned for their fine and slender shapes."[37] Throughout "the Indies," the women he encounters are in his estimation "very beautiful."[38]

Travels in the Mogul Empire might be considered a proto-racist text. It was, after all, written prior to the first-ever racial treatise. That text, *A New Division of the Earth*, would be authored by Bernier some thirteen years on. A mere four pages long, the vast majority of the work is taken up with describing the "beautiful slave women of Georgia and Circassia"; the pop of lovely in Persia; "Greek beauties"; plus more slavering over the women of the Indies, whose faces he describes as "yellow."[39] He moreover wants audiences to be aware that "[the] Turks also have many very beautiful women."[40]

Here, too, Bernier finds it within himself to fawn over the "Black" women he sees in multiple places in Africa. In Egypt, he runs across women whom he claims "put me in mind of the fair and famed Cleopatra." In the East African village of Moka, he claims to have encountered several slave women "completely naked, waiting to be sold," the caliber of their figures apparently unparalleled: "I can tell you, there could be nothing lovelier in the world to see."[41]

These are the only two tracts on geography and beauty laid down by Bernier. And yet, his approach to the topic has left an indelible mark on the field, setting the stage for what constituted a priority concern in future racial articulations. An incredible number of subsequent racial theories written by a slew of authors followed Bernier's example, allotting significant space to describing the beauty or ugliness of women by race and region.

And crucially, if Bernier was stunned by the magnificent beauty of the Black women he encountered in several locales, later theorists doing race work would not be. Bernier had entered the conversation during a time in which French philosophers were questioning whether there existed "natural slaves," such that the transatlantic slave trade might find a moral justification from the heavens. By the eighteenth century apex of race-making, few theorists questioned the legitimacy of a racial hierarchy with a Black bottom.

The result was that, by the mid-1700s, Black women were overwhelmingly described in racial science sourcebooks with derision and disgust. Their forms, once praised as peerless, were increasingly described as big bellied, a stand-in for grotesque.[42] Their sexuality was said to be crudely ardent and undiscriminating, as many argued that Black women would lie with anything on two legs, man or ape.[43]

In other words, the eighteenth century marks the genesis of well-known racist tropes about Black women. Scientific racists asserted that they were ugly but/and hypersexual, undesirable yet DTF. It was a creeping dehumanization that saw the characterization of Black women move from beautiful and (owing to colonization) accessible, to grisly strumpets. These were psychically useful tools; they helped to justify Black women's degradation, which intensified with the progression of chattel slavery.[44]

This turn of events was to have lasting implications for Black women's romantic chances. For while race scientists were not largely concerned with romance, they did concern themselves with key features of a woman's suitability for a romantic partnership: beauty and virtue. Which is to say that the buildup of race science had as one of its lasting effects the inching removal of Black women from the category of romantic eligibility.

This meant that white women, the implicit standard for such from the outset, found fewer female rivals for romantic partnerships, discursively and practically, after the early 1700s. But they were not to be without them completely. After all, wherever a group of women are put on a pedestal, there is always the expectation that other women, on the rungs below, might effectively jockey for position should those above let themselves slide. In this respect, the enduring fantasy of Asian women, too, has proven useful to white supremacy. The fetishizing of their (stereotyped) nearer-to-white skin and sweet manner has continued largely unabated among many European men since the late seventeenth century.[45]

To put a fine point on the matter, race has always been about sex.[46] That is, it has always served to regulate knowledge about women's appearance for the purpose of adjudicating their sexual opportunities and men's sexual priorities. Once used by the likes of Bernier to serve as a geolocator for hot mostly non-white chicks, by the mid-eighteenth century, it served a new purpose: To suggest the diminished desirability of certain types of non-European women. Women with darker skin, larger bodies, and curlier hair were, by that time, unsightly, making them unacceptable as romantic partners for upstanding (white) men.

In other words, whiteness became shorthand for a woman's romantic suitability.

SEEDS OF CHANGE

The Romantic Ideal has always been an ideal about more than just finding love. At the time of its flowering, it was meant to goad men to be honorable and to shoot for the love of an attractive noblewoman. By the eighteenth century, it had evolved into a principle for seeking a marriageable partner for white men and women of the middle and upper classes. White men were inspired to look for a partner with the right qualities according to the new aesthetic and behavioral netting that was race. Light skin, straight hair, a polite mien were all factors that, while long-considered desirable in Europe, were given a new meaning and a new mandate in the search for a life partner.

A century further and these patrician wives were expected to create a quiet "pleasant and restorative environment" for their husbands. It was the dawn of the "cult of domesticity." The husbands, for their part, were, following the Industrial Revolution, now expected to be the primary breadwinners.[47] This was the state of affairs for white persons of the cultured classes in the US, and much of the Western world, heading into the middle of the nineteenth century.

The early twentieth century, it seems, was when seeds of the dissolution of romance between (white) men and women—that which we are now experiencing in full swing—began in earnest. In white men's own words, as you will read in the chapters to follow, romance was already dying out by the first few decades of the twentieth century. What killed it, according to these men, was the first wave of the feminist movement.

The Romantic Ideal had been predicated on an agreement: men would be heroic so long as women were attractive, sweet model domestic helpmates. When women began to challenge the idea of continuing to polish what Mary Wollstonecraft calls their "gilt cage," men started to question whether and if they should sign up for a life of matrimony.[48]

If the seeds of change were planted with the first wave, they were beginning to bear fruit by the mid-twentieth century. During the 1960s, a vocal cadre of influential men were up in arms about women's making demands for equality in the public sphere while still expecting to enjoy the rites of courtship in private. It was a situation these men were not poised to accept for long. The move toward equality on the part of largely middle- and upper-class educated white women played an integral role in white women's increasing frustration while seeking white men as partners.

For Black women, who by virtue of their racial desecration had been placed outside the scope of the ideal of romance since the eighteenth century, a different push further hurt their hopes for long-term loving partnerships and marital relationships: the civil rights movement. As a result of this insistence on racial equality, a number of straight Black men expected to enjoy the same rights and privileges as white men. This included the right to screw around with or settle down with white and other non-Black women, opportunities that had been denied them by race science and its attendant anti-miscegenation laws.[49]

I am not the first author to describe the ways some Black men used the civil rights movement as an opportunity to sow their seed in lighter pastures. Black feminists have written extensively about how many men used the movement as a vehicle for picking up white women.[50] Some Black men sought equality not of all beings but between Black and white men. They wanted the same rights and *privileges* as white men, including the (continued) ability to use and discard Black women as they saw fit and to have intimate relationships with white women.

It is this confusing collision of competing demands for equality that has landed us in our current hellscape. Homing in on the nature of sexual relationships between men and women—largely but not exclusively in Black and white—in America since the era of slavery, this book will reveal the ways that Black and white men have been more aligned on the "woman question" than has been previously appreciated. That is, straight white *and* Black men since slavery in America have been relying on the rubric set forth by the Romantic Ideal as a guiding principle when selecting female partners. Women who are compliant, fair-skinned, and preferably upper-class, or at least upwardly mobile, have been considered desirable by white men, and Black men have been following their example, in the absence of others.

In the chapters that follow, I show that after the movement era, white and Black men held fast in their search for these traits in women. I call women bearing these qualities "sufficiently white." Women who are judged to lack some or all of these qualities, the "insufficiently white," have seen their opportunities for lasting partnerships diminish, especially since the 1970s.

Importantly, I use the term "insufficiently white" instead of simply "white" as a reminder that white is a manmade social category that is in constant flux. First, as explored above, many lighter-skinned Asian women have been fetishized for the very traits noted here. Some scholars have claimed that Asians are treated as "honorary whites."[51] But for our purposes, I will show that many white and Black men have treated Asian women in particular as if they are sufficiently white.

Second, some groups who are categorized as white today would not have been even a few decades ago, while others have found themselves expelled from that category.[52] That is to say that some women, for example many Jewish women who might currently be categorized as white may, as I show in this book, still experience problems associated with insufficient whiteness.

The final harrowing reality that I disclose in this book is that when men began to walk away from the Romantic Ideal, they did so under the shelter of a new ideal, one that I am calling the Pornographic Ideal. Rather than being at odds with romance, the Pornographic Ideal has been its wingman. It has advised men that hot and sweet "good girls" are still worth marrying. But women who are considered too sexually available, dark-skinned, fat, or low-class—attributes attached to insufficient whiteness—are deserving of the relational debasement articulated by Capellanus, a form of mistreatment I call "w/horification."

MEDITATION ON METHODOLOGIES

I am a Black queer-identified cis woman who is millennial-adjacent (or, my preferred term, xennial). It happens that many of my peers—and the men I have dated—have been millennials. However, my aim here is not just to interrogate the heterosexual courtship practices of one generation of men and women. Instead, this book encourages folks to explore and analyze, maybe for the first time, the peculiarly racialized dating landscape that has resulted from the mid-twentieth-century movement era.

As you might imagine, this book is deeply personal. It is partly a written response to the many people who are constantly asking me anxiety-filled questions about my relationship status (*Are you married? Getting married? Dating someone?!*). Additionally, it is a critical reflection on the curious romantic situations in which women, especially millennials and millennial-adjacents, find ourselves at this time. This is arguably the first time period in American history during which both intra and interracial dating are considered socially acceptable, and yet they are both still underwritten by sexual racism.

In an effort to unravel the legacy of racism that has placed Black and other insufficiently white women (B/IWW) in the position we are in, I have decided to veer from the beaten methodological path. Instead, I am employing what I am calling a "renegade methodology." I define renegade methods as those that do not conform to disciplinary regimes. To the extent that they refuse to uncritically follow methodologies sanctioned by any one field, they can be considered as practices of discovery that fall under the rubric of feminist methodologies.[53]

Renegade methodologies distinguish themselves from traditional feminist social science inquiries in that they do not necessarily attempt to establish a new "feminist" research imperative. Any project to create a new "normal" for research will inevitably contain within it the tendency to police, to enforce, to establish, and to regulate, *how* so-called feminist research can be collected, analyzed, and measured. Renegade methodologies are instead attuned to the rapidly changing nature of our social world and to the manifold (and evolving) contingencies framing the experiences of marginalized persons. They are not "objective" and widely applicable but site-specific. They do not summarily dismiss all existing methodological principles, and indeed they may build upon them in novel ways. But they are not beholden to them. They may be reproducible, but they are not to be *fixed*.

In this way, renegade methods reject many of the tenets of scientific positivism that were founded by cishet patrician white males during the eighteenth-century Enlightenment and that have, in the hundreds of years since, largely failed to capture the experiences of persons not fitting into this select group. They do not require the scientific method as the means but instead sanction the fugitivity of intellectual curiosity. They foreground revelation as the desired end.

My method of exploration for this topic is a blend of historical narrative, media analysis, and personal testimony. I have chosen to combine these seemingly disparate forms of inquiry for two reasons: First, to reveal the trajectory and general parameters of culturally sanctioned cishet behavior, as well as representations of Black women—and other insufficiently white women—in mass culture. The media play a tremendous and often unacknowledged role in shaping our perceptions. Indeed, it was medieval media—in the form of romantic stories and epic poems that were routinely sung by traveling artists—who popularized the Romantic Ideal in Western Europe. And, as I show herein, magazines, newspaper articles, books, and rap songs helped to further the aims of the Pornographic Ideal.

The second reason I have chosen this methodological approach is to reveal how certain behavior shows up in real time by scrutinizing how it has impacted me, a Black woman who has endured many nightmarish relationships and situations over the years. My brown skin and kinky hair and feminist bearing have long been considered disqualifiers from lasting affection for many men across race. Through a series of short autobiographical stories about a variety of my own dating scenarios—which have been alternately humorous, inconsiderate, and violent—I illustrate the behavior and cultural structures in question. The intimate level of detail regarding motivations, mishaps, and lessons is rarely available from informants who are not oneself. But more to the point, I am working to undo the notion that all women (or even all Black women) share the same dating trajectory—a fallacy enabled by the overreliance on dating statistics—in favor of exposing factors that structure a given experience. That is, I am attentive to the fact that my experience may be dissimilar to that of other women, especially if they are phenotypically distinct in ways that may induce better (e.g., light skin and straight hair) or worse (e.g., large-bodied) treatment from cishet men. In this way, I am not suggesting that my experience is generalizable—only that it is facilitated by the cultural messages about dating and romance that are transmitted, amongst other mechanisms, by the media.[54]

Last, I was moved to splice historical artifacts with a reading of the media and personal essays by the insights of feminist foremothers such as bell hooks. In her classic essay "Theory as Liberatory Practice," hooks reminds us that theorizing involves thinking critically about our roles in the social world, our own biographies, and what has shaped them.[55] We can extrapolate from personal experience the worth our culture has placed on our lives. And, by bearing witness to our own astonishments as Sandra Cisneros has so skillfully done in her writing, we allow others the space to the find the mutual resonances (and many departures) that constitute the human condition.[56]

This book includes seven empirical chapters. Each chapter explores how historical events in the US from slavery through the feminist and civil rights movements of the twentieth century influenced male-female relationships. Personal narrative and key developments in media are integrated into the discussion.

The first chapter, "Black Is The Commons," examines in detail how developments starting with colonization prevented Black women from being considered viable long-term romantic partners in the US. I argue that slavery converted Black women into sidepieces for both white and Black men. Post-emancipation, several Black men fought Black women's maltreatment as such, while a host of others did not. Many were allied with white men in the notion that Black women's bodies should remain easily accessible or that Black women should remain a form of "commons" for the pleasure of straight men. By the arrival of the civil rights movement (CRM), some Black men were eager to integrate with white men on the basis of jobs, freedom, and the pursuit of "normal" patriarchal relations with women.

The second chapter, "The Blacker the Berry. . . the Less Loveworthy," explores how on the heels of the CRM, the Black Is Beautiful movement endeavored a reclamation of Black-on-Black love and a celebration of the beauty of Black women. These ideas were picked up by a new art form known as hip hop, which arrived at the tail end of the movement era. But as rap music, a subset of hip hop, started to amass more white and male fans, the message swiftly transitioned from love and communal uplift to the popular (originally white and male) admonition against loving "ho's," who were overwhelmingly coded as Black.

Chapter 3, "Black Women Are Not to Be Trusted: Gold Diggery," details how, in addition to painting Black women as unlovable "ho's" in rap during its Golden Age, the Golden Age of rap also saw artists advising men not to marry "gold diggers." These gold diggers were routinely depicted as Black women, with one Black woman in particular being featured in dozens of songs as archetypal. As I show, there is, of course, no truth to the notion that Black women are quintessentially gold diggers. In fact, the term and the idea behind it—dating or marrying for money—were invented by white women to describe themselves, an ideology that coincided with the tail end of first wave feminism.

Chapter 4, "Enter the Fuckboys," takes us into largely white spaces to explore how (white) men in the twentieth century responded to the coincidence of feminism and gold digging. Their response, conveyed in newspapers and men's magazines like *Esquire*, was to counsel men to be more careful in their selection of wives or to avoid getting married altogether, lest they end up with a gold digger/feminist harpy. A number of men used their platforms to tell women that if they wanted equality, they should give up the expectation that men will pursue them or pro- vide for them. These men were laying down the principles of fuccboism, which I argue began to take root on the heels of the movement era.

In chapter 5, "Women as Sex Workers," white men find their sea legs. Feeling ripped off by the Romantic Ideal under the onslaught of feminism, they create a new ideal. This new ideal, instead of focusing on the conditions for building a loving partnership, had as its aim teaching men to w/horify insufficiently white women. Its figurehead was a newly divorced Hugh Hefner. Its vehicle was *Playboy*.

Chapter 6, "Sex Trafficking (a.k.a. Pimpin')," returns to Black com- munities. I show how a new generation of rap artists intensified the diminution of Black women. These (mostly Black) artists fused the trappings of Black pimps—long a feature of rap music—with ideas from white pornographers to further w/horify insufficiently white women and praise those meeting the feminine standard.

Chapter 7, "Masturbation Generation/s," tracks the effects of decades of porn on men's sexual functioning. I show that the widespread avail- ability of porn on the internet has contributed to an explosion of male sexual dysfunction, as many men appear to have abandoned the notion of committed relationships in favor of masturbation, at least partly out of the fear that real women will not measure up to our culture's (racial- ized) beauty standard.

The coda, "We Are Love," provides a few final insights into the problem of pornography as it pertains to women's hopes for romantic relationships. It also contains a shocking revelation about romance. It concludes with the view that we are all love. Getting out of the racist romantic/ pornographic quagmire will require us to embrace ideas by feminist and queer folx and to abandon practices inaugurated by elite white men.

CHAPTER 1

BLACK IS THE COMMONS

I n 2020, comedian and actor Aisha Tyler was interviewed by *Access Hollywood* about her stint on the hit TV series *Friends*. Tyler, a Black woman, was put through a series of rapid-fire questions about the cast and characters' habits, preferences, and idiosyncrasies. The lightning round was followed by questions about the intimacies she shared with two of the male leads, Ross and Joey. The interviewer, Scott Evans, queried who was the better kisser? Tyler, with characteristic grace and diplomacy, intimated that both actors were easeful and professional when it came to their on-screen affection and that it was she who, by the time it came to the rendezvous with Ross, had to relax into the role to make the affair more believable.[1] Evans came back with a question: If given the chance in real life, who would she date, Ross or Joey?

"It would absolutely be Joey," Tyler responds without hesitation.

"Really?" Evans probes.

"Yeaaahh," Tyler replies.

"We called it!" Evan screeches, elated.

The titillation expressed by Evans may seem extra. After all, they are discussing the pretend possibility of an interracial relationship based on Tyler's guest appearance on a show that ended its run over fifteen years prior. And yet for Tyler, this line of questioning—and the overblown reaction—is par for the course.

Tyler made her debut on the show in 2003, an unfashionably late hour for televisual romantic integration. Yet not only was it heralded as a landmark event at the time, but the gleeful reaction to this supposed racial milestone (a Black woman as a serious romantic partner for a white man on a sitcom!) has continued to receive intense media attention.[2] In 2018, it was the subject of an interview Tyler did with *InStyle*. A few months prior, she had discussed it on *The Late Show with Stephen Colbert*. In 2019, she made the rounds on *Bustle* and MSN. Tyler's exposure over these *Friends* episodes was such that by 2020, when she was interviewed on the set of *Access Hollywood* about the possibility of a *Friends* reunion, the question about who she might prefer, Ross or Joey (?!) still carried the intense libidinal power that it had seventeen years prior.

Along with the number of years that have passed since she appeared on the show, three other things strike me as peculiar about the Tyler-on-*Friends* frenzy (and yes, the double entendre here is intended). First, I notice the fleeting run of Tyler's character, Charlie Wheeler: a nine-episode arc. This, for a show that was on-air for ten seasons, logging a total of 236 episodes. This makes Tyler far from a series regular; were it not for the interracial aspect of her plot arc, her character would likely have been long forgotten, swallowed by the black hole that consumes all sitcom romantic foils.

Second, and more telling, Tyler was not the first Black woman to date a major character on the show. That honor belongs to Gabrielle Union. In 2001, during the seventh season of the show, Union played Kristen Lang, a new resident in their apartment building who both Ross and Joey meet and date briefly while helping her move in. When the two men find out that they are both dating her, they proceed to engage in aggressive and manipulative tactics to win her over, the end result of which is that Lang grows wise to their deceit and drops the two of them. Union was only on the show for one episode, and there has been considerably less discussion about her character. Still, what is most telling about Tyler *and* Union's appearances is that each of them dated not one but *two* of the white male leads.

Not being a *Friends* truther, I cannot say for certain that none of the other female guest stars dated multiple leads. (Although it is clear that actor Lauren Tom's character, Julie, the one Asian female character to date a male lead, dated Ross exclusively.) For me, it's significant that *both* of the Black women with speaking roles on the show did. The conceit of their appearances was that the characters (and by extension the show) was colorblind and that these Black women supposedly had a chance not only to become the leading lady for one of the leading men but to be empowered to select which of the men best tickled their fancy. But both Lang's and Wheeler's desires were ultimately nullified, as two men on the show puzzled out how best to ignore (while paying lip service to) each woman's wishes while they tried to make her their own. The reality of Tyler's presence on the show depended on her character being passed between the white male leads—not even the first Black woman to occupy *that* role—which proves that neither Tyler nor Union were serious contenders for either Ross's or Joey's affections. Instead, they were the shared property of both.

                                                       ▪   ▪   ▪

America has a long and masticated history of treating Black women as the property of white men. There are countless examinations of white's men treatment of Black women under chattel slavery, a time period during which a white man could purchase a Black woman as a slave and exploit her being in any way he saw fit.[3] Many texts have detailed how Black women were treated as little better than farm animals whose lives and labor ought to be dedicated to the assurance of white ease.[4] Some have taken a more sex-specific approach, describing the physical impact of white men's routine sexual usury on the Black women who were forced to endure it, or limning the looming threat of rape as adding an element of psychic terror to the already grueling conditions of enslavement.[5]

These are undoubtedly important facets of the Black female–white male dynamic deserving of these, and future, investigations. Yet while many of these texts have examined the economic, sexual, and psychic damages (for Black women) and the wages (for white men) of these coercive entanglements, far less work has interrogated the romantic or sexual ramifications for Black women of white men's unfettered access to their bodies. In other words, limited attention has been paid to the effect that white men's normalized and legalized rape of Black women has had on Black women's collective sexual relationship with white men.[6]

In the realm of the sexual, the enslavement of Black women in the US achieved something profound. It converted Black women, as a class, into the communal property of white men. That is, it was not just her "owner" who owned her. Any and every white man who might fancy a go, and who was not in some way at odds with her enslaver, was given license to use and discard a Black woman at will. For white men, then, Black women became "The Commons," a readily accessible carnal resource to support their physical needs.

The conversion of Black women into The Commons did more than grant white men the opportunity to delight in one or even multiple sanctioned sexual assaults. It created a reserve sexual army. An unfussy place for white men to relieve themselves separate from the taxing rituals of romantic courtship they'd have to enact with any white woman who was not a sex worker. And again, since race science suggested that Black women were naturally salacious and white women inherently chaste, white men could exploit this reserve sexual army without upending the romantic economy between white men and women.

Slavery's end did not, of course, end white men's collective access to Black women's bodies. For if slaves were deemed, by dint of their being (collective) property, "unrapeable," the Thirteenth and Fourteenth Amendments (which freed the slaves and gave them, on paper, equal protection under the law) did little to stem the tide of white male assaults on Black female bodies.[7] As other scholars have shown, the end of de jure segregation in rape law had nothing to do with its ongoing practice.[8] To the extent that Black women were presumed promiscuous, the largely white and male prosecutors responsible for going after these white men couldn't get it up for the cause.

That is to say, anything resembling a change in this state of affairs was slow to arrive. Decades after the end of slavery—when racial segregation was still written into legal code in matters outside of sexual venality—it was nevertheless still the habit among white folk in law enforcement to not see the predatory behavior of white men.

■ ■ ■

The case of Recy Taylor proves illustrative. In 1944, Taylor, then a twenty-four-year-old wife and mother, was walking home from church in Abbeville, Alabama, when six white males between the ages of fourteen and eighteen descended on her. Holding her at gunpoint, they blindfolded and kidnapped her. They took her to an abandoned field, where they gang-raped her before, like Dr. Jekyll who had just let Mr. Hyde out for a stroll, gathering themselves and returning to their lives as socially respectable young white men.

The authorities were well aware of Recy's case. In this small town, they had personal relationships with the families of the boys who had perpetrated these heinous acts. None of them saw fit to arrest these white boys or charge them with a crime.[9]

The NAACP was notified. They dispatched a young Rosa Parks, who had been stationed in Montgomery, to investigate Recy's rape. By all accounts, Parks was rebuffed and then manhandled by the Abbeville police, who wanted to prevent outsider race politics from rocking their sleepy town.[10] Unwilling to yield to the local authority's apathy, Parks and Taylor cofounded the Committee for Equal Justice for the Rights of Mrs. Recy Taylor. The committee helped to get eyes on the problem. First through their letter-writing campaign to pressure the Alabama governor, Chauncey Sparks, to make a move. This led to the convening of a grand jury.[11]

The efforts of the committee were meticulously chronicled in the Black press, which turned out to be its most effective weapon. A Black woman being raped by a cabal of white males wasn't exactly front-page news in the white media. In fact, it rarely made the news at all. That there would be *any* press coverage of what came to be referred to as the "Abbeville Affair" meant white folk couldn't claim ignorance of the routine violations of Black women's bodily integrity.[12]

Still, Recy Taylor's intrepidity didn't lead to justice in her case. The grand jury had been populated exclusively by local white men who predictably failed to indict the boys they'd had a hand in raising.[13] Adding ambush to injury, the Taylor family would also survive a firebombing attempt in the wake of Recy's accusation—a common form of white terror visited upon people of color who had the gumption to stand up to white men.

Following the grand jury debacle, the Committee for Equal Justice for Mrs. Recy Taylor dropped its specificity. It became simply the Committee for Equal Justice. Parks and Taylor recruited members nationwide, setting up satellites in other cities and towns, including, notably, Montgomery, Alabama.

The Committee for Equal Justice amassed supporters that included some of the most illustrious names in Black politics. Mary Church Terrell, Langston Hughes, and W. E. B. Du Bois are just a few of the fabled members. The committee continued its work fighting sexual violence against Black women for years, eventually morphing into the Montgomery Improvement Association (MIA). It was the MIA that in 1955 would instigate the notorious Montgomery bus boycott.[14]

That is to say the activism instigated by Recy and Rosa in response to the banality of white men's gang rape—countering the treatment of Black female bodies as The Commons—was one of the major catalysts of the civil rights movement (CRM).[15] Black women's sexual exploitation was, in this way, central to the early machinations of the movement. It would prove consequential for later rape cases, such as that of Betty Jean Owens in 1959. Betty Jean had been a student at Florida A&M University. Like Recy, she had been the pious sort. And while it was revealed in court that the four white louts who had raped her had made a pact to "'go out and get a nigger girl' and 'have an all-night party,'"[16] one might nevertheless imagine their surprise that they were ultimately convicted. Their conviction was a direct result of the mobilization of the Black community in the aftermath of Recy Taylor's rape.

■   ■   ■

This would be a neat place for the story of collectivized white male predation on Black women to end if it ended there. But it didn't. The civil rights movement gained steam, becoming an undeniable force that even the white people most prone to faux-innocent antics couldn't miss.[17] At the same time, the Black women who had been afforded center stage as a result of their claims of molestation had been pushed into the shadows. More men were getting involved in the movement, and many of them thought they should hold the reins. By the early 1960s, a great deal of the spotlight of the CRM was placed on its male figureheads.

Martin Luther King Jr., for his part, had a tenuous relationship with women leaders and with women's causes. Coming from the church, as celebrated historian Barbara Ransby notes, King and many of the other male leaders struggled to speak to the women leaders as social equals.[18] King and others decried police violence, economic inequality, war, and a lack of jobs for Black men. King's speech during the March on Washington carried notes in the key of each of these tunes. But he did not speak to the historical importance—to both the community *and the movement*—of white men's communal dominion over Black women's bodies. Perhaps this was owing to the contradictory nature of his own personal relationships with Black women, including his alleged extramarital affairs.[19]

But there was more to it than that. A growing chauvinism was creeping into the movement at the hands of its male leaders. A number of them tried to remind women of their gendered role in the US, this most civilized of places.[20] For some, the idea that Black women might finally take up the role of domestic servants to Black men was a tantalizing prospect. *This* was to be the true freedom: liberating the Black man from the shackles of racism that had prevented the full blossoming of his manhood. All the while, Black women would be reinscribed to the role of domestic goddess for *their own* nuclear families, as prescribed by the nineteenth-century version of the Romantic Ideal. In that way, they'd finally become real women.

For a cardinal sum of the male leaders, the idea that the movement would allow Black women to chart their own path to freedom was ludicrous—against God and normality. Not for nothing, such an idea was even against the supposedly radical position of Karl Marx, an idol to many in the movement. Within classical Marxism, capitalism thwarted the "natural" arrangement between the sexes—that of a male head of household and a female domestic support. Once capitalism was defeated, men of various ethnic groups could return to their native patriarchal practices.[21]

Leaders and Black nationalists like Amiri Baraka found a home within this strain of Marxist thinking. In the late 1960s, right as the movement was embracing a new chauvinism, Baraka intoned, in a text insultingly titled *Black Women*:

> We do not believe in "equality" of men and women. We cannot understand what devils and the devilishly influenced mean when they say equality for women. We could never be equals . . . nature has not provided thus. The brother says, "Let a woman be a woman . . . and a man be a man."[22]

Evidently, not everyone was on board with the project of attempting to lift Black women up from their racially proscribed status of sexual pliability to the Christian-patriarchal romantic status of respectable chaste woman turned wife and mother. Even as Black women continued to fight their conscription into old or new supportive roles, there were, troublingly, some Black men working to elevate their own status, all the while planning to leave Black women open to indefinite sexual profiteering. Stokely Carmichael, a leader of the Student Nonviolent Coordinating Committee (SNCC), famously announced at an organizing meeting in 1964 that the only place for a woman in the movement was "prone."[23] Given the prevailing restrictions of Jim Crow, as well as what kind of women would likely have been in the movement, these statements can only be read as a re-conscription of Black women's bodies as The Commons, and not just for white men.

In a short space of time, the gendered posturing of the movement had evolved dramatically. Only a decade prior, the movement had rallied behind Black women who'd been assaulted by white men. As recently as 1962, Malcolm X had delivered an unforgettable speech reminding Black America that the despoiling of Black women was an integral feature of these United States.[24] Looking at this speech from the vantage point of the late '60s, Malcolm seemed to be a man maintaining a posture from a bygone era. He had been one of the few Black male leaders from the

movement era to concern himself with Black women's physical security. Once other men took the reins of the civil rights and Black Power
movements, a lid seemed to be placed on the question of protecting
Black women from sexual predation, the very question that had been
in large part responsible for the growth and spread of the movement in
the 1940s and '50s.

The collective energy of the movement was largely placed elsewhere.
Stemming the tide of violence—centrally the lynching of Black men—remained a priority.[25] And yet concerns about something else increasingly
preoccupied the men at the top. They groused about access to America's
bounty of resources, ingress into its theretofore segregated institutions.
Were they not deserving of the same jobs, schools, and decent housing
as the white man?

"Integration" was on their lips. They wanted to be restored to their
rightful role as "men," which their racialization as Black had stolen from
them. By the late 1960s, prominent protests would feature men with
posters proclaiming "I AM A MAN" hanging from their necks like reverse
nooses.[26] Inevitably, this message was intended for white men, as the
protesters made their case for equality under the banner of manhood.

The movement may have begun marching in a different direction,
but Black women never forgot about the problem of their being The
Commons. Assata Shakur, the godmother of Tupac and a leading figure
in the Black Panther Party and the Black Liberation Army, kept the rape
of Black women and girls top of mind. In her memoir, *Assata: An Autobiography*, she writes extensively about the rape of Black women and
girls, wondering what her forbears must have felt "when they brought
their babies into this world, only to see them flogged and raped, bought
and sold."[27] Later, after her brief marriage to fellow activist Louis Chesimard dissolved over what she unsurprisingly described as his expectation that she take on a more traditional women's role in the home and
the movement, she pondered the probable number of Black women
the original Mr. Chesimard—her ex-husband's white slaveholder namesake—had raped.

Her concern about rape was more than mere speculation about historical events. Shakur's perturbation about the contemporary problem

of assault—especially the gang rape of Black women—was visceral. In this watershed work, she details her own terrifying experience narrowly escaping a gang rape in the mid-1960s after being duped into heading to a second location by a local boy she encountered at a party.[28]

.   .   .

I know firsthand what it is to be treated like The Commons. On Halloween night in 2011, I put on a short pink wig in the style of a blunt-cut bob with bangs. I threw on a pair of jeggings with high heels and a fitted top. Into the back of the jeggings, I'd stuffed a small pillow, giving myself the effect of major ass cheeks.

I met my friend Kiara outside our apartment complex. "Who are you?" she asked.

"I'm Nicki Minaj. Who are you?" I replied.

Kiara, who has long locs, was wearing a Grecian robe and carrying a staff. "I'm Black Jesus."

We set off toward a Halloween party in Hillcrest. The first thing I saw when we arrived was a white kid in a Tiger Woods costume, complete with blackface. I was disgusted. *How are white people still dressing up as people of color? Our skin is not a costume.* I started to address this idiot, but I didn't really know anyone at this party. Plus, it didn't make sense for me to pop off on arrival. I tried to ignore that dirtbag and enjoy myself.

In no time, I was approached by a couple of white guys. One of them was regaling our pod with a long if interesting story about Van Halen.

"Yah so, the band has it in their rider that they must have a bowl of M&Ms with the brown ones removed!"

"That's so weird!" I enthused. "The colors are not flavors."

"I know!" he added. We were vibing.

"Did you get that story from *This American Life*?" replied the other white man.

"Well, uh . . ." the first guy stammered.

"You got that story from *This American Life* and tried to pass it off as something you 'heard.'" He rolled his eyes, indignant now.

I smirked at this display of white male peacocking. They were Ross and Chandler. It only later occurred to me that the pillow in my jeggings probably played a role in their displays of bravado. This was before white men were openly admitting that they are into ass.

The first man skulked off, embarrassed. The second guy, let's call him Yanis, I later learned was a Jewish Yale man and a recent San Diego transplant. For the remainder of the evening, Yanis was never too far from my side.

At one point we were on the dance floor. Yanis turned to me and asked, "What does your real hair look like?"

"Short and curly, kind of like yours," I said, leaning in close. We smiled.

Black Jesus came to get me. I turned to Yanis like, "We're leaving."

"You should probably give me your number then," he replied, handing me his phone. I plugged my number in. Then I went to get my coat.

Before I left, I told him, "You better call me."

"I already did," he replied. I looked at my phone, and, sure enough, he had called me to make sure I had his number. We smiled at one another one last time.

Our text messages got pretty hot pretty quick. He spent several days constantly texting, giving the impression that he was truly smitten. I wasn't really looking for a serious relationship. But given what seemed to be Yanis's intense interest and the reality that we found each other smart and sexy, I didn't see the harm in us dating a little.

Yanis kept pressuring me to hang out with him and his friends—something my ex Cody had also pushed for. Déja fucking vu! I didn't think our first date should include his homies, but he seemed to think it was essential that I meet his friends.

My resistance was rooted in naïveté. I feared it would be boring to go out with him and a bunch of white bros. I hadn't been thinking about the other thing I ought to have feared. So when he asked me to a party his new female roommate was throwing at a restaurant downtown, I caved.

I was wearing a slinky orange shirtdress with my hair in a twist-out. When I walked into the party, he gave me that look. The look that men give women that says, *I will devour you.* I remember thinking it was sexy at the time.

When I met his roommate, she embraced me.

"Well, aren't you beautiful!" she cried. She, too, was Jewish. And beautiful. She and I had a lot in common. She also did yoga and was in fact a hip-hop yoga instructor. She was the kind of person everybody liked. When I glanced over at Yanis, who had been watching our exchange, I could tell he was in love with her.

It didn't take long for me to realize what I was doing at this party. I was the date for a man who was in love with a woman he couldn't have. His roommate was engaged to another man. It was clear what his con was: get close to her while always keeping another piece on his arm to deflect from his true intentions. He'd take the time to learn how the fiancé was slippin', be a bug in her ear about how he wasn't shit. Then, during one of the fights that all couples have, he'd be right there to console her.

I wasn't particularly in the mood to be a sidepiece. In less than an hour, I had my purse back on my shoulder and was telling Yanis I was leaving. He had been engrossed in a conversation with his roommate. He looked shocked by my intentions.

"Clearly I haven't been paying enough attention to you," he said. He excused himself from the conversation and tried to convince me to stay.

"Did you have enough to drink? Want another cocktail?" It seemed like he was working on getting me drunk.

"No. It's getting late. I need to be heading home," I replied.

"OK," Yanis said, relenting. "But let me walk you to your car. Did you park in the lot I told you about?"

"Yes," I said.

In the parking structure, before we could get out of the elevator, Yanis was suddenly grinding on me.

"OK!" I said several times, trying to push him off me. "That's enough." But he wouldn't stop. I was conflicted. I hadn't been looking for anything serious, but I also hadn't wanted a man to use me like a beard or a place to park his penis while he worked toward being with the woman he loved.

He eventually relented, walking me the hundred yards from the elevator to my car in the empty parking structure.

"This is it!" I sang, expecting for us to say our goodbyes and part ways.

"Let me into the car," he demanded.

"Why?" I asked.

"You'd better let me into this car," he said forcefully. His face changed. Amorous one hundred yards ago, he was now enraged.

"There's nothing to see in it," I said. He didn't reply.

When I unlocked the car doors, Yanis slid in and immediately pulled down his pants.

"What are you doing?" I yelled.

"C'mon. Just give me some head," he cooed.

"No! Get out of my car."

"You know you want it," he replied. He started feeling me up.

A struggle ensued. I was trying to remove myself from the situation, but Yanis, seeing as he couldn't force me to give him head, thought it better to climb on top of me. I screamed and fought him off. He gave up on the plan of penetrative assault.

"I'm not leaving. You'd better do something with this," he said, gesturing toward his erection. So I did. I didn't want to find out if he would make good on the threat in his voice. In the middle of all this, he yelled, "I love having sex with hot chicks!" I wondered if nonconsensual sex was his specific kink.

I felt empty inside.

I texted him the next day.

We had previously made plans to hang out, so I was following up. I suppose I wanted to make sense of this indignity. If we were still going out, what happened was a man's apish uncontrolled groping. Men have to have sex! Nothing more.

His reply to me read, "Sorry, my ex just called. We're planning to work things out. I hope you can understand."

Understand? I couldn't even think.

In my daze, I replied, "Oh wow, yah. Well, best of luck!" I imagined him smirking at this response. I went back to sleep. I slept a lot in the aftermath of the incident in the car in the nighttime.

Within hours I realized that the entire production had been a con, down to him telling me where to park, and being sure to make plans for additional dates well in advance. I was lucky I hadn't agreed to hang out with him and his friends, as he had insisted I do multiple times. That had been an invitation for something much worse. He *and his friends* would have tried to remind me that in their eyes I was The Commons.

When I told my friends what had happened, none of them knew how to react. None of them would say the word. Until my Jewish-Buddhist friend Lin did. Lin did not shy away from reality. Decades before we met, she'd been one of those hard-as-nails 1970s lesbians, active in all the movements for Black, queer, fat, and women's rights.

When I described the night's events, she said softly, but with conviction, "Well, you were raped."

I didn't reply.

I never saw Yanis again. Once I became more resilient in my own mind and body, after years of therapy and mindfulness, I thought to report him to the police. But I can't remember his real name. I've looked through messages on old phones and old Facebook posts. But I haven't been able to find a single remnant of this man anywhere. It seems that ten years ago, after he raped me, I purposefully deleted every trace of him.

■   ■   ■

If the writings of Assata Shakur, and my own testimony, serve as evidence (and they do), the end of the civil rights movement did not signal an end to Black women's susceptibility to rape, to our status as The Commons. But this is not to say that no inroads have been made since the early days of the CRM. For while BIPOC (often insufficiently white) women are routinely more likely than white women to be subjected to sexual violence,[29] such forms of sexual exploitation are not as readily sanctioned as they had been. Nor are they as easy to get away with, owing to a renewed intensity in the fight against women's sexual exploitation that was a main tenet of second-wave feminism.

In the 1970s, a multiracial group of feminists banded together, then flooded the streets. Their message: stop raping us. By 1976, feminists began organizing Take Back the Night marches, guided by their belief that women ought to be able to walk the streets at night without fear of being violated.[30]

Between 1975 and 1993, a series of legislative maneuvers added new legal protections against rape. As of 1975, prosecutors could no longer look into a victim's sexual history in an effort to determine the likelihood that she hadn't, indeed, asked for it. During that same period, all fifty states adopted laws specifying that yes, wives, too, had a right to refuse sex with their husbands—effectively moving the concept of marital rape from myth to crime.[31] That is to say that between the 1970s and the 1990s, America started to take the problem of forcible sex seriously.

My assault occurred in 2011. By that time, white men knew that the days of curt rape of a Black woman before returning to the warm hug of white family life without any aftereffects belonged to a bygone era. It's the reason Yanis bothered to concoct a plan to invisibilize my assault; he'd made it seem like we were going to be dating for a while to hide his predatory intent.

Which is to say that after the movement era, white men could not expect to unceremoniously use Black women as The Commons. The cultural and legal statutes preventing interracial congress having been overturned, Black women now had the right of entry into the romantic economy previously reserved for white women. That is, Black women now had the right to be long-term partners to white men.

This, the threatened removal of Black women as The Commons, was the price of integration for white men. Black women, too, now had to be convinced that they were being courted. This requirement undermined white male sexual prerogatives, and many white men devised to massage the situation through mimicry. White men hoping to get their rocks off with B/IWW found that it worked to go through the motions of persuading these women that they were in the first stages of a relationship, even if one was never on the billing.

This meant that women in America—who regardless of their rating on the whiteness index will be well aware of what is expected, historically, by men who court women—found themselves in faux-courtship situations like those I have weathered countless times. A (white) man will approach an (insufficiently white) woman in a way that appears to be forthright, chivalrous, and invested. The woman may believe a relationship is budding and agree to take the connection to a sexual level. Later, the woman will realize she was never a serious contender for the role of girlfriend and that the man was walking her through a feigned version of courtship in order to get the sexual favors he was actually seeking. Once he got them, he was gone. It was the same play Andreas Capellanus describes in his twelfth-century treatise *The Art of Courtly Love*, when a man tricks a woman who is obviously his social inferior into sex. Today, when a (typically insufficiently white) woman believes she is dating a man, but the "relationship" feels nonreciprocal, she is called a "sidepiece."

Urban dictionary defines a sidepiece, or a side chick, as a mistress. She is the other woman in relation to the girlfriend or wife, who is the so-called main chick in a heterosexual coupling. "Side" and "main" are clever if degrading metaphors for a satisfying meal. For a man can love a nice helping of meat, but sometimes he's going to want to get the side of mac 'n' cheese, since this new dish will add a richness of flavor to the experience. In a similar way, a sidelined woman adds piquancy to the humdrum.

But in my reading, the strict definition of "mistress" does not capture the full suite of possibilities for being sidelined. In reality, many sidepieces have no way of verifying if they are technically a mistress, or if a main chick even exists. And, if you listen to one of the top Black + queer podcasts on iTunes, *The Read*, you will know that many men have several side dishes, all of them hoping to one day be made the main.[32]

In my estimation, a sidepiece is any person (typically a woman) trapped in a nonreciprocal "situationship." A situationship is an unofficial entanglement with someone in which there is no clear path to matriculating to the status of partner.[33] The true litmus test, then, for being a sidepiece is that you are in an emotionally vacant (or sometimes emotionally manipulative) nonrelationship with a person who tries to keep you around to fulfill their sexual and emotional needs, while denying you the same fulfillment. Often, they are holding out for a woman they deem to be a better, more sufficiently white, partner.

The unspoken truth about sidepieces is that they are regularly of lower status than a woman who this same man would choose for a committed partnership. The would-be partner's appearance, class background, and/or other indicators of social status reside below the threshold meriting an actual relationship. To the extent that the factors under consideration are overdetermined by whiteness, we can understand why so many women relegated to the role of sidepiece, those hanging out in situationships, are B/IWW.

Black feminist theorist bell hooks recognized in the 1980s that Black and other insufficiently white women had become quintessential sidepieces. Unflinching as ever, hooks describes what it was like during the '80s and '90s to witness cultured young white men living out their fantasies of sexually and romantically exploiting B/IWW. In her iconic essay "Eating the Other," she recounts her real-life experience as a professor, listening to the white male students create an ethno-sexual hierarchy that included no-strings sex for insufficiently white women:

> While teaching at Yale, I walked one bright spring day in the downtown area of New Haven, which is close to campus and invariably brings one into contact with many of the poor black people who live nearby, and found myself walking behind a group of very blond, very white, jock type boys. . . . Seemingly unaware of my presence, these young men talked about their plans to fuck as many girls from other racial/ ethnic groups as they could "catch" before graduation. They "ran" it down. *Black girls were high on the list*, Native American girls hard to find, Asian girls (all lumped into the same category), deemed easier to entice, were considered "prime targets." Talking about this overheard conversation with my students, I found that it was commonly accepted that one "shopped" for sexual partners in the same way one "shopped" for courses at Yale, and that race and ethnicity was a serious category on which selections were based.[34]

There is nothing in the articulation of desire witnessed by hooks that spoke to these white men's plans to sincerely date or in any other fashion be in relationship with these non-white women. Clearly in the view of these men, B/IWW weren't girlfriend material. They were for the emotionally vacant rutting of a situationship. And, to the extent that any and all women of color around campus were fair game in this sport, the collective pool of B/IWW was being shared by the enterprising white men clamoring to get some.

These observations would later be borne out in the data. Christian Rudder's best-selling 2015 book *Dataclysm: Love, Sex, Race, and Identity—What Our Online Lives Tell Us About Our Offline Selves* delivers crucial insights into the enduring value of sufficient whiteness in white men's partner selections. Rudder, cofounder of the app OkCupid, and his team of researchers investigated the racial preferences of straight folks on three dating apps: Match.com, OkCupid, and DateHookup. The team found that white men gave their best overall rating to white women on Match.com, the site supposedly targeting people looking for meaningful and long-term connections. On this site (see chart 1), they rated white women a whopping 47 percent above average. This was the highest rating white men gave to any group of women on *any* site, suggesting a greater interest in white women when looking for relationships. By contrast, they reserved their lowest esteem for Black women, whom they rated 68 percent *below* average on this same app.[35]

		HER RACE			
	OkCupid	*Asian*	*Black*	*Latina*	*white*
	Asian	+18%	−27%	+2%	+7%
HIS RACE	*Black*	2%	−1%	+3%	−4%
	Latino	+5%	−25%	+13%	+7%
	white	+8%	−24%	+5%	+11%
	Match	*Asian*	*Black*	*Latina*	*white*
	Asian	+50%	−68%	−14%	+31%
HIS RACE	*Black*	+9%	−13%	+8%	−3%
	Latino	+4%	−67%	+33%	+29%
	white	+13%	−68%	+8%	+47%

	DateHookup	HER RACE			
		Asian	*Black*	*Latina*	*white*
HIS RACE	*Asian*	+11%	−24%	+9%	+4%
	Black	+7%	−9%	+9%	−7%
	Latino	+12%	−27%	+ 10%	+6%
	white	+18%	−30%	+6%	+5%

Source: Christian Rudder, *Dataclysm: Love, Sex, Race, and Identity—What Our Online Lives Tell Us About Our Offline Selves* (New York: Crown, 2015).

Celeste Vaughan Curington and her coauthors, in their 2021 text *The Dating Divide: Race and Desire in the Era of Online Dating*, found something similar. Their research into an anonymous dating site with reportedly millions of active users underscored white men's racialized dating and relationship preferences. Their findings showed that straight white men were most likely to make connections with white women. Asian women and Latinas were about 30–35 percent less likely than white women to be contacted by white men. *Black women were approximately 75 percent less likely to be contacted than white women.*[36]

If these data weren't damning enough, consider the current state of marriage. While marriage rates have seen a steep drop in recent decades, interracial marriage has been on the rise. However, it is *least* popular among white persons. A study from the Pew Research Center found that newlyweds of color in 2013 were anywhere from 5 to 54 percentage points more likely to wed a person of a different race than were whites. White men (and women) each married within their own race 93 percent of the time.[37]

These trends place a spotlight on the average cishet white man's intentions when pursuing B/IWW women. They may go out with non-white women, but white women sit comfortably atop their list of preferences for a long-term partnership. White men are least likely to choose Black women for anything that might be called "dating," meaning Black women are rarely in the running for a serious romance with white men.

It's doubtful that anyone involved in making the celebrated episodes of *Friends* in which Union and Tyler were being passed between white men was aware of this problem—that the transfer of these women between (noncommittal) white men was not progress but testament to Black women's status as The Commons. The creators simply used the materials already present in the master's house, in the domain of (white) male logic about relationships, to re-present for us Black women as sidepieces.

Ironically, one of the reasons Tyler's guest appearance on *Friends* two decades ago remains a current topic of conversation is that the show's legacy is at risk of being marred by the growing, vocal choir of people questioning its overwhelming whiteness. Tyler has literally become the franchise's "Black friend," her presence used to combat charges of racial exclusion. And yet even these protestations have had the adverse effect of reifying the white supremacist logic underlying American ideas of romance. They tout their attempts to expand the universe of non-white women who might have given the male leads a taste, but because the series ended long ago, its arc is wholly visible. It is clear from the repetitive story lines for Black women, and their being jostled between characters, that their "romances" with the white male characters were never real.

In a 2020 interview with *The Guardian*, David Schwimmer was asked about the lack of diversity on *Friends*. Schwimmer stated that he'd advocated for more diverse casting throughout the show's ten-season run, but only for one role:

> I was well aware of the lack of diversity and I campaigned for years to have Ross date women of color. . . . One of the first girlfriends I had on the show was an Asian-American woman, and later I dated African American women. That was a very conscious push on my part.[38]

This article, curiously titled "David Schwimmer: 'I'm Very Aware of My Privilege as a Heterosexual White Male,'" was reprinted on multiple news and magazine sites, from *Vulture* to *Essence*, each unquestioningly reporting on his self-characterization as a champion of inclusivity.[39] His statements suggest that it would have been impossible to have actors of color work on the show who were *not* cishet women willing to share intimate affections with his character. His statement also underscores the ethno-sexual dynamics historically at play between cishet white men and women of color. The only role for women of color on *Friends*—as it happened and as it was fantasized by one of its leading men—was one of minor sexual intrigue. They were fleeting distractions that served as little more than an interlude between Ross's first white wife and his second white wife.

White men, while historically responsible for Black women's treatment as The Commons, have not been the only ones to benefit from Black women's degradation. Black men, as noted above, have also engaged in sexual profiteering at Black women's expense. And with Black men, as with white men, when dealing with Black women, there has long been the expectation that the homie should get a taste of it.

CHAPTER 2

THE BLACKER THE BERRY . . . THE LESS LOVEWORTHY

At a glance, nothing could be less harmful and
more entertaining than music, and yet this too
is used as a weapon of cultural domination.

—WALTER RODNEY,
How Europe Underdeveloped Africa, 1972

Broderick Steven Harvey was born in West Virginia in 1957. Having dropped the Broderick, Steve Harvey became known by Black folk for a variety of things, from the comedic to the regrettable. But any Black person who was sentient in 2000 will likely remember one of his most iconic works with reverence: *The Original Kings of Comedy*.

The film was a smash success and an instant Black classic. In it, Harvey offers a poignant observation about rap music: "Rap, man, they done quit singing about love. I'm telling you something: if you don't get into old-school, you done missed it."[1]

The beat drops, and Harvey proceeds to groove to a series of old-skool songs, all of which celebrate love. As a twenty-year-old viewer, I couldn't shake Harvey's assessment of rap music, an entire musical genus in which the songs that see the most commercial success are those that are anti-love—and specifically anti-loving Black women. His indictment of rap is delivered as if it were a fleeting, almost meaningless observation. And yet for me, his comments landed with intense urgency.

For most of the history of Black music, it would have been unthinkable for Black men to degrade Black women so openly and vituperatively as they do in so much late-twentieth- and early-twenty-first-century hip hop. Back in the era of "race music," roughly tracking from the 1920s to the '40s, radio airplay was segregated. Black artists were given a miniscule and regulated sliver of airtime for the immaculate gospel, blues, jazz, and proto-R&B tunes they crafted. The songs were made by Black artists for Black audiences.[2]

At that time, it would have been illogical for Black men or women to displace their ire and angst regarding the quality of their lives as second-class citizens onto one another as a musical strategy. For starters, there was the financial risk attached to alienating approximately half of your listening audience. There was also, of course, the visible reality that Jim Crow and white supremacy were the obvious drivers of their misfortune. There are, indeed, plenty of lamentations in these songs about the hardships of Black life in the Jim Crow South. So, too, is there much whimpering over romantic turmoil. But even as Mamie Smith lays bare the requiem for her scurrilous-cum-absent lover in "Crazy Blues," it was not the general policy during that period to suggest that either Black men *or* Black women as a whole were a problem or unworthy of love.[3]

The 1940s proved a turning point for Black music. With race records (inadvertently) crossing over to white audiences, a growing number of executives—white and Black—thought it prudent to lean into the popularity of Black art forms. After World War II, terms like "race music" and "race records" were abandoned, as industry leaders thought it wise to capitalize on the evident profitability of Black artists.

Rhythm and blues was born in the 1940s and with it a new voice for Black artists. For whereas gospel music preached salvation, and the blues regaled us with its guttural keening, R&B delivered a danceable bop and a catchy hook. It was the kind of music the young folks looking to uplift their spirits might gravitate toward in the postwar era. It inspired the masses to sing along, their limbs keeping time.

This differentiated R&B music from race music. From its earliest days, R&B was expected to cross over to white audiences. It gave people the

chance to jig to the feel of, for instance, a Fats Waller jazz-band composition.[4] Still, a great deal of R&B has been specifically about building,
keeping, losing, or regretting romantic affairs. Artists like Dinah Washington wondered aloud, "Am I Asking Too Much?" in expecting her
partner to love her back.[5] Nat King Cole, meanwhile, declared his lover
"Unforgettable."[6] These and other artists—such as Johnny Otis with his
well-received "Turtle Dove"—crooned what would become iconic tunes
about the ecstasy of love and what it felt like to have it, then lose it.[7]

All of this warbling about love was taking place in the Jim Crow era.
Loving v. Virginia—the Supreme Court ruling that legalized interracial
marriage, effectively decriminalizing cross-racial romance—was not to
be determined until 1967. This means that the messages of love, loss,
and committed partnership that Black folks professed publicly were
addressed to one another.

By the movement era, R&B and its sonic cousin soul music, which
saw its debut in the 1950s, were submerged in the twin narratives of
Black love and the struggle for Black rights.[8] There are too many incredible artists to name them all here. But, if we were to list the quintessential artists of R&B and soul, of Black love and liberation during
the 1960s–70s, we might point first to Marvin Gaye and James Brown.

The list of Marvin Gaye's biggest hits reads like a paean to love and
sex in its many forms. Gaye's musical career shot into the stratosphere
in the mid-1960s after a series of duos with acclaimed singer Tammy Terrell, including "How Sweet It Is to Be Loved by You," "Ain't No Mountain
High Enough," and "You're All I Need to Get By." These hits represent a
fraction of the pair's chart toppers, each devoted to the enduring power
and transformative potential of romantic love.

Gaye's 1971 album *What's Going On* would be his masterwork, expressing as it did so many of the urgent fronts of Black life. "Mercy Mercy
Me," one of his biggest hits, spoke to concerns about overpopulation and
environmental pollution. The title track "What's Going On" took a critical
look at the impact of war and police brutality. The LP served as a fully
formed reproach of the devastation wrought by racism and capitalism.
Gaye was particularly pained by their effects on Black people living in

what was then referred to as the "inner city," as expressed in one of his most revered tracks, "Inner City Blues (Make Me Wanna Holler)."

In his follow-up album, *Let's Get It On* (1973), he leans uninhibitedly into his status as a sex symbol. On this album's title track, he pleads with a woman to "let me love you" with his whole body, such that they might both experience the rapture of lovemaking. The remainder of the songs on this album solidify his status as a lover, with songs like "If I Should Die Tonight" and "Distant Lover." These love themes (sex, romance, and community uplift) were the dominant messages of Gaye's career—revisited on several albums.[9]

Gaye was heralded as the "Prince of Soul," although his music straddled the (invisible) line between soul and R&B. The undisputed "Godfather of Soul," James Brown, however, gave us riffs full of rhythm and funk. James Brown is rarely considered a love-crooner, yet some of his biggest hits were about sexual and intimate relationships. His debut studio album with the Famous Flames, *Please Please Please*, is chock-full of love songs, including the hit title track and "Try Me" which rose to number one on the R&B charts.

Brown's subsequent albums would take up, as Gaye's had, other themes of sex and love predominately among African Americans. His 1969 album *Say It Loud—I'm Black and I'm Proud* engages questions of Black self-love and community advancement. His subsequent album, *Sex Machine*, needs little in the way of introduction or deconstruction, although it is worth noting that here he refers to himself, prophetically perhaps, as "Brother Rapp."[10]

Gaye and Brown are but two of the beloved artists of soul and rhythm and blues who were popular during the movement era. We might also have spoken of Sam Cooke, Billie Holiday, or Nina Simone. Each of these artists lived out the creed that the personal is political. Singing about love, anger, pain, and the nonfungible spirit of Black people, their music was a reflection of their entire being. Their activism and their discographies are inseparable from the beautiful struggle for Black dignity.

And yet, even in these musical denominations thick with emotion and peopled with fabled artists, Brown and Gaye managed to stand out. They were two of the most popular and influential artists of all time. Their bodies of work were to serve as an inspiration for musicians who would populate the genre that was to dominate Black music—and mainstream music writ large—in the decades to come, that being hip-hop.

Marvin Gaye's work has been sampled by countless rap acts. James Brown, Brother Rapp himself, produced the song "Funky Drummer" in 1970. When it arrived, it was met with an absence of critical esteem. It would ultimately be vindicated as one of the most-sampled tracks in rap history.[11]

Within the container of the movement era, Black entertainers had been promoting Black love, community uplift, and solidarity. They rallied 'round the jubilee of Blackness. It was a time capsule of rebuke that set its sights on the nation's erstwhile white mania.

When the new musical genus arrived, it did so in old clothes—several layers of them. Hip-hop exploded first as a novel manifestation of the protest and resistance that still coursed through the streets in the 1970s. The shell top was later to be peeled back, revealing a core of (white) male proclivities. The unveiling was as unremarked as it was unrelenting, and it underscored the difficulties of sustaining a message of Black love in a country that has always been invested in white fetishism. It moreover disclosed the complexity of Black men's relationship with Black women.

The slow and incremental conclusion to Jim Crow that the movements wrought marked a new era for Black men. Finally, they would be able to regain some measure of the manhood that had been squeezed over the preceding four hundred years. For many rap artists, this renaming of Black masculinity was paramount. In the doing, it seemed, Black women had to be put down.

That is to say that the advent of rap was the instigating act to the (further) degradation of Black women, and thereby the (creeping) dissolution of their access to romantic affection. To understand this, it's important to consider the paces of emasculation that Black men have endured since slavery, as well as how the reclamation of Black manhood was figured on white terms.

■   ■   ■

The first blow to Black masculinity came with Black men's arrival on the continent. Disembarking from slave ships, Black men found that they had left behind more than just their homeland. Here, in the so-called New World, they had been stripped of any and all freedoms that ought to attach to a human being. Among these were two qualities that many throughout the world up to that point deemed inherent to manhood: the ability to choose a mate and form a family.

A significant corpus of literature describes how Black families under slavery could exist as family units only insofar as they had white approval. Black men were routinely denied the ability to find their own partners.[12] When they were allowed to do so, there was no guarantee that, should they want to formalize a union, they would be granted that right. Further, even when the master gave his blessing to a union, there would be nothing stopping him from selling one or both partners, or their children off to distant pastures.[13]

Black women's conversion into The Commons was another strike to Black masculinity in the Americas. That is, Black men's inability to protect the women of their ethnic group—another long-vaunted characteristic of masculinity—added a second layer of damnation. There is also, of course, the reality that they may have been sexually assaulted themselves with no means of recourse.[14] Being able neither to cultivate their own relationships, nor to protect themselves or the women in their ethnic group from unwanted sexual advances, Black men under slavery were in the peculiar position of being males denuded of manhood.

Scholars have depicted how this emasculating chain of events deprived them of their male role and, critically, their identity.[15] As a form of the psycho-sexual fallout of slavery, that is important to comprehend in its own right. What is missing is any scholarship that addresses the social effects of slavery on Black men as a group in their ability to relate to Black women as a group.

Collectively, Black men had a handful of common responses to their situation that affected their relationships with Black women. Despite its seeming futility, there were nevertheless those Black men who did their utmost to shield themselves and Black women from harm. Some were even willing to risk their own lives in the effort.[16] Those who were fathers might have leaned into their paternal instincts, working to the best of their ability to protect and care for their children.[17] The information about these valorous Black men, which has only relatively recently made its way into the historical record, has done the critical work of restoring a sense of agency and honor to the Black men in question.

Yet these were not the responses of all Black men. A number of them were determined to capitalize on Black women's sexual exposure as The Commons. Oxford University professor Brenda Stevenson recounts in her 1997 landmark work *Life in Black and White* how some enslaved men made efforts to "gain control of and manipulate Black women's sexuality."[18] More recent work has expanded upon this premise, showing that not only did enslaved men regularly take advantage of their female counterparts but that these men frequently cooperated with white men in the doing. One of these Black men could simply indicate to "massa" that a particular woman was to his liking and inquire about making her his own, despite any objections she may have had. The result, as witnessed by enslaved women, was a collusion between Black men and their white owners to force Black women into sexual submission. It was the enforcement of a certain type of male prerogative over Black women's bodies that transcended race.[19]

It's difficult to comment with any accuracy on the frequency of each of these strategies—protection versus exploitation—on the part of Black men in relationship to Black women during slavery or its aftermath. But we do have more definitive evidence of the regularity of a third ramification of slavery and white dominion on Black male and female interactions. There is abundant evidence that these institutions worked in tandem to generate an aesthetic orientation among African Americans that would have lasting implications for Black-on-Black love. It is called "colorism."

Colorism describes the preference for lighter skin. If you were a slave, light skin might have garnered you a bevy of benefits, from a reduced workload to the less arduous tasks landing in your lap. You might have even had a better chance of getting free if you were light. That is to say, white people often played favorites with the lighter-skinned slaves who were likely to be their progeny.[20]

As psychic colonization goes, light-skinned people gained a certain currency within the slave population as a result of the good turn white folks showed them. This endured post-emancipation. So-called "mulattoes" had enjoyed decades of distinction from darker-skinned slaves, especially those mulattoes who were free. When emancipation came, it leveled these distinctions among Blacks in the eyes of white southerners, who resented the new reality. Light-skinned Black people, too, did not take this lying down, rare as it is for anyone to willingly accept a loss of privileges. Wanting to maintain an air of superiority, light-skinned Blacks, loosely known as "the mulatto elite,"[21] set up their own private institutions; clubs, school, churches, businesses, and whole sections of neighborhoods were exclusively "light."[22]

While this new color line was one of the most vigorous defenses against the dark-skinned, some churches and clubs took the added measure of instituting a "comb test." If a person had nappy or kinky hair that a comb wouldn't glide straight through, they were denied admission into places of light entertainment or access to congregations observing God's universal love of mankind.[23]

And yet the privileges of lightness were not gender neutral. White supremacy shapes norms of beauty, and beauty has long been a more important factor in men's esteem of women than the reverse. So while colorism affects Black men, both light- *and* dark-skinned men have described being rejected on the basis of their skin tone.[24] By contrast, there has been a constant and enduring high valuation of fair-skinned Black women. Light-skinned Black women have enjoyed favor in the Black community (and broader society) for a practically uninterrupted period of time stretching back to slavery.

Consider the bar for entry at the Cotton Club. This infamous Harlem haunt opened its doors near the front end of the Harlem Renaissance, the twentieth century's first fête of Black art and aesthetics. One of the major attractions of the club were the "Copper-Colored Gals," Black women dancers whose skin had to be lighter than a brown paper bag in order

The Copper-Colored Gals, ca. 1920–30s.

to dance on the line.[25] Passing the paper bag test was not a prerequisite for the Black male entertainers who frequented the club.

Evidence of light-skin fetishism was not limited to the field of entertainment. The fetishizing of light-skinned, or "high-yellow," girls meant that light-skinned women had the best romantic prospects with Black men. Consider this paean to light-skinned women—described here as "yaller"—penned by Levi Pollard, a formerly enslaved man from Virginia:

> *Yaller gal fine,*
> *She may be yo'ne, but she oughter be mine,*
> *Lemme git by En see what she mean by de cut er dat eye.*[26]

In the 1920s, an anthropologist by the name of Melville Herskovitz wanted to find out about the prevalence of Black men's preference for lighter-skinned women as romantic partners. Harlem being an epicenter for the celebration of Black culture and achievement during that period, he decided to investigate the color match of successful Black couples in the neighborhood. He found that only about 15 percent of the couples were of nearly the same skin tone. In about 30 percent of the couples, the wives had skin that was darker than their husbands'. However, in the clear majority of couples at 56.5 percent, Black women were noticeably lighter-skinned than their mates.[27]

Taken as a set, these findings reveal how the institution of slavery impacted Black men's orientation toward Black women. Two of the three most prevalent forms of managing its attacks on their manhood involved the adoption of white men's attitudes (e.g., skin color preference) and behaviors (e.g., treating Black women as The Commons). The former served as the precursor to the contemporary moment in which Black women are increasingly thrown off completely by Black men in favor of women who bear no formal relationship to Blackness. Or, said differently, in favor of women whose skin offers better visual confirmation of white sufficiency.

▪   ▪   ▪

By the mid-twentieth century, Black activists, many of them men, started working in earnest to excavate the virulent strain of white preference within Black communities. Many encouraged Black women to reject hot combs and chemical hair straighteners. They searched for brown-skinned models of beauty from within their own spaces, models that were not marked by their proximity to the hegemon.[28]

The 1960s witnessed a "Black Is Beautiful" movement hitting its stride. Within the movement, Black men and women celebrated and attempted to elevate Black looks. Heeding Malcolm X's reminder that "the most disrespected person in America is the Black woman," there was a particular emphasis on restoring an appreciation for Black *women's* looks.[29]

In this spirit, activists held beauty pageants that centered Black aesthetics.[30] The objectives were manifold. Partially, such pro-Black messaging was to show white America that they did not have a monopoly on

Saundra Williams, the first Miss Black America, 1968.

beauty. But for many Black leaders, the more pressing and urgent message was to instill a sense of self-love and self-worth in Black Americans that had been largely deflated by centuries of living under white rule.

The success of these efforts was undeniable. Within the space of a few years, Black people throughout the country embraced Afrocentricity.

Short Afros or "naturals" were in vogue, and thiccness was openly celebrated. Dark skin, wide noses, and thick lips—once subject to ridi-
cule—were symbols of pride and signals of being "down."[31]

This revolutionary aesthetic might have carried the day, but it did
not conquer old habits as they pertained to courtship. Private lives and
partner choices weren't keeping pace with the hullabaloo about Blackness on the streets. At least those were the findings of a study released
in 1984 in the *American Sociological Review*, on the heels of the Black
Is Beautiful movement's dissolution.

The paper's authors investigated the skin tones of a sample of Black
couples who had at least one partner make the list of *Who's Who Among
Black Americans* in 1978. They found that Black men on the list were
more likely than Black women to have light-skinned spouses. Moreover,
the female ancestors (mothers and grandmothers) of the folks on the list
too were more likely to be fair-skinned than their male ancestors, speaking to the intergenerational effects of light-skin privilege, specifically for
Black women searching for Black men as partners.[32]

■   ■   ■

I scoured the depths of my memory searching for a story, some evidence,
of colorism in my dating life. There was no story to tell. This is not because colorism has had no impact on me but because of the opposite.
It has been so common for Black men to overlook me, forming a line
instead behind lighter-skinned women, that I have only dated a couple
of Black men.

I have only one story related to intra-Black dating aesthetics: When
I was in graduate school, I linked up with a Black man I met on an app.
He was about five years younger than I was, and he was in the military.
I was surprised by the entire proceedings—here was a Black man who
was checking for me, and we seemed to be enjoying our time together.

We were in San Diego, on the beach. He made some comment about
us running carelessly into the sea together—something real corny like
that. I gestured toward my head.

"What?" he said. He seemed confused.

"My hair," I said. Now *I* was confused, because surely he knew that a Black woman's hair plus water equals not the hairstyle she had a minute ago. I mean, no less than the figure of Beyoncé in *Austin Powers: Goldmember* revealed this to the entirety of America within his lifetime. He rolled his eyes in disgust. That was our first and last date.

These are tangible aspects of Black life. They are rarely discussed in front of non-Black persons. But they have been well known among Black women for more than a century.

▪   ▪   ▪

Mullins and Sites published their research in the early post-movement era, a period marked in Black circles by the ongoing thrust of colorism among Black men. It was also marked by a critical innovation in Black culture and history. It was the moment at which rap music was just starting to make its mark.

The period from ~1980 to 1995 came to be known as the golden age of hip-hop. The music itself had come into being as a direct result of the movement era. As chronicled in the film *Rubble Kings*, hip-hop was born at the intersection of Black and Brown resistance and creativity in the late 1970s.[33] Birthed in the choked housing developments of the Bronx, where poverty and police brutality were endemic, Black and Brown youths started hosting DJ parties and dance-offs to settle rivalries over who owned what "set" (or hood). The contest tested who was the best at scratching, mixing, and b-boying. It was only later that hip-hop beefs became largely about MC (i.e., rap) battles.

If battles were native to rap, so, too, was a certain Afrocentricity. A disproportionate number of MCs were Black men—whereas Latinos were more active as b-boys. These golden-age rappers regularly affected a conscious vibe.

The whole attitude was pro-Black. It was not uncommon to see rappers during the era sport dashikis and nappy locs. Africa medallions and references to the tenets of Black liberation abounded.

The first rap record to see any real commercial success, Sugar Hill Gang's 1980 bump "Rapper's Delight," is a testament to as much. The

De La Soul, one of the premier rap groups during The Golden Age, repping their characteristic Afrocentricity.

song is an extended lamentation of the state of affairs in the ghetto. The video has the aesthetic appeal of a documentary. The lyrics are populated with references to state-sanctioned violence, low-income housing, failing schools, and the explosion of cocaine and crack in their communities. It was a stance toward radical Black politics that picked up the strain put down by folks like Marvin Gaye only a decade prior. Now, sweeping melodies and crooning vocals were replaced by the hard-hitting staccato of the immiseration that the movement hadn't cured.

Being a genre dominated by men, and straight Black men in particular, there was a lot of talk about "girls." The only girls judged worthy of mentioning were typically "fly" girls, young Black women deemed beautiful by dint of their swag and general hood stylings. They were women just like the ones LL Cool J paid homage to in his first *Billboard* top-ten single, "Around the Way Girl."

But the talk about girls is where the Afrocentricity of the artists was to meet with their internal colonization. During the Golden Age, a new subspecies of the genre arose: "gangsta rap." To be clear, "gangsta rap," or sometimes "gangster rap," is a term popularized by journalist Robert Hilburn in 1989 in a story about N.W.A for the *Los Angeles Times*.[34] It was not a label generated by, or for much of its tenure used by, rap artists themselves.

Still, with the mainstream success of N.W.A in the late '80s, there was a new ghetto rawness that spoke about gangsterism in a way that was political in its own right. It was a politics that did not abide by the terms of what was increasingly seen as the assimilationist/integrationist rhetoric of the Black middle class.

Which is to say these artists did not expect to achieve success through protests, inclusion, or integration. Most didn't use their music to talk about the high stakes of fighting for Black love, life, and liberation like many of the hip-hop originators.[35] A slew of gangsta rap artists kept a nearly single-minded focus on amassing wealth, status, and, of course, sexual conquests.[36] Compared to other types of Black music, one of the main things missing from gangsta rap songs is the conventional orientation toward love and romantic partnerships. In its place is a celebration of the Black woman as The Commons.

N.W.A's 1988 song "Gangsta Gangsta," from their paradigm-shifting album *Straight Outta Compton*, gives us the new rap formula: "Life ain't nothing but bitches and money," raps Ice Cube on the iconic track. The rest of the song is consumed with other familiar aspects of ghetto living: smoking, drinking, and running from the police—all important elements of post-industrial hood life. Like many N.W.A songs, this one tells a story about life in their racially segregated environment. The "bitches" in question—the ones they roll the streets searching for, the ones "with the big butts," the ones "in the biker shorts" who appeared to be dead ringers for the "Around the Way Girl" LL was to praise in his 1990 chart-topper only two years later—are Black women. Per the song lyrics, finding, accosting, and "fucking" these women are top priorities. From Cube's verse, we find that they are first on the list of things life is about.

N.W.A were pioneers of this attitude. This view of Black women was alive in their bodies, needing no external white input. And yet, with rap music taking off in the mainstream among a growing number of white people, and especially young white men, the music industry saw an opportunity to capitalize anew on what might have once been called "race music."

Of course, the white dollar rarely arrives in Black hands with no strings attached.

As artfully portrayed in Dr. Dre's 1993 "Dre Day" video, white music executives had an investment in steering the talent in the most lucrative direction for the industry. Controversy might be good for sales, but not all content was going to be equally profitable. Record executives were thirsty for rap acts that would sell big. Sexism in the music industry sells.[37]

With rap, beyond simple discussions about sex, defining (Black) women as places for men to get off, before they take off, sold big. These songs sold especially well among young white males. The gangsta attitude went gangbusters in part because it reminded both white and Black men that Black women were The Commons. It evinced a certain thug white supremacy. A curious marriage to be sure, but also one that helped gangsta rap reach new heights on the record charts and in profits.

So it was that right at the moment when rap music was reaching its apex, an increasing number of mainstream rap songs neglected to concern themselves with the politics that had birthed the genre. Rather than concerning themselves with Black love and community uplift, a growing number of artists were out for "bitches and money," which besides being an Ice Cube bar was also the name of a popular 1991 song by Master P.[38]

The rhymes of Notorious B.I.G. (often simply called "Big"), my favorite rapper growing up, are also illustrative. Big's lyrical poesis, as he details each element of the planning, execution, and aftermath of his hustles on the album *Life After Death*, is a master class in off-the-beaten-path bootstrapping. In his verse on the mid-'90s smash "Notorious Thugs," for instance, he sets a new standard of success for hood niggas. He shades the type that aspires to inclusion in high-class white spaces, the middle-class Black strivers "[u]p in restaurants with mandolins and violins." Real niggas like him don't make such efforts to ingratiate themselves: "We just sittin here tryna win . . . steadily counting them Benjamins." The path to success for Big involves remaining a true hustla, a street nigga who makes money rapping and selling drugs, and who protects his own through an unapologetic willingness to pull a gun when the situation calls for it.

And for Big, like many others affecting this gangsta attitude, the role of Black women in his life amounts to scattered instances of rutting ("Fucked a few female stars or two").[39] Big even advises listeners *not* to fall in love with a (Black) woman, cautioning (Black) men not to be the simps who fall into that trap. According to Big, many Black women are checking more for money and status than love: "Know the bitch 'fore you caught yourself loving it, Nigga with a Benz fuckin' it." (We'll take up the question of what many people believe to be Black women's romantic intentions in the next chapter.) For Biggie and others in the genre, there's no room for the (integrationist) expectations of success through good jobs and romantic love with a woman poised to be a domestic goddess. Instead, success comes through stacking cash, toting guns, getting high, and fucking Black women, pejoratively described throughout his discography as "bitches."

Of course, no one stands as a bigger figure against loving Black women than Snoop Dogg. Introduced to the world as a friend of Dr. Dre—who was by then already a rap icon, owing to his status as a member of the rebel group N.W.A—audiences got a first taste of Snoop's style in 1992. That year, he was featured on the single "Deep Cover," recorded for the soundtrack to the Lawrence Fishburne film of the same name. A year later, Snoop's debut album *Doggystyle* hit airwaves to much fanfare and critical acclaim. The album clinched the number-one spot on the *Billboard* 200 before going on to claim quadruple platinum status.

Two of the most memorable songs on the album generated chants that were to help swaths of young people appreciate Snoop and his friends' positions on sex and love with the Black women around his way. In the first, "Gin and Juice," one of my favorite songs as a young person, he tells listeners that after he cums, he gets going. He tells any woman he leaves in his wake not to get upset, because, well, she should have known Snoop "don't love you hoes." Later on in the track, this statement is reformulated to the unforgettable mantra *"we* don't love them hoes" (emphasis mine), a move that invites the listener to agree with his "toot it and boot it"[40] strategy for handling the women in his neighborhood.

When I first heard the song, the refrain redounded through my marrow with unease. But that didn't prevent me from blasting the song day and night. Surely *I* wasn't one of the hoes in question. I heard the same avowal from every Black woman within earshot. *Snoop doesn't mean all women. Just those ghetto women he knows. These songs aren't about us.* "Us" being polite Black women who may not have started out with much but who were nevertheless upwardly mobile. There was a ball of twine forming at the edge of my consciousness. I followed the lead of my elders and leaned into the naiveté. I lowered my eyelids, nodding off to the beat.

The second legendary chant generated by *Doggystyle* arrived courtesy of the track "Ain't No Fun." This song, featuring Nate Dogg and Warren G, advises men not to trust (Black) women, not to love them, but definitely to go on and fuck them. But whereas "Gin and Juice" observes a solo rendition of knocking boots, "Ain't No Fun" tells the listener that sex with an (implied) Black woman is better when the homies can partake of this same woman: "It ain't no fun if the homies can't have none."[41] It is the clarion call for a gang-bang. A reminder of Black women's legacy as communal male property. Sex with a (Black) woman is most enjoyable, the song announces, when several Black men can have collective access to her body.

■   ■   ■

During recess one day in 1987, me and my best friend Shanae pledged our allegiance.

"I'm going to Harvard," she stated.

"OK," I said. "I'm going to Berkeley."

As playtime activities go, this one had to be unusual. Still, at the age of seven, having been in gifted classes for years by that point, we were two proud Blerds with our whole lives ahead of us. Lest they pass us by unawares, we figured we'd better start planning for the future without delay. We passed the kickball between us, discussing the merits of each school and what drew us to make our respective choices.

Ten years later, on a sunny afternoon in 1997, my mother went out to get the mail and came back with an envelope for me.

"It's from Berkeley," she said.

"It's a large envelope," I said. We both knew what that meant. In the predigital age, when admissions were revealed by the post, everyone prayed to get the legal size. A letter-sized envelope was bad news. They'd deliver your rejection neatly, on a single page.

I opened the envelope and read the contents aloud: "Congratulations! You have been accepted to UC Berkeley."

My mother, who at the time was thirty-five years old, squealed with glee as we jumped for joy.

I blinked. My parents were dropping me off for Black Admit Weekend. It was organized by senior Black undergraduates. I would stay with the host of the program, an affable brown-skinned girl with a mop of curly black hair. I remember thinking how beautiful and poised she seemed alongside my abject terror at the thought of being away from home.

That first day, the older students organized an event for us. It was part meet-and-greet, part rap session. About fifteen of us occupied the student lounge. They separated us into two groups, girls and boys, for a structured conversation. There were about twice as many girls as boys. The girls' group was to go first. We sat in the center of the room, fishbowl style.

One of the seniors tossed out the question, "What happened to love in the Black community?"

I don't remember much outside of our timidity. *How were we to respond to such a question?* Mostly, we just sat with it awkwardly. We didn't make much headway on this, or any topic.

It was the boys' turn in the hot seat. They sat in the center of the room, slouching and uncomfortable.

Then, someone said loudly, "I wanna know why a bitch always gets mad when you try to pass her to the homie?"

Uproarious laughter from the boys. Oh, they found it! Many abandoned their slouched positions and sat with a more upright and dignified bearing. Their loud attestations about the merits of needling one's way into a gang-bang filled the room.

The ideas from the music, from the culture, that were supposed to be about those *other* Black women, the ones who I was told were *deserving* of such a label, were being thrust into our faces. Us! The good, smart, clean girls. There was no denying anymore that any one of us young women in that room could have been a part of the group of "bitches" to whom these good, smart Black boys were referring.

I was one of a handful of girls trying to signal to the seniors that we thought this was inappropriate. None of us believed that seventeen-year-old boys were having rampant group sex with scores of Black girls. But that was their aspiration for "relationships" with us.

They had steered the conversation to this place as a way of rejiggering the terms by which Black boys would have conversations about Black girls. *Love? Who cares? But can me and my friends hit it though?* They were staking their claim to a fully American form of masculinity.

The seniors, including my host, let the boys talk. They said this was "real." They implied that these young men had a right to air their grievances about Black girls who don't agree to—or, more accurately, do not *consent to*—group sex.

This part of the program was followed, weirdly, by introductions. I and most of the other girls were shell-shocked. We fell mute after the boys' little confab. Still, we were required to introduce ourselves to the whole group, saying our names and describing ourselves using one word that begins with the same letter as our first names. A small game, a bit of light entertainment to get to know one another as individuals right after the boys had reminded us that we were The Commons.

When it was my turn, I stood up and said,

"My name is Sabrina. And I am . . . SOMEBODY." This got laughs from the right people—including my host, who was like, *She's with me! That's my mentee!,* and a football player who had arrived already popular and was there compounding his notoriety. It blanketed me in a whiff of fame that lasted for the remainder of the event.

What I'd said was taken from a speech by Jesse Jackson about respect for Black personhood. I said it as part joke, part protest. I and the other seventeen-year-old Black girls present were human beings worthy of respect. Some folks needed reminding.

I left that weekend and told my parents I didn't want to go to Berkeley. If *that* was the kind of Black experience *Cal* was offering, they could keep it. My parents, who had no formal education past high school—my mother having been pregnant with me at her graduation—were, all the same, two smart young adults who understood the currency of a school like Berkeley. They rallied all their forces for weeks. I had conversations with relatives they knew I trusted and their successful friends who had gone to college. They all said the same thing: Those kids are not the only ones you'll meet there. Don't let people who you won't spend time with anyway ruin this for you. So I didn't.

■   ■   ■

That Black women should be thingified, that we should be for "fucking," preferably collectively, instead of for loving, was only part of the appeal of hip-hop for young Black (and white) men beginning in the late '80s. The other issue was one of tone. That being skin tone. The movement era insisted that dark skin be acclaimed as a counter to whitewashed beauty standards, and the same dark hue formed the basis of Heavy D's 1994 classic "Black Coffee" from his *Nuttin' but Love* album. But over the years a creeping preference for light-skinned women emerged and it soon came to dominate the genre. It was undeniable by the mid-00s.

The colorist mien of rappers has been noted by fans and journalists alike.[42] That Kendrick Lamar was clapped on the back for choosing a dark-skinned lead for the video for "Poetic Justice" gives further insight into the problem: its rarity. Far more commonly, light-skinned Black women—and increasingly non-Black fair-skinned women—are represented as dimes, worthy of pursuit. Consider A$AP Rocky's position that "light skin is the right skin" or Young Jeezy's brag that he was just "[t]op floor chilling with some light-skin girlies" on his track "Do It for You."[43] Or how about Lil' Wayne's verse "Eat a red bone like red velvet cake" on the "Cyeah Remix"?[44] Kodak Black, a dark-skinned man known for sporting gangsta grills and nappy knots, declared that dark-skinned women are "too gutter" for his taste—a view shared by many white men since the founding of this nation.[45]

The spoken word is not the only evidence of this predilection. The stunning visual array of rap video vixens leaves nothing short of an archive of light-skinned dancing beauties, glorying in what long constituted sufficient whiteness for many Black men. It's an orientation to skin color that would give the Cotton Club a run for its money.

Consider the visual montage in Drake's "Hotline Bling." The video opens on a racially ambiguous woman with fair skin and long, straight hair. She is in a deep bend, a Pavlovian cue for sex, doggy style. She walks over to a set of cubicles peopled with an assembly of light-skinned lovelies, all with long hair—most of it straight. This scene sets the, well, tone for the type of woman Drake moons about. The type who used to hit him on his celly but now seems preoccupied with things other than Drake's feelings. To be sure, there is one thicc brown-skinned woman he romances in the nearly five-minute song. But the majority of the girlies he croons to and about are light.

Rapper J. Cole reflected on the problem of colorism in hip-hop: "I can't say it for sure but I just think we're still in America. We're still Black Americans. Those mental chains are still in us. That brainwashing that tells us that light skin is better, it's subconsciously in us, whether we know it or not . . . still pursuing light skin women."[46]

Cole here is more thoughtful than most rappers. And still, he's only addressing one-third of the problem. The fetishization of light-skinned

women has to be discussed alongside the frequent hymns reminding
Black men to fuck Black women—preferably collectively—and to avoid
loving us or committing to us in any fashion. They are a set of priorities originally set by white men but soon imitated by Black men under
slavery. They made their way into the DNA of hip-hop, deposited as
they had been in the bodies of the men who would act as its MCs. But
whitewashed dispositions in the lineage would show up in ways beyond
the learned habits of Black masculinity. Almost since rap's inception
another concern about Black women was being stated and restated as
a warning to Black men: they are gold digging. Funnily enough, it was
white women who started that ball rolling.

CHAPTER 3

BLACK WOMEN
ARE NOT TO BE TRUSTED

Gold Diggery

In 2018, *Refinery29* released a YouTube explainer on the mythology of the gold digger. In it, host Eliza Kreisinger sits down with social media influencer and author Sesali Bowen to unpack an undeniable, if underdiscussed, feature of the women most commonly maligned as gold diggers: They are Black.

Titled, "Debunking the Black Women Gold Digger Myth," the explainer names Kanye West's 2005 single "Gold Digger" as a critical referent. Yet Bowen points to other cultural productions, specifically the TV series *Love and Hip-Hop* as among the more recent vociferous sources of the tarnishing. There's often, the two women concur, a conversation about a Black woman's intentions with a man that implies they are inevitably nefarious. Says Bowen, when people see a Black woman in a relationship with a man of any standing, there's usually one niggling question: "What is it that she is trying to get from him?"[1]

Bowen's analysis here opens up new questions. Namely, how is it that men, and, in the case of hip-hop, largely Black men, have grown so suspicious of Black women's "intentions" within relationships? How

47

is it that Black women became the flag bearers of gold diggery? And perhaps more to the point, how is it that men feel justified questioning whether Black women's ambitions are crudely pecuniary in a genre of entertainment wherein men regularly equate the pursuit of money and sex with the pursuit of happiness?

Curiously, the gold digger archetype was once nearly exclusively applied to white women. It was foisted on Black women only in the post-movement era, amplifying the modish view of Black women as fiduciary leeches. Among the budding coterie of wealthy Black men, few challenged this stereotype, electing instead to build on it. Effectively sharpening the blade of their masculinity against the skein of Black womanhood, a rising number of Black men publicly questioned if Black women were not, in fact, rapacious in their desire for unearned sexual benefits. And these men used hip-hop as a vehicle to voice their wariness.

■   ■   ■

It's rare that Black people induct a term into the Black patois that was invented by white people. Even rarer is said adoption after a neologism has spent decades being tossed around in white spaces. And yet that's precisely how the term "gold digger" made its way into the Black vernacular.

The first recorded use of the term dates back to the 1910s. According to Virginia Brooks, an activist and friend of Ida B. Wells, it was a term she'd heard spilling out of the wild and rowdy Chicago dance hall scene of the early decades of the century. Brooks herself, it bears mentioning, was white. While she regularly crossed the rigid color line to support African American enfranchisement, the term "gold digger" was most familiar to—and appears to have originated with—white women.[2]

Additional evidence pointing to white women as the term's originators comes from American playwright Avery Hopwood. Hopwood was chatting with a female friend named Kay Laurell, a dancer who commanded a coveted spot with the Ziegfeld Follies performers. As one of Laurell's friends walked by, she greeted her by saying, "Hello, gold digger." Bemused, Hopwood inquired about this term. Laurell replied,

> That's what we call ourselves! . . . You men capitalize on your brains, or your business ability, or your legal minds—or whatever other darned thing you happen to have! So why shouldn't we girls capitalize [on] what nature has given us—our good looks and ability to please and entertain men? You men don't give something for nothing—why should we?[3]

Implied in Laurell's explanation is the differential ability of (white) men and women to make monetary gains in America. In the 1910s, there were limited options for women of any race to secure their economic futures outside of getting married. This was in contrast to the position of (white) men, who could apply themselves in any industry in which they could gain entrée as a result of their social networks, tradesman's skills, business acumen, or intellectual savvy.

In 1910, only about 23 percent of women over the age of ten—an age by which we would certainly not mark womanhood today but was used for these early statistics—worked outside of the home.[4] The barriers to employment were numerous, the largest of which was that women were deemed to lack the willingness and aptitude to enter the workforce. As a result, when women did take work, they aggregated in a limited few professions, mainly domestic service, teaching, and nursing.[5]

The jobs in the caring professions paid less than the jobs men did and were generally thought to be viable for the short run. Women's limited job opportunities were attended by the prejudicial notion that the most important job for a woman was that of wife and mother. Therefore, it was not uncommon that women with the means, those of a certain class standing—all of whom would have been white—were never expected to work outside the home. Other (mostly white) women were only expected to work until they were able to marry and have babies.[6]

What Laurell was speaking to, then, was the reality of a life hemmed in by domesticity. There is no evidence that gold digging was a widespread tactic employed by white women looking for a petty come up.

The offhand way in which Laurell describes this little game—mixed with Hopwood's obliviousness to it—delivers the impression that this was a small-time con orchestrated by a few cunning ladies. Laurell surely could not have imagined the tremendous generative capacity of such a revelation in the hands of the white men of the time.

It just so happens that the early twentieth century saw a revolution in the way Americans—and especially white Americans—found partners. For decades, courtship had been the primary way that men found mates. Under the rules of courtship, a man would initiate a series of outings with a lady of his choosing in the hopes that such interactions would lead to marriage. Sometimes in this form of courtship, known as "calling courtship," he would begin by first asking the permission of his intended's family to take a woman out. With familial approval, the couple would be granted time alone or with a chaperone. In other iterations, the young couple's parents might arrange a string of meetings for them as a mechanism of judging their compatibility, constituting a more commonly recognized form of courtship.[7]

Calling courtship started to lose its hold over American youth when more of them abandoned their rural homesteads for the pulse of city life in the early decades of the twentieth century. Without parents around to keep a watchful eye, young people frolicked in the streets as they saw fit. They went to movies and shows or simply had dinner with friends. It was a much more informal, and in many respects more intimate, way for a young couple to get to know one another. This was the genesis of "dating" as we have come to know the term. It gave young women and men more say in who they might choose to marry. In the doing, it also removed the controls put in place to prevent various dangers. For women, foregoing chaperones and parental approval, going out and finding a mate now carried with it a greater risk of sexual exploitation.

It's not immediately clear if sexual assault became more common due to the diminished societal controls on men's and women's sexuality, or if the laws were finally adjusting to things long known. But we do know that between the late nineteenth and the early twentieth centuries, rape prosecutions shot up. During the same time frame, laws against statutory rape—historically defined as sex between an adult male and an underage girl—emerged in states across the US.[8] Public concern about the sexual exploitation of (white) women and girls reached new heights.

It wasn't just white women seeking partners who had new freedoms and liabilities to contend with at the turn of the century. The discovery of self-described gold-digging white women on the dating circuit left white men, too, feeling as if they had something to fear. *What about the damage this "dating" thing was doing to a man's finances?* If dating was the order of the day, and if there were no laws preventing a woman from dating around casually without any plans for sexual affection or a marriage contract, well then, some men argued, they'd better start creating their own game plan.

The practice of dating itself arrived coterminous to a new wariness among white men and women. Women became more vocal about rape. White men, too, had concerns; they now feared the kind of women who might be trying to use *them* for their own wicked purposes.

There was another concern about gold diggers that men rarely put into words. The women who were best positioned to exploit the new dating structure were the attractive ones. That is, gold diggers were likely to exist in the same strata of women who men were supposed to be pursuing.

Kay Laurell made this plain when she effectively introduced the male sex to the gold digger's creed: girls ought to be able to "capitalize" on their good looks. That the women trying to get one over on men this way would be the good-looking helps us better digest the power of the specter of the gold digger.

Beauty was (and still is) regulated by the terms set forth in race science: tall, straight hair, fair skin, slender build. The (insufficiently white) women who were unappealing by this standard were low on the scale of those considered desirable for partnerships. If they also happened to be Black women (a.k.a. The Commons), they were poised to endure more appeals for screwing than dating or marriage in any case, so there was little fear of gold-mining Black women then.

The gold diggers American men feared most were bewitching white women, the kind of woman a (white) man wanted perched on his arm for the long term as a statement to other men about *his* status. This is the reason the recognition of the existence of this breed of woman bred terror in the hearts of (white) men. Gold diggers were upsetting gender and racial hierarchies by trying to use men's objectification of them for personal gain.[9]

The timing couldn't have been worse for white men. It wasn't just relationships that were being upended with the advent of dating and gold digging. Other strongholds of masculinity were also being rattled. After 1910, women started gaining ground in the workforce.[10] By 1919 (white) women would even get the vote. That same year, with the United States in WWI, more women than ever before decided to enlist.

Women were making inroads into spaces that had once been the nearly exclusive purview of men. Now, gold diggers were violating the tacit terms of the romantic agreement too. Women were supposed to look good to lure partners, then be responsible for maintaining hearth and home. Men were supposed to be providers, working outside the home to amass the financial means that would allow their families to live comfortably. Each had to pretend they were only coming together for "love." Gold diggers' bald manipulation of this equation, in the eyes of many, posed a threat not only to white manhood but to the white American family and its attending social structures.

Understanding gold diggers as yet one more hit to masculinity at a vulnerable point in history can help explain how the mere idea of an entire class of women who might behave in such a way immediately captured the popular imagination. Inspired by his conversation with Laurell, Hopwood promptly set to writing a script about these crafty creatures. In 1919, he released the play *Gold Diggers*. It was a roaring success. In 1929, it was adapted into a film with the same name, starring the iconic Tallulah Bankhead.

The 1930s saw a spate of movies featuring gold digger characters, each production more popular than the last. Arguably the most famous cautionary tale about these purportedly unscrupulous (white) women is the Warner Bros' film *The Gold Diggers of 1933*, starring Ginger Rogers. This film gave us the enduring cultural ditty "We're in the Money," sung by Rogers.[11] It was also one of the highest-grossing films that year.[12]

For nearly two decades, America witnessed a stampede of visual spectacles featuring gold diggers. The productions made it plain that these

An image from Gold Diggers of 1933, *showing nearly nude pretty white gals covering themselves with silver coins. An inescapable reminder of the common exchange of white women's looks for white men's cash.*

women were beautiful but of a class below their social aspirations. They hoped to make their looks work for them by attracting moneyed men.

The women who ignited this trend may have left conversations about marriage on the table. But the public was gripped by a gnawing panic that gold diggers weren't just dating for fun and gifts but committing in the name of money. Not the least reason for which was all of the pageantry suggesting this was so. But there was a second reason: new alimony laws.

Marriage had long been deemed "a permanent economic and procreative institution . . . grounded in larger networks of kin."[13] With dating, its economic aspects were supposedly receding. In reality, however, they were obscured by men obsessed with finding women with elite white looks, and women seeking men with good jobs. These were the unstated socioeconomic benefits for each gender. So, the final straw in what many saw as men's sliding grip on the benefits of partnering was the flowering of divorce in the early decades of the twentieth century. More women than ever were dissatisfied with their marriage partners—presumably found through the spreading practice of dating. Divorce claims doubled between 1910 and 1920. The number of women seeking alimony from these upended unions also soared.[14]

Then, in the early '20s, an actual Ziegfeld Follies star, Peggy Joyce, sought alimony from her third millionaire husband. This news lit a fuse inside an already explosive situation. Joyce was considered a knockout of the highest order. Ziegfeld himself was known to engage a certain type of "eugenic thinking" when it came to his girls, preferring women with "straight noses . . . blond hair, and creamy white skin."[15] However, Joyce's divorce from yet another rich man made national headlines. There was a stench of outrage, as Americans could now put a perfectly molded face to the gold digger archetype. Peggy's divorce proceedings were so spectacular they garnered her a mention in one of the most legendary films about gold diggers in US history: *Gentlemen Prefer Blondes*.[16]

The iconography of the peak white woman as gold digger arguably reached its zenith with this 1953 vehicle for the leggy, buxom Marilyn Monroe. The movie teams her up with her brunette equivalent, Jane Russell, in a tale about the trials of beautiful women and the rich men who love them. In it, Monroe, plays the loveable gold digger and Russell her more straight-shooting counterpart, as together they navigate the manipulative games of rich and attractive men.

The two make a charming pair, both honest in their intentions. When questioned about her pursuit of lavish gifts, Monroe delivers the classic line "Don't you know that a man being rich is like a girl being pretty? You wouldn't marry a girl just because she's pretty, but my goodness, doesn't it help?"[17] She admits she goes hard for the cash, and in the doing, she forces her intended's father to admit to the well-known political economy of the sexes: men need to have money; women should look white-hot.

At the time, the movie was the most humane treatment of self-styled gold diggers yet. But shifts in racial and gendered politics in 1960s and '70s America would ensure that this would not be the final word on the

*The stunning and lavishly adorned couplet of Marilyn Monroe
and Jane Russell in* Gentlemen Prefer Blondes.

supposed threat posed by women who were thought to be profiting
unfairly from men's earnings. As the movement era waned, America was
to be rocked by a new understanding of the kinds of women who were
supposedly looking to get something for nothing. These women were
of an altogether different hue.

‡   ‡   ‡

In Black communities throughout America, the period of the late '60s and into the '70s marked a peculiar period of expansion and contraction that would play its part in establishing new ideas about Black womanhood. For starters, some of the most prominent male figures of the movement era—John F. Kennedy, Malcolm, MLK, and, later, Fred Hampton—had been murdered. Their killings generated despair and confusion among those who remained in the struggle regarding where to go from there.

The confusion owed in part to the divergent approaches of those who had been steering the vessel. The orientations of these men (and many other movement leaders) to the so-called Negro Question,[18] were distinct one from the other. While some had sought integration, others were in favor of a more separatist approach, such as that pioneered by Marcus Garvey.

Malcolm had wanted Black people to have their own spaces, their own businesses. He had advocated for the right of Black people to develop their own identities and communities free from white overseers.[19] Fred Hampton, too, had leaned into the question of Black self-determination. A Marxist-Leninist, Hampton believed that capitalism was the font of Black immiseration. To achieve liberation, he said, Black people had to reject integration into capitalist society and instead work to transform this society into something more egalitarian.[20] Which is to say that both Malcolm and Fred were critical of the possibility of a desultory "integration" of Black people into white hetero-capitalist society.

JFK and MLK had thought differently. JFK was not widely considered by those in the movement to be a "leader" so much as an occasional sympathizer. Nevertheless, describing civil rights as both a constitutional and a moral issue, he drafted the Civil Rights Act of 1963, which was supposed to end segregation in public schools and facilities. It was also supposed to guarantee all adult Americans the right to vote—a particularly glaring omission of the US Constitution.[21]

MLK is of course best known for advocating an end to the color line. In 1963, at the March on Washington for Jobs and Freedom, he delivers his paradigmatic speech about the stumbling block of skin color in America. If, by the time of his death in 1968, he had pivoted toward a greater concern about war and poverty, his most bandied goals were still the end of segregation and racial discrimination.

With each of these pillars of the CRM resting in the hereafter come the late 1960s, lesser-known figures attempted to rise to the challenge of local and national leadership. The uncertainty about what was next offered the perfect opportunity for politicians from both parties to step into the void. Perhaps it goes without saying that neither party was particularly interested in the aims of Malcolm X or Fred Hampton. Malcolm for one had articulated the specific ways white liberal Democrats—naming JFK among others—leaned into the integrationist aims of King and the like, as a means of undercutting the revolutionary ambitions of the era's more radical Black figures.[22]

Lyndon Johnson—succeeding JFK to the presidency in the wake of his murder—continued his predecessor's efforts, when it was not a foregone conclusion that he would do so. For the first twenty years of LBJ's time in Congress he opposed every civil rights bill anyone put up for a vote.[23] But, by 1957, he'd begun to align himself with several of the movement's causes.

Seven years later, following conversations with MLK and other civil rights leaders, Johnson, declared a "War on Poverty," an idea in line with his Great Society program. Central to its aims was the expansion of social welfare programs, including Head Start for children and supplementary aid to poor families.[24] Between this program and his push for civil rights—by some accounts Johnson "saved" the Civil Rights Act by getting it signed into law in 1964—and his efforts to get the passage of the Voting Rights Act in 1965, LBJ is remembered by many as an essential figure in the gains made during the movement era.[25]

And so it was that the diverse goals of a movement to liberate African Americans from racist rule was boiled down, in the eyes of many and especially white liberals, to a few legislative maneuvers. When describing the gains of the civil rights movement, these two legal actions feature prominently in the historical record. They continue to be celebrated as landmark achievements, despite the fact that one was never fully realized, and the other has been repeatedly subverted.[26]

The same folks who champion LBJ's achievements here might fail to notice that the man who declared a War on Poverty, the man responsible for getting civil rights laws passed, had also signed the Law Enforcement Assistance Act of 1965. This act would, in his own words, begin "a thorough, intelligent, and effective war against crime"[27]—what we now know as the War on Crime. Advocating for these two types of legislation was Johnson's calculated attempt to uphold and uplift the ideas of prominent integrationist civil rights leaders, while also punishing the insurrectionary acts of the Black masses protesting in the streets. These three acts—expanding civil rights, voting rights, and the power of law enforcement—were passed in the span of about eighteen months, and meant that the time of the greatest political achievements for African Americans also carried the seedlings for what might be reasonably called the Great Destruction of Black communities in the decades to follow.

As LBJ made his plays, conservative politicians responded to a movement that never achieved widespread support among white Americans.[28] So it happened that white Americans grew more vocal with their dissent. They lifted their voices to the tune of drawbacks set to undermine the legislation so prominently heralded and so recently passed. They found a friend in Congressman Richard Nixon.

Nixon, disdainful of the rebellious nature of the movement era, sought something new for America: law and order. The call for law and order was a discursive strategy that would reinvent the terms for discussing the Negro Question. It maneuvered the question onto new terrain by adding a third rail. Rather than debating the merits of separatism or integration, Nixon argued instead for containment strategies.

Nixon's was a veiled attack that treated protesters like rioters, looters, and enemies of "the public."[29] His use of law-and-order rhetoric in his 1968 campaign for president—an extension of Johnson's Law Enforcement Assistance Act—was so effective that it became an incantation for the next few generations of Republican politicians.[30] Three years later, in 1971, Nixon declared a War on Drugs.[31] Taken together, these policies— alongside the deindustrialization that diminished economic prospects for Black Americans, and especially Black men—ushered in a new era of poverty in many urban communities. This period saw Black men and women struggling anew to form and provide for their families.

Ronald Reagan, the man now recognized as the standard bearer of the Republican party, continued the call for law and order to counter insurgent demands for racial justice well into the late 1970s. But Reagan did Nixon one better by electing to be more gender-specific in his race-baiting practices. Nixon hadn't said much about how the gender of African Americans played a part in their unsettling of the national fabric.[32] But Reagan made it clear that Black men and Black women each played a distinct role in the undoing of American social mores. Reagan claimed that Black men were peddling poison, meaning drugs, to innocent and unsuspecting (white) citizens. Black women, he contended were another type of threat: they were fast becoming a public charge.

In 1976, Reagan riled up white voters on this score with the tale of a Black woman living in Chicago who made a living taking advantage of American welfare policies. This woman "used eighty names, thirty addresses, fifteen telephone numbers to collect food stamps, Social Security, veterans' benefits for four non-existent deceased veteran husbands, as well as welfare."[33] Referring to this real woman, Linda Taylor, Reagan established the racist trope of the "welfare queen."

A welfare queen is a woman—coded Black—who supposedly dodges work at all costs, preferring instead to find ways to exploit the welfare system—and in this way the goodwill of the (white) voter. Her main weapons in this con job? Her cunning and her ability to attract men to impregnate her, all the better to file for a heftier payday.

Reagan's reason for sensationalizing this tale of a real-life Chicago woman was to imply that Black female welfare defrauders were the norm. These Black women were suckling at the teat of the (white) American taxpayer. It was only a matter of time, so the logic ran, before welfare queens sucked them dry.

The scandalous image of Black women—who had long served as mammies to white families—sucking *white people* dry had to be part of the salacious appeal of this lie. And a lie it was.[34] Linda Taylor was indeed involved in a scurrilous misappropriation of welfare monies. Yet her criminal activity was by no means representative of all—or even most of—the Black women on welfare, much less all of the African American women in the nation. Nevertheless, the image of indolent Black women as welfare queens stuck.[35] They were little more than barnacles, benefiting from their parasitic relationship with honest, taxpaying white citizens.

There is another important aspect to the Linda Taylor story that is rarely mentioned: Taylor could pass for white.[36] She was born to a white mother who'd had an affair with a Black man.[37] Having been peremptorily excluded from the same spaces her mother could occupy must have felt like a slap in the face. And so it was that much of the time during which she ran her cons, she did so while passing as white.

Taylor would tell people that she was white, Hawaiian, or sometimes Mexican, depending on her goals in the situation. In one of her many marriages in which she was passing as white, she birthed a baby with skin dark enough to give the game away.[38] It had to have been a scene right out of the George Schuyler classic *Black No More*. Her white husband promptly filed for divorce.

Taylor's capacity for graft, it seems, relied on her racial ambiguity. On her ability to rally the support, belief, and protection generally accorded a *white* woman. While for one of her grifts she posed as the sole heir to a wealthy Black man's fortune,[39] it was usually her light skin and proximity to whiteness that opened doors.

This ability to pass complicates the story. It raises the question of whether a woman who was not light enough to pass could have had half the career in crime and welfare fraud that Taylor enjoyed. Which is to say that her pass-ability, her near white sufficiency, inevitability made it possible for her to bilk her white male lovers and the government system of social support.

Reagan had manipulated Taylor's image into one of a risible "Black" scourge. This characterization had palpable negative implications for Black women in the wake of the movement era. Because Reagan had firmly labeled Taylor lazy, greedy, and "Black," in spite of her racial ambiguity, several representations of the so-called welfare queen in the popular media presented her stereotypically, as a heavy and dark-skinned woman.

Through the phantasm of the welfare queen, Reagan had made Black womanhood in the mainstream all but synonymous with the idea of a shiftless Black woman, racking up boyfriends and babies in the interest of securing a payday.

*   *   *

It wasn't as if no one in Black communities by the 1980s had ever heard the term "gold digger." The folk devil of a woman using a man for his money—a reversal of the common practice in a white capitalist hetero-patriarchy of men using money to attract and control women[40]—had accumulated several Hollywood productions in her honor by the 1950s. Any Black person who had been alive at the time of these smash hits would have been well aware of the idea. The 1933 production starring Ginger Rogers even featured a Black woman in a first-ever nonstereo-typical role of a lovelorn widow mourning the loss of her husband to the killing fields of WWI.[41]

By the 1990s, a few pop culture touchstones indelibly changed the color and shape of the gold digger. The twilight of the twentieth century marked the dawn of her blackening. And when she was blacked up, the image combined elements of the sleazy welfare queen *and* of the high-class attractive money grubber.[42]

It was an intriguing combination to say the least. The welfare queen Reagan had conjured was represented in the mass media as fat and Black. The original gold diggers were thin and white. When the gold digger became a Black woman, she retained several of the features of sufficiently white women (in matters of size and hair style or texture), paired with the behavioral traits of the welfare queen, which were derided as "Black." In this respect, the image of Black women as gold diggers involved the creep of Reaganomics, stirred together with the elements of attraction that largely appeal to Black men.[43]

Media coverage of the new gold digger began with Robin Givens. In the 1980s, the New York native was already a highly successful actor, having appeared in the iconic 1978 production *The Wiz*. In 1985, she occupied the spotlight in a controversial episode of the epochal TV program *The Cosby Show*. One year prior, Givens had been enrolled in Harvard Medical School at the tender age of twenty. Having been something of an academic prodigy—she'd started her undergraduate studies at Sarah Lawrence at fifteen—the striking young woman had left academia behind altogether by the time she landed a costarring spot on *Head of the Class* in 1986.[44]

She met world heavyweight champ Mike Tyson in 1987. The two started seeing each other, tying the knot in February 1988. Months into their marriage, the two went on *20/20* to discuss with cohost Barbara Walters their very public, very volatile relationship.

With Tyson sitting silently by her side, Givens describes their relationship to Walters as "torture . . . pure hell . . . worse than anything I could possibly imagine."[45] Walters asks Givens if Tyson ever hits her. She nods. Later, holding back tears, she explains that she doesn't want to divorce Tyson: "He would be alone. . . . And I don't want that to happen. . . . He would have gotten so, so bad that I think maybe one day he would have been more deliberate and killed himself or hurt somebody else."[46] A few months later, in early 1989, she decided she'd had enough, and left Tyson.

Tyson, for his part, never shirked the accusations. The 1989 book *Fear and Fire: The Inside Story of Mike Tyson*, written by his former friend Jose Torres, offers up the following Tyson quote: "I fought Robin in Steve Lott's apartment. She really offended me and I went BAM. She flew backwards, hitting every wall in the apartment." Tyson concluded this reflection nostalgically: "That was the best punch I've ever thrown in my entire life."[47]

Months prior to the finalization of the divorce Givens sued Tyson to the tune of $125 million for libel, saying that he had been orchestrating a public smear campaign, calling her "slime." It's not immediately clear how she arrived at such an eye-popping total. Seemingly, the sum constituted her estimation of her current and future lost wages due to Tyson's aspersions. She claimed to have never wanted alimony from her ex. She also claimed that he had pinched one million dollars of her money. Tyson's lawyer fired back, "Mike didn't make those statements with the intention of defaming her. Saying she's a slime is an opinion. He's entitled to his opinion."[48] The situation somehow got messier from

EXCLUSIVE!!!!!

ROBIN GIVENS

Life After Tyson

In first major interview since divorce, star talks about 'roughest year' of her life and says her name doesn't rhyme with rich

SHE has been called the most hated woman in America. Her very name is emblematic of the glamorous glacial gold-digger. Though she appears every week as Darlene, the brainy student on ABC's *Head of the Class*, her role in the hit series is *not* her claim to fame. No. To most of America she is the drop-dead beautiful temptress who made her name and fortune by making a fool of Mike Tyson; the one and only person who, gossips say, played the champ for a chump.

Since Oct. 7, 1988, the day she announced she was divorcing the heavyweight champion after only eight months of marriage, the furor surrounding her has grown in intensity. By the time she and Tyson were granted a Valentine's Day divorce in the Dominican Republic last year, their story had become a part of our folklore, a national legend.

To be despised so widely and so publicly is a profound burden for a 25-year-old to bear, and there is no question that the past year has done a number on her psyche. "Without question this past year has been the toughest of my

Cover story for EBONY *magazine's March 1990 issue.*

there. Givens ultimately received a $10 million judgment. She insists, however, that Tyson never paid one cent of that money.[49]

It's hard to parse the various claims made by the two parties, but one thing is certain: In the wake of their nuptial dissolution and Givens's big-bill lawsuit, the model and actor was framed as a prime example of a gold digger. In 1990, when she graced the cover of *Ebony* magazine's March issue, she was described as "the most hated woman in America" and "emblematic of the glamorous glacial gold-digger." Many Americans believed she was the very essence of the beautiful yet unscrupulous woman feigning interest in a man in an effort to turn his pockets inside out.[50]

Tyson has long maintained that Givens was after the mean green when she said her marriage vows. But Givens was reportedly devastated that this is how the story played out on the world stage. She maintains that she married Mike for love. That the lawsuit was her attempt to re-coup her losses and end his campaign to defame her.

Givens and Tyson's wild romance became fodder for hundreds, if not *thousands* of articles at the intersection of celebrity, domestic abuse, and wily women.[51] It has been the subject of multiple books, TV interviews, and docuseries. And yet within this crowded cultural space, rap music was one of the earliest and most prolific venues for the dissection of Tyson and Givens.

Rappers, overwhelmingly Black and male, sided with Tyson. In 1989, Kool Moe Dee (KMD) dropped the song "They Want Money," in which he raps that he doesn't have money, a new car, or any new kids, be-cause a lot of ladies are out to make money from a relationship with him. He mentions the Givens-Tyson affair by name, "You're holdin' a flame for my name and my fame/Livin' like Givens schemin' on Tyson." Outrageously, given the abuse Givens suffered—abuse Tyson gleefully corroborates—KMD infers that she was lucky because she'd met a "nice one" in Tyson. He closes the song with the sentiment "But I ain't nice, and I don't play that."[52]

One of my all-time favorite rap songs, "Jingling Baby" by LL Cool J, takes a similar, if more subtle, approach to the controversy. It happens that LL and KMD had a years-long feud in which they traded battle raps. "Jingling Baby" is one of LL's many diss tracks targeting Kool Moe Dee. In it, LL describes himself as a legend and compares KMD to Givens, saying, "Now you look booty like that bum Miss Givens."

I was in elementary school when "Jingling Baby" came out. It wasn't until I began the research for this book that the line about Robin Givens even registered. If I didn't know how men use the idea of gold diggers as an excuse to bash women—and in this case a fellow rapper as well by association—I wouldn't understand why she had to be mentioned at all.

LL and KMD may have been early hip-hop entrants into the discus-sion about Givens's alleged love of the dough, but they would not be left lonely. Between 1990 and 2021, the following musicians mentioned Robin Givens in their songs: Rick Ross, Jay-Z, Bun B, Lil' Wayne, MC Eiht, 2 Chainz, Chris Brown, Master P, Beanie Sigel, Common, Kid Rock, and Erick Sermon.[53] This is far from an exhaustive list.

Mere months after the Tyson v. Givens debacle, hip-hop group EP-MD—a duo featuring the Long Island–bred rappers Erick Sermon and Parrish Smith—released their own backhanded tribute to women perceived to be looking for a come up. EPMD stands for "Erick and Parrish Making Dollars," presumably by scrupulous means. Their song "Gold Digger" appeared on the twosome's 1990 album *Business as Usual* on the Def Jam label.

It's hard to imagine that this song was inspired by anything other than the scrutiny and condemnation raining down on Givens that had captivated the media only a few months prior. But when questioned about the motivation for the single in a 2012 interview with *Vibe* magazine, Sermon offered the following reflection: "I don't know who came up with the original idea for 'Gold Digger.' But that record was huge for EPMD."[54]

It was, in fact, one of EPMD's most successful tracks. The video was, for me, one of the most memorable of the golden age. It opens on a group therapy session—"Suckers Anonymous"—filled with Black men. One of the men stands up to recite the first lines of James Brown's 1970 song "It's a New Day." The man delivers the lines with the thrust of a manifesto: "Fellas, things done got too far gone. We got to let the girls know what they got to do for us."

The scene cuts to attractive Black women in bras and panties sporting hard hats and wielding pickaxes, an allegory for gold mining. Sermon relates his (fictional) experience, playing the part of a man blithely getting married like it is "no big deal, no sweat." Quickly, but nevertheless far too late, he realizes that he should have signed a prenuptial agreement.

Sermon's fake wife spends his money freely and without his input during the course of their video relationship, including buying a brand-new Jaguar while he is away on tour. She taps into his bank account, "gettin' more and more money," always without consulting him. He's afraid to get divorced, thinking it will mean he'll lose half his cash. He curses himself for his mistake; for him to have forgotten something so elementary as a prenup means his "brain-locked, my whole damn head was malfunctional." Now he feels obligated to stay in a (s)hell of a union, all the while, "wishin' she gets hit by a Mack truck."

Smith has a similar story to tell. He meets a lovely lady with "green eyes, thunder thighs, and a def body." When he meets her, she is already stuntin': "she drove a black Maserati/Chrome kit" and had a smile he couldn't resist. Based on this woman's specs, he steps to her, thinking, "Yeah, I gots to get this." They get married. In no time flat, she starts spending up all his money. Just when he's ready to get out of this relationship, she announces that she's pregnant. Smith is regretful about this turn of events. All he wanted to do was cuddle up with a fly chick, but instead he is "stuck with alimony payments." He loses his house and car in the (pretend) divorce. In the end, he's "eating TV dinners in a one-bedroom apartment." If that weren't enough, "she wheels the Benz" while the Smith rides Greyhound.[55]

In his *Vibe* interview, Sermon says that he and Parrish's fictitious treatment of gold diggers was inspired by the number of money-minded women he and other rich Black men met during their rise to stardom. But there are a few critical misconceptions in the song. First, when Sermon claims, "Ladies of the 80's got hip and went for self/With the new divorce laws, which entitles them half," he was riffing on a perception about alimony that did not match reality.

In fact, US divorce laws between the 1970s and '80s made it easier for women to petition for divorce, but they did *not* make it easier for women to get alimony or child support. In 1979, the highest court in the land ruled in *Orr v. Orr* that gender-based alimony statutes were unconstitutional.[56] This meant that all fifty states were required to revise their alimony laws such that "maintenance," a term which replaced alimony in many discussions, could be awarded to either party in a divorce. Maintenance was generally granted based on the likelihood that the lower-earning party's quality of life could be significantly diminished by the divorce.

In 1975, the US had enacted federal legislation to establish a child support system. It was originally intended to support the growing number of divorced or unmarried women with children.[57] Still, between 1977 and 1986, the federal government passed a variety of measures to enforce child support laws that largely involved garnishing the higher earning spouse's wages.[58] By 1987, another statute stipulating that payouts to

one party would be "based on the standard of living the child would
have enjoyed" had the marriage continued.[59] The combined effect of
these measures on alimony and child support was that women were not
necessarily entitled to *any* payouts, much less half. At the same time, a
growing number of men have requested—and received—maintenance
and child support from their former spouses.

Indeed, many of us may be familiar with high-profile cases of men tap-
ping into their ex-wives' bank accounts. Halle Berry's $16,000-per-month
payments to her ex, Gabriel Autry, spring to mind; these payments
were belatedly reduced to $8K monthly.[60] Some of us are still reeling
from Kevin Federline's $1.3 million-dollar spousal support ruling against
Britney Spears. Federline also requested $60,000 per month for their
two kids, which felt to many Britney fans like shots fired; it appears he
was awarded $20,000 per month, total, in child support.[61] While these
female celebrities' pricey maintenance and child support payments to
their ex-husbands are relatively well known, fewer of us may be aware
of the fact that, according to research by Stephen Jenkins, a professor at
the London School of Economics, men's incomes rise about 30 percent
after divorce.[62]

There are other reasons for us to flat-out reject pop culture representations of (Black) gold diggers. When gold diggers in the popular imagination were white, their behavior was met with public finger shaking
and tongue wagging, to be sure. Still, there was a certain playfulness,
too, like that witnessed in *Gentlemen Prefer Blondes*. These lovely ladies
were entertaining men's affections under false pretenses and perhaps
were even willing to accept a ring from a man if his bank account was
deemed sufficient. There was usually some backstory to this woman's life
that could explain her willingness to use a man to escape her financial
straits. Rarely, if ever, were white gold diggers characterized as plotting
to cold-bloodedly hollow out a man's economic reserves.

But when the gold digger was blackened, she became a cold calculating aggressor in hot pursuit of someone else's pocketbook. We know
this not just because of the obscene amount of press coverage devoted
to Robin Givens or because the incantation "Robin Givens" was used
by rappers as if she were Gollum after the precious. Black female gold

diggers were said to be looking for opportunities *to get married and have kids* as a means of exploiting men. The latter feature in particular, involving children, was not a common attribute of white gold diggers.

It was Black women who were supposedly using marriage and kids to access their former (Black) male partners' money (e.g., Robin Givens) or state benefits (i.e., the welfare queen), and there was nothing cute or farcical about their purported gold diggery. If their songs are to be believed, rappers thought that Black women's agenda included searching for a baller and marrying him and/or having his kids—not for love but for purely mercenary reasons involving the rapper's cash. This widely held opinion was not only motivated by their perception of Tyson and Givens's relationship. It was also a direct descendant of Reagan's exploitation of the image of Linda Taylor in his condemnation of so-called welfare queens. And in this respect, it was anti-Black.

The treatment of Black women as gold diggers engages white supremacist criteria for who makes a good female partner and mother. When it is argued that Black women (unlike white women) have been using marriage and motherhood for selfish reasons, it places them outside the bounds of "real" womanhood as structured by the cult of domesticity that has influenced Western culture since the nineteenth century.[63] It is another reminder that Black women are, in general, judged insufficiently white to occupy the role of domestic goddess. It is a category intended for only the best women as defined by scientific racism, those being elite white women.

Though a cloud of suspicion descended over Black women after 1989, in reality there have been many obstacles in the path to glory the gold-digging way. For starters, in order to attract a (Black) man, they have to be considered fly enough in a white-centric visual economy, not easy for any woman browner than a paper bag. Second, this man has to be wealthy enough to be worthy of the scheme. This, too, is no mean feat. While civil rights legislation promised an end to job segregation, it neither promised nor delivered on actual jobs or living wages. Deindustrialization in the late twentieth century battered Black men's economic prospects, and their wages did not climb appreciably between 1970 and 2000, despite civil rights legislation.[64] Recent analyses of domestic wages show that Black women and men in America make nearly identical sums, each being less than *either* white women or men.[65]

Despite the suspicion with which (Black) men regard Black women as prospective romantic partners, most of these women will never have the opportunity to mine for a Black man's money, much less a rich one's. This reality is due both to the white supremacist perception of Black women as undesirable partners—seeing as they are regularly deficient in whiteness—and the limited number of wealthy Black men that exist. These verifiable facts haven't stopped a number of rappers, such as Jay-Z and Ja Rule in "Can I Get A. . . ," from making songs asking (Black) women if they would be with a man who has no dough? The answer, of course, is yes. Black women continue to seek out Black men as partners at a significantly higher rate than Black men seek them out.[66]

With all this in mind, we arrive at our discussion of the most popular rap song ridiculing (Black women) gold diggers. The one Sesali Bowen named in her explanation of how the relationship between Black femininity and gold digging was forged. The one by Ye.

·   ·   ·

Late Registration was Kanye West's second studio album. Following on the heels of the massive commercial success of his debut album, *College Dropout*, this sophomore project from the producer-rapper had much riding on it. Any fears that West wouldn't be able to replicate his initial success were soon quashed. The album, which dropped in the summer of 2005, generated five hit singles, including the juggernaut "Gold Digger."

The song was originally written for Shawnna, a female rapper, and was slated to be released on her debut album *Worth Tha Weight*. When she rejected the song, West retooled the lyrics, making them suitable for a cishet male. The song's hook, "I ain't saying she a gold digger. . . . But she ain't messin with no broke niggas," is tongue-in-cheek. As West regales us with (imaginary) interactions between himself and an unspecified woman, it becomes clear that he is indeed saying what he professes to not be saying.

If West is farcically unwilling to come right out and call the subject of the song a gold digger, he describes the woman's behavior in ways that make the label the logical conclusion. There is no greater evidence than that found in the second verse. Here, Kanye offers a delicious vignette of a man who pays his ex-girlfriend child support for eighteen years. During that time, his baby mama uses "his" money to buy herself a car and a home, bigger and better than those the man himself can afford. She also reroutes child support checks that were supposed to go toward meeting the child's needs and uses them to pay for her own surgical enhancements.

Hers is more than a little light embezzlement. We learn later in the verse that the man is wealthy, a football player, in fact. In Ye's tale, the dogged forlorn fella wins the Super Bowl. But due to the money he's been putting out for child support, he's too broke to flex right. Instead, he is forced to "drive off in a Hyundai." The final injustice comes when, after enduring eighteen years of such indignities, the man finds out that the kid he was supporting is not his biological child. For men hoping to avoid this pathetic fate, Ye has the following advice: "If you ain't no punk, holla, 'We want prenup! We want prenup!' (Yeah!)"[67]

Despite West's affected uncertainty about applying the label of "gold digger" to the woman in his story, he leaves little room for a different interpretation. The woman is shrewd in getting what she wants from the man, i.e., the duckets. The man, being unaware of the probability that a relationship with a (Black) woman might be transactional in nature, is a simp. West issues a rallying cry to all cishet men who do *not* want to file behind "punks" like this one: get a prenup!

In a career heavy with accolades, West's "Gold Digger" stands out. It was the artist's first single to reach number one on the *Billboard* Hot 100. It displaced songbird Mariah Carey's "We Belong Together" in its ascent. The song also won a Grammy. It has been recognized as the single biggest hit in Ye's illustrious career.

This brings us to another irony: songs and videos about (Black) gold diggers generate a fortune for rappers like West. The popularity of songs about gold diggers and the lure of scantily-clad jiggling Black women in the music video means that the sum rap acts command by producing such a combo is, to borrow from Kendrick Lamar, "persuasive."[68] According to *Complex*, artists can earn on average $1,000–$2,000 per million views on a music video.[69] West's "Gold Digger" has over three hundred million views on YouTube—equivalent to $300–$600K in revenue from this site alone. When rappers cry "gold digger," they profit from both the verbal demonization and the video sexualization of Black women.

In the wake of the Tyson v. Givens fight over finances, no media product has been a more successful or powerful venue for the visual and lyrical for the pairing of Black women with money schemes than West's version of the song. Like the EPMD treatment before it, the song contains the language of Reagan's welfare queens backed by an 808 and tight rhymes. Its status as a hip-hop titan discloses something about the power of racism and misogyny when conveyed through music. In a genre that was once a vehicle for the ongoing discussion of Black liberation (and still is for some artists), several Black male artists became talking points for (white) men's views about Black women.

■ ■ ■

There are a few final ironies on the rise of the suspicious Black woman, qua the so-called gold digger. They involve the curious circuit of the melodies used by EPMD and West. Each artist sampled tracks that originally had very different relational politics than those the current songs are selling.

West's version of the song samples Ray Charles's 1954 smash "I Got a Woman." In the original song, which made it to number one on the R&B charts, Charles details the qualities of a "good" woman and what constitutes a fine relationship for a man such as himself.[70] Per Charles, a good woman is one who gives *him* money: "I got a woman, way over town. . . . *She gives me money when I'm in need*." This sounds like gold diggery coming from a man, and yet I have never heard anyone describe it as such.

There are other qualities of a good woman on Charles's list, for example, she gives him all the nookie he wants morning and night, but she only gives it to him. She's "never runnin' in the streets." She doesn't ask anything of a man but gives him everything: her body, her time, her attention, no bitchin, and legal tender. She is, moreover, a woman who knows her place is in the home. It's a depiction of femininity that calls on the cult of true womanhood. It also generates questions regarding where her money is coming from. The race of the woman who keeps the speaker's pockets padded isn't disclosed, but his description leads me to believe she may have been white.[71]

West's sampling of this song effected a curious reversal of fortune. The speaker in Charles's song celebrates his own gold diggery, vaunting his selfless lady's patronage. West uses the same tune—replete with the same hook—to denigrate Black women who are arguably accumulating similar romantic benefits.

EPMD, too, sampled a track in their iteration of the song, a 1981 jam by Jamaican artist Denroy Morgan titled "I'll Do Anything for You." This song, a success in its own right, features Morgan professing his willingness to do anything and everything for his love interest: "I'll give you the world/If you want me to." Morgan was an old-skool romantic, it seems. The artist finds this kind of sacrifice merely a reflection of their shared willingness to go the extra mile to please one another. Per Morgan, other men don't see the many sacrifices his partner makes for him. She makes him strong, stands by his side, relaxes him, and in general does what she can to make his dreams come true.[72]

In the space of fifteen years, two iconic rap acts, Kanye West and EPMD, sampled songs by other Black artists. The OG versions of these melodies describe the speakers' love for and compatibility with the women in their lives. The subsequent sampled versions reframe their narratives to describe Black women as bloodsuckers of low moral standing.

Ye, to my knowledge, has never been seen publicly cuddling up to a woman with skin as dark as or darker than his. With the exception of a short-lived relationship with a woman named Vinetria in 2021, his romantic affairs have been with white women almost exclusively for more than a decade.[73] Perhaps there is a hint of autobiography in West's claim that when a Black man makes it, "he'll leave yo' ass for a white girl."[74]

But West is far from alone in evolving his former predilection for "light-skinned girlies" to a desire to sup at the source. Nor was he a pioneer in this regard. Already by the 1980s, a number of men across race and ethnicity were changing their standards for partners, many seeking women with a higher white quotient than they might have expected to enjoy in the past.

Curiously enough, the number of men demanding sufficiently white partners rose in direct response to women's post-feminist-movement social gains. Suddenly, insufficiently white women began to encounter newfangled men on the dating scene who were extra skittish about commitment. Today we have a word for them: fuckboys.

CHAPTER 4

ENTER THE FUCKBOYS

In the early days of the change, American women weren't sure if they were being paranoid. Many of them discussed the problem quietly amongst themselves, confirming that they were not alone in their experience or hadn't misperceived something. Somehow, all of a sudden, there weren't any men left.

The *New York Times* was among the first to report on this problem, which had been dubbed "the man shortage." Ron Alexander, in his 1983 article for the Gray Lady, set out to investigate the mounting sense among women that a "good man" was becoming damn near impossible to find.[1]

The women of interest for Alexander's reporting happened to be Jewish. They were described as "bright, good-looking, and successful."[2] And yet, their prospects for marrying equally attractive Jewish men were dim. They wanted to know why, and what to do about it.

Worriment led them to cram into the tight space of the 92nd Street YMCA for a lecture on the state of relationships. About 350 people packed in, around two-thirds of whom were women. There, they were to be instructed on the purported root causes of, and solutions to, finding themselves at a firmly marrying age without any requisite desirable male counterparts in the offing.

Their guiding light was a man by the name of William Novak, the author of the recently released book *The Great American Man Shortage and Other Roadblocks to Romance.* The women in attendance led with their laments about the fetid dating pool. They called the men in it "not emotionally mature" and "[in]capable of a relationship."[3]

Novak aimed to temper these, what he considered unhelpful, judgments. The real problem, per Novak, was that the standards of these admittedly high-achieving women were too high. Instead of feeling disillusioned by the bounty of men that were available, the ones they didn't want, Novak argued that women should change their attitudes toward the seemingly undesirable. Women, he instructed—for the advice was almost exclusively targeted to the women in the audience—should be willing to date the kinds of men they usually scoffed at. They should be more open to dating younger men. Less affluent men too. Women should accept more of the qualities they hadn't wanted.

To Novak's advice was added the unsolicited opinions of men who'd ambled in. One claimed that good Jewish men hadn't vanished, they'd just been in hiding, or, as he put it, "camouflaged themselves in self-protection." Precisely why these men had found it necessary to go underground, or what they were protecting themselves from, hadn't been belabored. Regardless, the advisement was for women to make an effort for a change. That, the male audience members claimed, could bring these purportedly worthwhile men out of their hiding places. If women were so liberated, why'd they still expect men to do all the asking out and the work of initiating a relationship? If women were so big on equality, it was high time they started reaching out to men and being straightforward about *their* interests and intentions.

For women, the lecture had to have been illuminating to the degree that it was humbling. Self-reflection, it seemed, was in order. Rather than being all high and mighty, they ought to take it down a notch. It was time to roll up their sleeves and get to the business of actively finding a partner rather than passively waiting for one to show up. Hadn't they, after all, been angling to break into opportunities previously reserved for men?

The outline of this strategy, of course, did not answer the question of where all the marriageable men had gone. There were noticeably fewer of them to choose from, and women were fairly certain they had not been raptured. Instead, it turned out that the men in question had adopted a new position on hetero relations. Frustrated by alimony, fearful of gold digging, and, above all else, turned off by feminist agitation, eligible men were working a code. They had recalibrated their expectations in response to feminism, changing their standards for a partner to those better meeting the (racialized) feminine ideal. It was a stealth attempt to reinforce heteronormativity. The tactics they employed would only find a name decades later.

▪   ▪   ▪

The *New York Times*' provocative 1983 announcement of a "man short-age" wasn't to be their only statement of the problem. Later that year, more advice appeared for women having difficulty finding a suitable partner: double up. Kenneth Noble, in his article "One Approach to the Shortage of Men Is Sharing," profiled a woman in her late thirties, a Ms. Audrey Chapman, about her dwindling prospects. Chapman was a trained therapist working at Howard University. When she'd moved to DC, she claimed, "The first thing I noticed was that many of the women behaved in a manner that had an air of insecurity, tinged with an overcoating of desperation."[4] The men she'd met, she claimed, were garrulous to the point of arrogance.

To help women cope with this treacherous situation, Chapman formed an on-campus workshop titled "Man Sharing: Dilemma or Choice." (It should go without saying that Chapman and the women she counseled at Howard were Black.) Chapman herself, it seems, was not advocating for women to go halvsies on a man. Rather, she was speaking to the reality of many women she'd come across at Howard who, at some point in their relationship with a man, discovered that he had another woman—potentially making them a side chick. These women didn't know what do to. Instead of holding out for the elusive dream of a happily ever after with one man, Chapman counseled them to consider serial dating or seeing several men at a time.

Curiously, Chapman didn't want this life for herself. Like many of the women whom she counseled, what she wanted was the opportunity to date until she found someone with whom she felt a connection and then work toward becoming exclusive. It was the script for dating under the aegis of the Romantic Ideal that had been in vogue for decades up to that point. "I'm an old-fashioned girl," Chapman explained. "I like to be wined and dined. I like flowers."[5]

Three years later, clearly owing to the number of Black women experiencing this problem, the issue of the man shortage was increasingly framed as a *Black* man shortage. *Ebony* addressed the problem in both its May and August 1986 issues.[6] They came back around to concerns about this presumptive deficit in several issues in 1987, as well as in 1992, 1993, and 1994. The latest issue in which I saw this concern mentioned was from 2007.[7] In almost all of these articles and letters to the editor, the verdict was the same as the one delivered by Novak in 1983: stop being so picky and *try harder*.

What's interesting, however, is that two of the earliest entrants in the "man shortage" literature actually provided helpful contextual information that was inexplicably left out of the vast majority of later writings on the topic. The first is a piece published in *Ebony* magazine in 1973, ten years before the *New York Times* and other mainstream publications picked up on the trend. Its author was Robert E. Staples, a Black man and a professor at the University of California, San Francisco.

Staples had noted that there were about "a million more females than males in the Black population." He doesn't expend prime real estate endeavoring to explain wherefore this gap exists. But historical evidence suggests that it was due, at least in part, to the War on Crime and the War on Drugs, which had been legislated in the midst of the movement era to derail Black progress. The unequal enforcement of these new policies meant that many Black men were in prison.[8]

Apart from the role of the state, Black women had Black men's own predispositions to contend with. Staples suggested there was a growing preference among Black men for interracial digs. Black men, Staples says, took an intense interest in white women. He argues that this was one anticipated result of America having recently ended racial dating taboos. Newly "liberated" white women were venturing into darker terrain, some of them intent on investigating the legitimacy of the Mandingo claims.

The aftereffect of white women's new sexual openness and Black men's own sexual curiosity was that "the black woman [was] seriously disadvantaged in competing with white women for the few black men available."[9]

But Staples's analysis seems to be missing a piece. How had he leapt from opportunity-meets-curiosity to a Black male "preference" for white women? For Staples, it was about sexual accessibility: Black middle-class women were less likely to give it up so easily, looking as they were for long-term partnerships. Black men could go around with white women for a few casual kicks and avoid the question of commitment.

Staples was right on one front: Black marriage rates were beginning a precipitous decline by the 1960s.[10] But he was studiously ignoring the rest of the data. Turns out that even as Black marriage rates dropped, the intermarriage rates for Black men soared.

In 1990, M. Belinda Tucker and Claudia Mitchell-Kernan reported on the considerable variation in intermarriage rates that existed within the Black community. Their findings were striking: For the period covering 1916–1964, between 41 and 90 percent of Black mixed marriages involved a Black man. 1970 was one of the few years on record revealing equal outmarriage rates for Black folk across genders. But the period of 1970–1980, the very period during which Staples was writing, revealed that Black men were three times as likely to outmarry as Black women. By 1973, the year Staples took up his post at UCSF, Black men on the West Coast were four times as likely to outmarry, with a surprising 16.5 percent of their dwindling marriages being to non-Black—and presumably more sufficiently white—women.[11] This was a detail Staples failed to mention.

It was not the only time critical information had been foregone. Intriguingly, author William Novak, in his 1983 appraisal of the man shortage, had also curiously vacated a few of the key facts in his appeal to Jewish women. He had ignored the reality, for instance, that men of the old guard continued to exist—the kind of men who wanted their wives to be seen and not heard. To be sexy as hell while staying mute and putting together a little something for their men to nosh. Some of these men would have been threatened by these newly successful and (at least partially) liberated women. Other men, seeing an opening, would have been scrambling to escape the traditional marriage-and-family plan. These men didn't necessarily think the purpose of dating was to find "the one," the love of a lifetime to settle down with. The existence of these men, too, appears to have been suppressed.

With Jewish women, as with Black women, there was another quiet fact softly spoken about, that no one allowed to linger: Jewish men were more than twice as likely to outmarry, mostly with non-Jewish white women, than were Jewish women. Jewish women, too, were being silently pulverized by the mounting whiteness of their men's choices. What a curious sleight of hand that made Staples's and Novak's presentation of the "man shortage" as largely about women's gendered choices instead of men's racial ones. Accordingly, it was framed in the media as a *women's issue*. Society agreed: Women had to chill with their list of relationship goals and standards for the kind of man they wanted. If they were so hot to get married, they'd better take stock of their real-time pickings, and then pick.

By coining a term to describe a phenomenon that didn't exist—a "man shortage" whereas men had simply trained their eyes on the great white interior—these self-styled experts had a hand in knocking newly liberated women back into their traditional place. But more than that, their work at once papered over and amplified a new men's politics of the post-movement era.

The man profiled in the *New York Times*, the one attending the lecture by William Novak at the Y, was emblematic of the surplus of men women didn't want, men who were unwilling to initiate relationships, men who wanted to hide from women in an effort to protect their own feelings. In a move that Michel Foucault would certainly tip a hat to, these men were constantly in the process of divulging their emotional state to women as a means of explaining their emotional unavailability.[12] Nor were they the "New Men," the vulnerable, lucid, and egalitarian types, whom the media had suddenly grown so fond of depicting but who appeared to be quite rare.[13] Unlike the New Men or chivalrous men of yore, these surplus men were mercurial. They betrayed a callow fear of commitment, delaying marriage as they awaited the arrival of the women they had fantasized about, those who would accept them just as they were. This passivity, this waiting on the right person, had been women's role. It was a curious gender reversal that all the talk about them being "missing" had missed.

So, while (Black and Jewish) women were being told to be more expansive and aggressive when casting their nets into the dating pool, these surplus men folded in on themselves and narrowed what they were willing to accept in a long-term partner. They were delaying matrimony while also raising their sights toward women whose appearance better met the demands of "Beauty," with a capital B.[14] It took women several decades to identify and label these men "fuckboys."

There is no single definition of the term fuckboy. But there is nevertheless wide agreement among analysts that the biggest problem with fuckboys is their inability to commit. There are other qualities also regularly observed in these men: feigning intense interest, running hot and then cold, being cheap, trying to move quickly into a purely sex-based relationship, masquerading as sensitive when they are actually emotionally withholding.[15] Here, I would also add a preference for sufficient whiteness to the list. Exhibiting any one of these behaviors in isolation does not a fuckboy make. What makes a fuckboy is the deployment of many (or for some men all) of these behaviors in romantic situations.

This brand of behavior, this "fuccboism," which is readily apparent to women across America today, was, in hindsight, already visible by the wane of the movement era. But, like many things in our culture, fuckboys didn't just spring up fully formed. No, as it turns out, much of this behavior was actually encouraged in young men by powerful male elders.

Long before fuccboism became a widespread phenomenon with its own title, even before the movement era that cultivated this behavior reached its apex, there was a subterranean rumbling of disaffected men. They denounced the sad state of American romance and the gross errors of "women's equality." These men decided on new relationship rules to protect male power. Central to them was one axiom: do not commit.

■   ■   ■

Few could have imagined the turn that Merle Miller's life took. A novelist and dramatist, Miller penned a prodigious number of books and plays in his multidecade career. And, if you were to ask his contemporaries, he was nearly as well known for his rancorous relationships with publishers and producers as for his writing.

Miller led with his politics, and he was unapologetic about them. In the 1950s, he found himself on Senator McCarthy's notorious blacklist as a probable communist.[16] In retaliation, Miller decided to investigate the communist investigations, publishing a book about his findings, *Blacklisting: Two Key Documents* in 1971. That same year, in one of the most influential stories ever to make its way into the *New York Times Magazine* up to that point, Miller came out as gay.[17]

Miller publicly rejected the suppression of forward-thinking calls for a more equitable society. He himself refused to remain a silenced sexual minority. Perhaps these stances are what made his discordant anti-feminism all the more telling.

In 1954, he submitted a curious entry into the annals of history with his essay for *Esquire*, "The Suicide of the Sexes: The Wife Who Works." In it, Miller wastes no ink on niceties, propelling himself headlong into an excoriation of working women. Describing their careers as the quintessential threat to American nuptials, he intones, "Those who insist on having a husband and career" are doing "their damnedest to wreck marriage as well as home life in America." These women, he adds, "are a menace, and they have to be stopped."[18]

The piece was authored prior to the peak of the second wave of the feminist movement. But Miller was a perceptive kind of guy. He was anticipating something. He described it as the "trouble [that] began considerably more than a century ago with those sexless fanatics who, since they were without femininity, called themselves feminist." Miller felt the press of what he called an "increasing and strident minority of women," those inspired by the damnable machinations of female activists of yore.

His solution to this as-yet-unnamed new wave of feminism was simple: Men should deny these women any form of commitment. "I propose a simple solution," he began, "that henceforth no man propose marriage until he has found out whether or not the girl he thinks he wants to marry is willing and happy to give up any thought of a career outside the home." It was a firm stance to be sure. One that was intended to make clear to this new group of upstarts that the vote was one thing, but if they wanted equality of opportunity in the workplace, the price was the end of marriage. What Miller was proposing was nothing short of a war on feminism. This much he avows without hesitation, calling what he is advocating for a "counterrevolution" and claiming that any women foolhardy enough to try and work in the face of it would be sufficiently chastened, so that this war on feminism "wouldn't take long" to win.

Miller's comments were incendiary, but they were not singular. In an essay running side-by-side with Miller's, the writer Maggie Smith offers her view of women's attempt to mix marriage and career, and her verdict is the same: men ought to avoid these women, as the heartiness of their masculinity is on the line. Fearing the feminization of men that supposedly results from partnerships with career women, she opines, "A whole new genus of human males has come into being. The species is composed of the husbands of successful career women, the do-nothings, say-nothings, contribute-nothings who pose as modern married men." Smith argues that these men are "[i]neffectual, lethargic males willing to exchange their manliness for a life free of responsibility."[19]

Yes, this is a men's magazine, and inevitably the perspectives are curated just so. But interestingly, in response to this tart pair of essays, *Esquire* also published multiple angry letters to the editor composed by women and men, most of whom found Miller's and Smith's ideas asinine. Per one man who wrote in, "Mr. Miller's treatise on career wives is unquestionably excellent material for the cylindrical file," adding, "Mr. Miller seemingly clings to the rather outmoded idea that men are the Lords and Masters of the households, to be catered to, but never questioned by their combination concubine, maid and cook. Unrealistic? Very much so."[20]

If those letters moved the editors, it wasn't in the direction of ceasing the incriminating assessments of feminists and career women. Instead, they softened the blow. In a bevy of essays targeting married and single men alike, *Esquire* repeatedly presented working women and marriage like puzzle pieces that just didn't fit.

One of the first was a 1956 screed reminding men about the price of divorce when a relationship heads south. Author S. Jay Lasser slams the so-called feminist assault on men and marriage that, he argues, alimony had recently become. Quoting a 1955 book written by a Judge Morris Ploscowe titled *The Truth About Divorce*, he asserts,

> The dominance of man in the matrimonial union has been largely elim-
> inated under the assaults of the feminists of the nineteenth century. . . .
> However, the feminists, while they took away the privileges of a hus-
> band in his wife's property, still left him with the same common-law
> obligations to support his wife as heretofore. Equal rights for men and
> women, the battle cry of feminists, did not extend to the curtailment
> of any of the husband's obligations of support. But the feminists in
> this country have gone one step further . . . under pressure of feminist
> opinion, a husband's legal obligations to support a wife, based on the
> fact that he had control over her property, came to be extended to
> the duty to furnish support not only to a wife but also to an ex-wife,
> despite the fact that he had lost all control over her property.[21]

Whether or not this testimony represents actual legal changes that benefited women in divorce is subject to debate, given the terror and rebuke surrounding alimony that regularly led to outlandish claims. For that reason alone, the claim is suspect that this purported trans-formation ought to be attributed to feminism. Still, Lasser insists that feminism should be on trial. He offers a few tax solutions to married men to avoid the worst of the damage engendered by the presence of "cupid on Capitol Hill."

Dragging in the undertow of this piece is a backlash against marriage itself in a feminist environment. To Lasser, these new women are per-verting the institution. He implies that they would eschew a gold ring for a brass one, meaning that if they could be assured of a lifetime payout from one man, an ex-husband, in the form of alimony, they'd "[shy] away from marriage" altogether in the future. For Lasser, it's a tale of "bear traps in the alimony thicket," and he is dismayed at women's seeming gaming, or even besiegement, of marriage. It is the same note of terror that would appear in rap songs in the years to come.

The pearls of wisdom kept dropping. By the 1960s, writers in *Esquire* were describing feminism and its attendant career women as a full-blown domestic liability. Women, they argued, were taking up roles that were rightfully men's, bulldozing over tradition with their demands for reform. Such is the tone of a 1962 article by Dan Wakefield, "The Outriders." Calling women reformers "the internal female threat," Wakefield suggests that these educated and sloppily dressed career women were converting political life, especially in the Democratic party, into a "matriarchy." The worst bit of it, to Wakefield, is that these rough women were relying on the domestic aid of their overly solicitous husbands to get their political work done. Reporting on women involved in the League of Women voters, he writes that league husbands are "usually cooperative" and "do their bit by babysitting while wives are out on league business."[22]

Wakefield's complaint is ostensibly about the state of politics. And yet it is expressed as a fear of men's roles beside their wives, these "women pols." Interestingly, one of the issues lamented by Wakefield and at least one of the women he profiles in his article, is that these new accommodating men aren't really men at all—they're unchivalrous, self-satisfied "boys." That the future of politics might be tough-talking women married to devil-may-care "boys" ignited Wakefield's animus.

This concern, what some called the feminization and others the boyification of men, was lampooned in another *Esquire* piece from 1962. This one is defensively titled "Women of America, Now Is the Time to Arise: 'No!'" Its author is none other than the writer and producer Robert Alan Aurthur, known for his critically acclaimed films, as well as for his marriage to comedy legend Bea Arthur.

Aurthur presents a futuristic conversation among men, in which a speaker identified as "Old Man" reminisces about the days before *men* were disenfranchised. In an altered timeline in which men no longer have the vote, the Old (married) Man cries, "I remember when I first began to realize that we men were all leading ourselves into a desperate trap by accepting Women's demands for equality." Feminist demands for equality, Aurthur implies, are at once a slippery slope and a ruse; once such equality has been realized, women will turn their sights toward dominating men.[23]

The suspicion that feminists had ruined marriage—and had as their real goal control over men—reached a fever pitch by the 1970s. Several articles, penned by men and white women, described feminists as "crazy," or "man hating."[24] However, the most consistent theme of all, witnessed since Miller's 1954 philippic, was that feminists and career women (or, heaven forbid, women who are both) make for unhappy wives and unhappy lives. If a man found himself in an unhappy marriage with a feminist career woman, he was done for; best to stick it out or face the social death brought on by alimony. But, by far, the best and easiest solution to the problems caused by these types of women? Do not to marry them.

With this anti-marriage proposal, American men were in open revolt against the old sexual order. For the first time, they were questioning the aims of the Romantic Ideal, which, while created in the Middle Ages, had been tied to the tradition of marriage for the past two centuries. American men—beginning but not ending with white men—were throwing off the yoke of history and announcing that the Romantic Ideal could not stand in the face of feminist incursions into men's domains.

The Romantic Ideal turned on there being unblemished women to protect and defend, women who were keeping up their side of the bargain. Feminists didn't need as much protecting and defending. To the extent that men believed feminists were denying them their vision of themselves as heroic saviors, a budding number of them argued that the correct response was retaliation. They argued that men could end women's threats of stealing men's social and political power by abstaining from partnerships with the more bullish individuals in their number.

Esquire was one of the top men's magazines by the middle of the twentieth century. And yet, its influence in the domain of sexual relationships was quickly overshadowed by a magazine that was in many respects its offshoot: *Playboy*. If the idea of refusing to commit to feminists and career women as presented in *Esquire* proved both popular and contentious, *Playboy*'s romantically scarred founder managed to make this idea, and the pursuit of sufficiently white women, integral to the magazine's success.

CHAPTER 5

WOMEN AS SEX WORKERS

It's hard to imagine Hugh Hefner getting up to the straight life. But, by the age of twenty, he was well ensconced in a heteronormative lifestyle. It was, after all, 1946. Hefner had just completed two years of military service. He took the stipend he received from the GI Bill and enrolled in the University of Illinois alongside his high school sweetheart, Millie Williams. By 1949, the two fresh-faced college graduates were also new-lyweds, starting their married life in Hef's family home.[1]

He had made these choices without hesitation, and yet something was gnawing at him. Perhaps on some level it was the certainty of the whole thing. Up to that moment, it hadn't occurred to Hef to reject the script of a work-a-day fellow with a polite wife and a sprouting brood of children. This is largely owing to the reality that there were no options outside of the circumscribed for bright, hopeful youths at the time. In the postwar environment, young white people met their matches at the altar for a life preloaded with bourgeois markers of achievement. The alternative was to enter the underground economy and find themselves shunned by their middle-class families and friends.

The humdrum had him cornered. His life felt as though it had already been pre-lived, dictated as it had been from birth to death. Dedicated to others and not to oneself, lives like his could feel lifeless.

Hefner was ultimately able to revitalize his life and in the doing re-write the rules for men entering heterosexual relationships in the latter half of the twentieth century. *Playboy*, with Hefner at the helm, expanded the rationale for rejecting commitment. In the doing, the magazine helped create an entirely new man: an anti-feminist, anti-career-woman kind of guy who views all women who don't meet certain standards (a.k.a. insufficiently white women) as intruders into men's spaces. With this, *Playboy* was creating a certain type of fuckboy playbook. It positioned all but a small fraction of elite and traditional "good girls" as potential sex workers whose bodies could be used for unpaid and nonconsensual sex work.

.   .   .

Underneath Hefner's dissatisfaction with the way his life was unfolding was an intense desire to know more about sex. In the beginning, this manifested as a wholly acceptable academic enterprise. After years of fascination with sex researcher Alfred Kinsey's work, he enrolled in the graduate program in sociology at Northwestern University. There, he planned to study sexual practices and mores. But one semester after settling into the grim realities of grad school, Hef let go the academic pretense.[2]

He decided to explore his interest in sex through art and pop culture. He took on copywriting work at a local department store. While working there, he started making naughty cartoons intended to take the piss out of the phony politics of respectability that governed public sexuality in his hometown. That was headed in the right direction, but it still wasn't quite right. It was then that Hef took on a gig as a promotional copywriter for *Esquire*.

This was anything but a small deal. It had been *Esquire* that had first given Hef a glimpse of a debonair and gutsy masculinity. As a teen, he'd studied its pages with acute interest. But the realities of working for the publication left much to be desired. It was as if working there was no more exhilarating than pursuing a PhD in sociology, which is saying something. After a brief and somewhat demoralizing stint, he left *Esquire*.

Esquire was, after all, a magazine for "gentlemen." It told of a life where men were successful and powerful, and usually married. But Hef's time in the military had exposed him to the possibilities of a manhood that wasn't on the straight and narrow. There, he and his fellow soldiers slavered over photos of scantily adorned actors and other busty, pliable, doe-eyed women whose posters made a diaphanous wallpaper that covered the surfaces of their barracks.

Hef wondered what a life infused with sexual excitement and freed from the bother of marriage and family might look like. For the time being, he postponed the question of whether or not such a life was for him. Instead, he set about creating a cultural product that would give his idea of sexual intrigue free rein.

He decided on a magazine. His zine would be unapologetic in its pursuit of sensual fulfillment. It would highlight his dream of the high life: The men depicted there would be high-powered—executives, athletes, covert government operatives. They were the kind of men who might swirl an eighth of scotch in a diamond-cut glass before picking up a sexy young thing who was just looking for some kicks. Marriage, if it were on the docket at all, wasn't by any means pressing.

The lifestyle Hefner imagined was described in detail in Ian Fleming's James Bond series, first in the UK in 1953, and in the US in 1954. Hefner would later claim that Fleming's famous Bond girls were inspired by the women who worked in his clubs.[3] Later still, the high life Hefner imagined would be spoofed in the animated series *Archer*. But these events were years away. For now, the mag needed a name. He chose *Playboy*, which invoked a frisky ease but didn't immediately disclose its bawdy content.

Playboy launched in 1953 and was an instant hit. By contrast Hefner's marriage, which had left him with a ten-year-long out-of-body feeling, was terminated in 1959. In a 1974 interview for *Playboy*, he explained that at the time he'd felt as if he were dying inside.[4] The confines of marriage had begun to hollow him out. He hadn't spoken about it much publicly, but he had been a virgin when he'd said his vows. Millie had not. She'd slept with another man while he was in the service. She'd offered him a long leash to explore sexual encounters with other women, but it didn't make up for her betrayal. For the duration of his marriage, he'd been living with that truth. After a decade, he could no longer stand it.[5]

The magazine seemed to be his way of writing himself into a new existence, one in which men were freed from the notion of "matrimony, no matter what." In point of fact, Hefner wanted his magazine (and by extension his life) to be explicitly at odds with so-called family-oriented rags. *Playboy* was instead suffused with a hedonistic joie de vivre. It hit newsstands in a postwar setting in which scores of (white) Americans were finding new disposable income filling their wallets. Rather than doting on a wife and kids, Hef wanted to encourage men with a new heft of discretionary income to spend it on themselves. To enjoy life a little.

This being his aim, and young men eighteen to thirty being his target audience, mid-century *Playboy* articles were bursting with stories on the ills of marriage for men. In a 1963 article ominously titled "Love, Death & the Hubby Image," author William Iversen opens with a fake advertisement:

> Tired of the rat race? Fed up with job routine? Well then, how would you like the chance to make $8,000–$20,000—*as much as $50,000 and More—each year*, working at Home in Your Spare Time? . . . Yes, an Assured Lifetime Income can be Yours now, in an easy, low-pressure part-time job that will permit YOU to spend most of each and every day as you please!—relaxing, reading, watching TV, playing cards, socializing with friends![6]

This phony ad, Iversen averred, presented an offer "addressed solely to single American women, and represented the unspoken, undefined, but strongly subliminal sales appeal presently contained in the age-old male proposal: 'Will you marry me?'"

Iversen's was a representation of wifedom that suggested women only wanted to marry for a type of financial security that entailed not working very hard. It anticipated the welfare queen—that most dastardly public charge—only the problem with wives was a private problem. Its hard line on marriage—that it benefited women at a steep cost to men—would later animate the rap lyrics of men against gold diggers. But whereas the latter two concerns were about women who were Black, or otherwise suffering from a deficiency of whiteness, the time period and the author suggest that it was *white women* who, in Iversen's view, were using marriage like it was their very own trust.

▪   ▪   ▪

Playboy was, at that time, overwhelmingly white. Consider the findings presented by Elizabeth Fraterrigo in *Playboy and the Making of the Good Life in Modern America*. She notes that in the 1950s, when the magazine got its start, "*Playboy* assumed a white middle-class audience and represented a world of white affluence."[7] Indeed, throughout the 1950s and early 1960s, Black women were largely excluded from the magazine. This occlusion was challenged by some Black men, who argued that *Playboy* was by that time the "premier arbiter of American beauty,"[8] and that by leaving Black women out, Hefner was issuing a statement of open white fetishism that Black men (however briefly) could not abide. In response, Hef pointed out that there had been a "Negro Playmate" in 1957. The woman, Linda Vargas, was fair-skinned and described as "restless" and "lithe," like a "satiny, black cat."[9] Later, in a series of developments that should surprise no one, Hef oversaw the inclusion of a handful of non-white Playmates and Bunnies, who despite their racial positioning could make the cut so long as they "had slender frames and ample busts."[10] Women who were fair-skinned, slender (yet buxom), and compliant: these were the sufficiently white women of *Playboy*.

Playboy's authoritative voice on identifying the right kind of women to incite arousal and inspire commitment was often little more than a twentieth-century regurgitation of eighteenth- and nineteenth-century racial beauty ideals, with more meat in the mammaries. The visual "masturbatory aids" the magazine proffered were dominated by slim, pliant fair-skinned women. The written word, too, offered a twentieth-century refashioning of things white men have long propagated about the ideal woman. Which is to say that despite Hef's post-hoc intervention, Black women were seldom featured or even mentioned in *Playboy* for the remainder of the twentieth century. Other non-white women were also rare. But the conversation about Asian women was that they still had the goods for (white) men who no longer wanted to deal with shrill feminist (white) women.

In a feature from 1968, "The Girls of the Orient," an anonymous author makes the case for traveling to Asia to meet the kind of girls who are now in short supply in America. Writing of the Maluku Islands—which he calls by their colonial name, the "Spice Islands," although he is writing after they won their independence in 1945—the author urges American men to travel there to meet goodly women possessing the coveted qualities of white sufficiency. The author giddily conveys the information that, there, one finds "slender, ivory-skinned maidens dedicated to serving man's slightest need."[11]

An American man could feel refreshed meeting different types of idealized Asian women, seeing as how, according to the author, they vary by country. In Korea, Japan, and Vietnam, "the Asian girl still devotes herself single-mindedly to pleasing her man" being that she is, as implied by the author, relatively removed from the Western influence of feminism. In Thailand, "forest maidens . . . keep their half-clothed bodies trim with hours of exercise—pounding rice in giant mortars." All told, American men can find sexual fulfillment in this feminist caesura, since throughout Asia, one can happen upon an "Eastern girl" who betrays a "[f]rank and untroubled acceptance of her role as a woman," which aids her in "the art of pleasing men."[12]

That is to say that during the movement era, American men were being told unabashedly and unequivocally to seek women who were slim, docile, and fair-skinned—although "toasty brown" women such as Filipinas were still deemed "seductive."[13] That men might need to travel to Asia for the kind of sex tourism that colonists of a prior century patronized serves as a form of justification or even encouragement for this behavior.

Tellingly, the author of "Girls of the Orient" advises that money is still to be used as a carrot on a string, banknote bait from men who despise gold diggers but still use their wealth to lure women for sexual purposes. It's a deceptive form of seduction and withholding that is still common among contemporary fuckboys. I like to call this maneuver "kitty entrapment."

●　　■　　■

William Iversen, like many *Playboy* contributors, kept implicit the understanding that whiteness and elite class status were central factors in the conception of female beauty. Initially, there was little pushback among its largely white and male readership to its racial exclusivity. In later years, some readers would curse and others praise Hef for including more women of color.[14] But for the time being, the race question was not of particular concern to *Playboy*'s content creators. Iversen, for one, was more taken with the question of what these feminist agitations were doing to the specter of romance.

Presenting an about-face to the common narrative of romance and marriage, Iversen claimed that men were the true romantics and that women were crude hangers-on who saw marriage as a path to a life of ease. The "very concepts of romantic love and devotion" he writes, were "masculine creations which have been sung and celebrated by male poets, novelists, composers and playwrights for at least 600 years." In Iversen's opinion, women have forsaken this legacy, becoming cold and calculating in their pursuit of partners. He argues that "the American girl seems to view marriage purely in terms of acquiring stuff and glomming on to a male provider."

Whereas *Esquire* slammed women who were attempting to "compete" with their husbands for jobs, *Playboy* at times despised the kind of women who didn't. Tellingly, for both men's mags, feminism was the root cause of the problem. Iversen charged "feministic propaganda" with turning women into opportunistic louts.[15] And now that women had their male caretakers and their feminist equality, men were left to do a growing share of the housework, in a new reality that, to Iversen, was just shy of criminal.

One of the worst abuses of feminism, according to Iverson, was how it had downgraded the role of the husband. Feminism, he asserts, had bespoiled the hubby image. Abraded it. Taken it from is valiant, heroic, Romantic Ideal, and turned him and other married men into bungling incompetents with their checkbooks out. Feminism had meant "the increasing erosion of rights and the growing magnitude of the sacrifice which American marriage imposes upon the male provider." In short, feminism had killed marriage as men had known it.

This state of affairs required some sort of coordinated response, and Iversen had the blueprint. Men, he suggests, might turn their attention to their *other* aim with women. Not the one that makes them the natural romantics but the one peculiarly enough at the opposite end of the spectrum. In a tacit plea, Iversen encourages men to recognize that settling down with one woman may not be best under the current circumstances and that they might consider obeying their "equally natural inclination towards polygamous sexual activity."[16]

Now, if you were to ask Hef, he would likely claim to be in favor of feminism, but he might also be playing fast and loose with the notion of "in favor of." In point of fact, he did support some feminist aims, like equal pay and access to birth control. But as articulated by other scholars, these features of feminism fit comfortably inside Hef's view that the new manhood should be about freewheeling fun with liberated chicks. Within his conception of masculinity, unplanned pregnancies and dependent partners were a real drag. They conflicted with a suave public image and unencumbered shagging with single independent "girls."[17]

As it were, a legion of *Playboy* articles denounced the ways feminism had transformed women, marriage, and even society writ large in any number of unsavory ways. Several articles decried what they called the "Womanization of America," a current of thought that first appeared in *Playboy* in 1958. The author who coined the phrase, Philip Wylie, sets out to warn young men about the reprehensible way feminism is remaking America. He uses a tactic that might these days be deemed Trumpian, that of recalling an earlier halcyon era of masculinity in an effort to incite men to work toward its revivification. "What I am about to describe here is a historical process . . . ," he begins, that has led to the current "sad condition."[18] It is a condition in which "a deadly distaff encroachment of what started as feminism" has "matured into wanton womanization."

Beside its superior tone, the first page deploys an outmoded anti-woman slur ("distaff," suggesting that women's place remains in the home) and signals precisely the kind of anger and misogyny to which the reader is about to be treated.

To Wylie—whose own name is a fitting homonym—the abominable creep of women began in the 1920s, just after they'd won the vote. Women were stepping out en masse, many of them marching uninvited into formerly all-male spaces. They'd arrive with their pocket change and, with the sheer force of the requests made with their little pennies, set about transforming male sanctuaries. Wylie writes,

> I myself recall the transition as experienced from that outpost of fad and fashion, Manhattan in the mid-Twenties. Saloons had been abolished; speakeasies had replaced them. The fresh-freed fair sex thereupon switched from nostrums for female complaint (which were laced with grain alcohol) to the honest beverage. But the beverage was not kept honest. Prior to those days, the thirsting male consumed a martini, manhattan or bronx—if he did not prefer straight whiskey with or without a beer chaser. After a few dozen months of Prohibition, however, speakeasy waiters would hand you an alphabetical list of cocktails beginning with apricot ambrosia and running with through orange blossom and pink lady eventually to zombie.

It was unconscionable to Wylie that "[d]rink became feminine" and that, worse, establishments for respite had followed suit. Because it wasn't just what was on order but the ambience that had shifted, as "speakeasies, now femme-thick, lost all resemblance to historic male drinking places," and "Little Chinesered tables you could tip over with a mere emphatic gesture were placed in front of banquettes upholstered in the hides of African beasts. Illumination was reduced to tearoom level."

Men were under siege. Nightlife had once been festooned with uproarious male laughter. If wives called, not a single husband was to be found there, even if he was sitting close enough to the phone to be overheard. And if one of the "panting beauties" took up space there, sexy young things who worked there or happened to stroll in off the street or on the arms of their paramours (because girls like this were always welcome), no one blinked an eye at the infidelity that was a release valve for the harsh realities of the male working world.

Those days were gone. Now there were "battle-axes" lurking in every corner. And it wasn't just men's old-haunts-cum-new-nightmares where women were pushing all the maleness out. These "she-warrens" had remade men's homes (their very homes!) with sickly sweet bubblegum fantasies, complete with "poufs big enough to lie on and ankle-deep rugs—resembling the parlor of a lavish brothel."

The women had taken over. Worse, they had used the idea of "equality" as a pretext for doing so. "The expressed feminist ideal of 'free and equal partnership' sounded fine," Wylie writes. "American men . . . assumed the ladies' lust for liberty would restore their proud, male being . . . its classic nature, demands, fantasies and lusty amenability." Curiously, Wylie suggests here that the role of equal women is to "restore men" to their highest state, their noble "classic" way of being. There is no equivalent press for men to lift women up to their greatest manifestations of themselves. That he might use the word "lust" twice to express one thought about men hits the reader like a dog whistle. It's a prompt, calling men to remember and respect their *own* desires.

Still, for all its misogyny and speak of "she-tyranny and pink-sequin shambles," the piece is not entirely without merit. Wylie offers a useful note on the way some women in the mid-twentieth century did behave, articulating how, "ladies won the legal advantages of equality—and kept the social advantages of their protected position on the pedestal." He is wrong in that this was not the strategy of all women. To be sure, there's no evidence it was even most women. But just as there had been a few avowed gold diggers during the time of his writing, so, too, were there those women who spoke of equality and independence, even as they expected men to treat them like European princesses.

In this respect, Wylie's condemnation of feminism was more than a hot take. It was an early salvo in the barrage of essays in *Playboy* articulating what he and many others perceived as the ills of feminism. His piece on womanization, women encroaching into every public place but still expecting to maintain their private romantic favors, started not a conversation but a convening.

In 1962, a handful of men were asked to sound off on the question of America's womanization. In a moderated panel hosted by and published in *Playboy* that included the celebrated playwright Norman Mailer, several men identified what they deemed the benefits and detriments of the so-called womanization of our nation. Most concurred: America was indeed being womanized by feminism. But how should they understand these developments? Were they exclusively bad news?[19]

Mailer, for his part, believed the media was the red-handed culprit spurring women's latest power moves at men's expense. Women had used their access to the mass media to compound their influence, he said, with the result being that "virility" was being destroyed, "slowly and steadily." Not all the panelists responded in this manner. Edward Bernays, considered the founder of the American public relations industry, understood women's political agitation, stating, "A lot of this so-called feminization is a direct result of a very healthy trend in society: simply that nobody wants to be anybody's servant anymore." Bernays's position notwithstanding, the general tone of the piece was one of consternation. That the women's sphere now overlapped with the men's was the primary concern.

But so, too, were some of the men worried about the rise of homosexuality that, they suggested, women's lib had encouraged through its breakdown of traditional gender roles. Panelist Alexander King, for instance, believed that a new apparent sissification of American men was afoot and that it was a troubling outgrowth of feminist machinations. Discussant Mort Sahl, the comedian, claimed that women played a more direct role in the flowering of gayness, arguing that women glorified gay masculinity by "dressing up in clothes designed by fags." Many feminist scholars have clocked anti-gay prejudice as a form of sexism. In this instance, feminist inching was identified as one cause of the rise and spread of an untenable and visible gayness in the country.[20]

Statements by Wylie and others indexing feminist trouble landed in the exact opposite way among *Playboy* readers as Miller's piece in *Esquire* had done only a handful of years earlier. In *Playboy,* the writings of Wylie in particular were less lamentation, more rallying cry. The men who responded affirmatively may not have called themselves anti-feminists affecting a men's movement. They didn't need to. They were simple restorationists. Their anger, hatred, and determination to place (hetero) men back atop the human pile in this country was a reaction to and a rejection of the new place in society that women had carved out for themselves. So now it was the men's turn to agitate for change.

                              ▪   ▪   ▪

I was sitting at a café, mulling over the latest useless hurdle that had been dumped in my lap. Another hoop to jump on the path to the PhD that prolly wasn't even going to get me a job. It was 2007. I hadn't yet started identifying as queer. That was three years away. So when a confident male voice broke through the din of my dissatisfaction with the paper in front of me, I found myself a willing recipient of his interest.

"Hi," came the voice of this stranger.

"Umm, hi," I replied.

"I see you here a lot," he continued.

"Yes, I work here," I replied.

"You work here?" he said, clownishly pretending to miss social cues.

"No," I said with a wan smile. "I do my schoolwork here."

Goffrey was an older man. He carried himself with an air of the Old World. The kind of man still bold enough to ask a woman out. The kind of man I'd soon meet—and fall in love with—when I moved to France.

He offered me his hand. I stood up to shake it. The thorough way he took in my entire body before speaking again should have been my first clue. If this had taken place today, that move would have been the end of this story.

But in my twenties, I was more pliable. Graduate school is boring. I wanted something, someone, to break up the monotony.

I wasn't expecting much out of Goffrey, just to hang out with him until he got on my nerves, or I found something else to distract me from the heart of darkness. So when he arrived at my threadbare graduate habitat in a brand-new cream-colored Lexus reminiscent of that Ye line ("I push Miracle Whips"), my bottom jaw fell off. I picked it up and greeted him.

"Hey, Sabrina." He smiled winningly.

"Hi, Goffrey. This car is amazing. I've never seen this model."

"It's just out," he said, his eyes unsmiling.

I hopped in his ride, and we headed to dinner. He didn't tell me where we were going. I didn't ask until we parked at the mall down the road about four minutes later.

"Uh," I began, "why are we at this mall?" At that time, this particular mall—which is now at a level of lavish befitting La Jolla—was as shoddy as my pad.

"There's a great sushi restaurant in here. C'mon, let's go."

In 2007, my palate wasn't as refined as it is now. But I was pretty sure that sushi in a low-rent mall—one that we could've walked to had his aim not been to floss his car—wasn't good, much less "great."

We crowded into a tight space that accommodated four leaning tables. The waitress came, and he ordered for the two of us. He explained that he knew what was good on the menu. As we waited, I was confronted with a group of people queueing for the movie theater across the corridor. There was a thin blond white woman in a pink velour tracksuit with "JUICY" splashed across her backside. She was cuddling her man. Seeing their intimacy in my present circumstance made me embarrassed.

The sushi wasn't good, because seven-dollar mall sushi is meant to be eaten when there are no other options, not sought out on purpose. I ate it without complaint.

I'm always willing to pay my own way, but Goffrey insisted on paying the twenty-dollar tab. I thought the cheapness was out of order. Why would a man roll up to my apartment in a fresh-off-the-lot cream-colored Lexus and take me to a nasty little dinner? I was growing impatient with whatever it was he was doing, but I had already agreed to head over to the San Diego Harbor for an evening stroll. I decided to wait and see if the mood might not shift in the night air.

On our way to the harbor, he was telling me about all the money he had and all the things he wanted to do for me, unprompted of course.

"I'm a dentist."

"Oh, really," I replied halfheartedly.

"Yah. Do you know how much money dentists make?" he asked. I glanced over at him wordlessly.

"We make *a lot* of money."

"Oh, OK."

"So what do you think about a trip to Barcelona?"

"Sounds expensive. I can't afford that right now."

He chuckled. "No, of course. *I* would pay for it." He turned a toothy smile in my direction.

"We just met," I replied. I also thought, *and so far, I think this ought to be one of our last meetings.*

"We can get to know one another on the trip."

I didn't say anything. I let him believe I was going to Barcelona with a stranger, knowing full well I wasn't. This was the point at which his demeanor changed. He'd been testing me. He wanted me to know he had money and could get a classy respectable woman. He was trying to gauge if I fell into that category. My disinterest showed him that I didn't care about his money and that I knew full well that whatever magic drew him to me would draw another him if he fell through. He liked this.

At the harbor, he was more affectionate. We held hands. I started to relax and settle into the idea of us. And even though I wasn't going anywhere out of the country with this individual, I could not deny the power of that ride. I'm from LA, and I do love a good stunt.

He ducked into a cigar shop, bought a cigar, and took a puff. Right afterward, he kissed me. It was disgusting. I'm sure he saw me flinch. But I didn't pull away. This pleased him.

"How old are you?" he asked.

"Twenty-seven. How old are you?"

"I'm thirty-seven."

I shrugged. Ten years is not an untenable age gap at that age.

Out of nowhere, he picked up one of my braids and rubbed it between his fingers. Feeling the synthetic texture, he rolled his eyes, then let the braid drop. Still, he didn't seem to begrudge me this aspect of my insufficient whiteness. Perhaps because he was Middle Eastern, he seemed to be less bothered by as much. Besides, I was still considered young and shapely. If I proved to be malleable, he might judge me a good enough catch to go the distance.

We held hands again as we walked along the pier. He was talking a lot about "our" future. He didn't try to get any more intimate with me than that one cigar-flavored kiss. Somehow, it seemed gentlemanly. I thought, *This is the benefit of being with an older man.*

■　　■　　■

Goffrey wanted an answer.

"Look, Sabrina. You hate where you live. Why don't you just move in with me? I have a huge home in Carlsbad. I'll set you up with a car. I have another car—a Nissan—that I no longer need. I'm ready to start a family. Aren't you?"

I didn't know what I wanted. I mean, women are *supposed* to want this, right? I mean, shouldn't I be pleased that an older Persian man, who had never pressured me into sex in our few weeks of dating, just wanted to do things the old-fashioned way? Tie the knot, start having kids?

"I'm not ready. We don't know each other that well," I said.

"We'll get to know each other," he replied.

"I have to finish my degree. And then with the job market, I don't know where I'll be able to get a job and . . ."

"You'll finish the degree and get a job around here." He seemed pretty sure of that. "Sabrina, let's be serious, OK? Let's not play games."

We hung up.

I walked, zombified, into the makeshift toilet closet they labeled "bathroom" in grad housing. Turned on the scarcely illuminating light and stared into the mirror. *Could I be with this man? Could I marry him?*

It just didn't feel right. I wasn't in love—and didn't think he was either. He seemed to find me pretty and nice, and I was younger, and that's all he seemed to want in a woman.

I didn't care about his money. I was getting a PhD. I figured I'd eventually have my own money—maybe. Something about the security he offered was seductive though. No more putting up with selfish, corny men my own age. And twenty-seven! *Such* a respectable age to get married. Not too young and dumb. Not so old I started to look it.

I wasn't sure if these were my thoughts or Goffrey's. He'd told me a cautionary tale about a few of his friends: *My friends are all about thirty-six, and they have tried to find women their own age and have children. They couldn't. The women were too old, couldn't get pregnant. You're young. This is a great time to have kids. Don't you want kids?*

I had always thought I wanted kids but hadn't really thought too seriously about having a husband. They'd seemed like a burden often.

My best friend at the time, Chartrese, could not believe I would even think twice about his offer.

"I would do it," she said firmly. "You'll be married; you'll have kids. You'll be comfortable." Four years later, Chartrese would find her own older man willing to put a ring on it in exchange for her compliance. True to her word, she moved in and became the kind of woman who knew how to listen to her man and support him. Chartrese's new beau didn't like me though. Thought I was a bad influence, owing to my strong will. One year after they moved in together was the last time I ever saw a woman who had been my best friend since we were thirteen.

I couldn't decide what to do. Goffrey kept applying the pressure. One day, we went for a drive up the coast in the Lexus. We had been together for many weeks by then, and the car didn't have the same hold on me it had once had. He could sense my growing dissatisfaction with our relationship.

"You know?" he began. "Feminism is the worst thing that ever happened to relationships."

"What?" I said. His assertion had seemed to come out of nowhere.

"I mean," he scrambled, "this is not my opinion. I heard this from my dental assistant. She said feminism made it so that men and women no longer know how to get along. No one knows their place anymore." He kept shifting his gaze from me to the road to see how this revelation was hitting me. I didn't say anything. I just thought, *What the hell does feminism have to do with anything? Feminists wanted the vote and equal pay. What does that have to do with us?* I remained silent.

"How old are you really?" he asked, suddenly skeptical of my infuriating non-cooperation.

"I'm twenty-seven."

He relaxed. This made *me* skeptical.

"How old are *you*?" I asked.

"Well, I'm actually forty-two," he cheesed. He kept looking from me to the road to see how the news of his lie had landed.

I turned to him with my mouth open, then closed it. Ten years was cool, but fifteen? Nah. I had not agreed to such a time lag. At that time, I was strongly against being with a man that much older. I'm sure I had never told him, but my parents had me when they were very young; my mother was seventeen when I was born. I was afraid of being with someone who was more my parents' peer than mine. This man could have gone to high school with my mother. That tore it.

I didn't say anything. I turned my gaze out the window, staring longingly at the scores of men in my own age group drifting past and thought how fine they all looked. I wished I could've tucked-and-rolled out of the vehicle that had once held so much promise and linked arms with one of them.

■   ■   ■

Goffrey didn't take the breakup well. He kept calling and calling and calling and calling. I had been advised by a male friend to never pick up, to just let him continue to fall on the voicemail. Eventually, he'd get the message.

I ran into one of my neighbors, Amira, and she asked about him. I explained the situation and how confusing it had all been. When she got the full rundown, she was blown to pieces that I had ever even entertained this jackass.

"Sabrina! You were considering marrying this man? He's a *dentist* and trying to act all *rich*? What does he have, like *one* million dollars?" Amira was a classically trained violinist. She too was from the Middle East. Which is to say Amira came from money. She thought her parents thought it was funny to try to "toughen her up a bit" by forcing her to live in one of the grad shanties.

When she said the "one" in "one million dollars," she half-heartedly unfurled her index finger in disbelief. She couldn't even bring herself to fully extend it, forming it instead into a question mark, so unbelievable were the circumstances. She blinked exaggeratedly and shook her head before looking back at me sternly.

I smiled sheepishly. I realized then the role race had played in my decision-making. *Would another man want me for his wife?*

In 2010, I ran into Goffrey, curiously enough, at that same mall where he had taken me to dinner. Being normal, I said hello. He was with a group of friends and pretended not to know who I was. His friends loved it. Oh, wasn't this game an uproarious delight! I turned on my heels and started toward the escalator. It was then that he remembered, paradoxically, that what he'd always liked about me was that I didn't need him and didn't put up with his shit. That is to say, my feminist bearing.

"Oh, hey, c'mon Sabrina. Hey, I'm sorry. I was just having a little fun. Hey!" He started yelling in the direction of my retreating frame. "You stopped talking to me, remember? Hey, Sabrina!"

Holding my head high, I strode, dignified, into Fry's Electronics without uttering another word.

*   *   *

Playboy's relationship with modern women was explored, and even encouraged, by prominent writer Helen Gurley Brown, author of the popular romance guide for women, *Sex and the Single Girl*, published in 1962. Well into her thirties, Brown had been a single gal. In the 1960s, this way of living inevitably opened women up to accusations of spinsterhood. But Brown, like Hef, had an entrepreneurial spirit. Instead of associating singledom with sadness, she sold the idea that the single life for a young woman could be an exciting adventure and should be considered preferrable to rushing to the altar.

Brown's position was not revolutionary, but it was radical. In encouraging young women, too, to hold off on marriage, *Sex and the Single Girl* "rejected gender roles that posited marriage, motherhood, and homemaking as the fruition of female existence."[21] Now, women too had a tome advising them against early marriage, a book in which self-reliance and personal autonomy through employment were fêted rather than feared. Independent experiences gave single young ladies a taste of freedom rarely afforded by those who went from father's house to husband's.

Yet even with Brown as a guide, women's lives in the 1960s were still circumscribed. So-called working girls were dissuaded from thinking of their careers first. Their jobs were supposed to provide at least enough money to pay the bills and keep a lady outfitted in the latest fashions. It was understood that paying one's own way could attract men, but competing with men for high-powered positions was not in a girl's best interest. The final destination for young women was still assumed to be a life shared with a male partner.

Brown believed women should take more time to enjoy single life *on the way to marriage*. In so doing, a single girl could be flirtatious with men. She would not have the kind of sexual hang-ups that would prevent her from enjoying a good causal romp. In short, she was the perfect playmate for the playboy.[22]

And, just as the playboy had rules, so, too, did the fancy-free single girl. The single girl was mysterious yet accommodating. She was coy in a way that men enjoyed. A way that got them amped for the chase and kept them coming back for more. She did not try to force her way through the glass ceiling—which would not have been accommodating.

Therefore, she had to be frugal with her undoubtedly meager earnings. Whereas *Playboy* advised young men to indulge in conspicuous consumption, Brown suggested that women spend wisely, pinching pennies and cutting corners on nonnecessities. An important way for the single girl to save money was to avoid spending a dime of it on men.

Men made more money. Thus, according to Brown, it was their responsibility to provide for the women they hoped to entertain. When it came to the growing costliness of dating, Brown insisted that men bear the brunt of that expense, as if it were a form of dating tax. "Reciprocity is not entirely in order with beaux," Brown wrote. "I think the correct ratio between times on the town and dinner *intime* in your apartment is about twenty to one!" This calculation, of course, only applied to men women expected to be able to reel in—the ones with whom a long-term partnership was desirable. For the men a woman was just going around with for kicks, there was no need to repay them at all: "If you aren't en-gaged . . . you don't really have to pay back dinner ever. Part of the price bachelors pay for staying single is to spend money taking girls out. No use making their bachelorhood easy by feeding them like little mother."[23]

It wasn't just dinners that single ladies should expect as compensation for their company. Young women should "Expect and encourage gifts from men," Brown wrote. "They are part of the spoils of being single."[24] Brown's entreaty could be read as a siren song for gold diggerism. And, critically, the woman issuing it, as well as those most likely to have heard and heeded its call, were white.

In the conversation between *Playboy* and *Sex and the Single Girl* we can see the genesis of the relationship rules that framed the latter half of the twentieth century, when love went from a feeling to a game. Men were advised by *Playboy* to hold out on marriage while banging the hottest chicks they could, before "the one" came along. The one would be good-looking, no doubt. But she would also be tender and giving, a "lavisher"[25] who was independent enough to make her own way but who was also not a feminist or a career woman—she knew a woman's role and did not step outside of it. *Sex and the Single Girl*—a book that sold millions of copies in over thirty countries and was on the bestseller lists for the *Los Angeles Times* and the *New York Times*—similarly encouraged women to date around until they found "the one." To work, but not too seriously. To keep up a desirable appearance and be on the lookout for a man attractive in face and figure, and handsomely paid.

On both sides of the aisle, women were being urged to be "working girls," a term now doubly signified. Men's and women's publications during the 1960s increasingly demanded that women be sexually alluring and independent financially but not careerist, while also telling them (for better or worse) to use their looks to attract gifts and favors from men. Both sides were working (perhaps unwittingly on Brown's part) to erode the distinction between "woman" and "sex worker." For whereas men were being encouraged by men's mags to see life as a series of acquisitions, and to use their money to give them access to the high life, which always included a lump of women's bodies to be used exclusively for men's sexual pleasure, a growing number of women, too, taking up this ethos, described how they expected men to "treat" them, buy them gifts on their dates, or sometimes outright pay for sex.[26] Which is to say women were expected to use their sexual capital to attract and please men.

So, despite the fact that Hollywood's new leading men were depicted as sensitive, the new men on the ground, those millions taking their cues from Hef and the like, were increasingly envisioning women's bodies as little more than places to relieve themselves. Women too—and especially white women—perhaps seeing no way out but through, were beginning to accept this as the reality and to rejigger their expectations to those of the "working girl." Which is to say that since the 1960s, an unquantifiable contingent of women—and in particular the white women that the playboys would have sought—did have gold digging as an ethos. They internalized the idea that a thinly veiled form of sex work was a means to laying hands on commodities they would never earn enough money to purchase if they stayed in their lane as uncombative noncareerists. So, too, could this new sexual capital, this lightly obscured sex work, be useful for finding and (maybe) keeping a worthwhile male partner. It was a reality that feminist reformers found alarming but perhaps didn't have the words to address.[27]

Helen Gurley Brown, the most visible proponent of the single girl as working girl, eventually did get married. She tied the knot at age thirty-seven, marrying film executive David Brown. It was Brown who prompted her to write her best-selling book. He was also responsible for developing the prospectus that launched Brown's career as the latest editor of one of the top women's magazines in history, *Cosmopolitan*.

In the aftermath of Brown's death in 2012, journalists wrote multiple think pieces about this woman whose cultural power has heretofore been underestimated. Many claimed she was "the original Carrie Bradshaw."[28]

＊   ＊   ＊

Ahhh, Carrie and Mr. Big. HBO's hit franchise *Sex and the City*'s most talked-about couple. Their notorious on-again, off-again ten-year saga was one of the most watched romantic spectacles of the early twenty-first century. For a decade, fans of the show reveled in the sumptuous garments and impossibly chic—if impractical for city walking—stilettoes worn by Carrie and her sexually liberated posse. Then, in 2008, we watched with bated breath as Carrie, played by Sarah Jessica Parker, had her fairytale wedding to Big, the emotionally withholding man of her dreams.

The show, which first aired in 1998, saw tremendous commercial success during its six-season run, winning an Emmy in 2001. During its six seasons on HBO, and even after the first film was released in 2008, many viewers and critics heralded the franchise as "feminist." It debuted at a time during which more women than ever before were becoming educated and choosing the single life. Its representation of independent, successful single women over thirty exploring their sexuality amid the jungle of New York City's high-end galleries and exclusive nightclubs had obvious cultural cachet.

In 2010, after the movie *Sex and the City 2* was panned for its racist depiction of Abu Dhabi (and, critically, of Arab women), fans began exhibiting signs of a post-show hangover. Feminist liberation, as depicted on the show, presented four white women in a cartoonishly white version of New York where women who were not millionaires blithely entered the social circles of the lavishly rich in the hopes of finding partners. It was not a new take on liberation. Rather, it was a rerun, decades later, of Helen Gurley Brown's *Sex and the Single Girl*.

The retrospective think pieces that have been written about the show point to as much. For alongside the presentation of Arab women as needing white (female) saviors from the twin "menaces" of Islam and Arab men, niggling questions have arisen about the portrayal of the "loving" relationships on the show, especially that between Carrie and Mr. Big. To poach from the show's narrator, *We all began to wonder, had we been rooting for a toxic relationship the entire time?*

The answer to the question is a resounding yes. The "will-they, won't-they" nature of their relationship was engendered almost exclusively by Big. Big is a prototypical playboy: He is a forty-something bachelor with a high-profile job in finance. He is handsome, aloof, and wealthy. His money gives him access to the finer things, and he shies away from the kind of commitment that might not benefit his "new man" lifestyle.

Carrie, the prototypical working girl, makes her desire for a committed relationship with Big plain from jump. Big, for his part, continuously gets her hopes up. He professes his love for Carrie approximately one year after she has told him the same, explaining that he didn't want to feel pressured and had to do it in his own time.[29] Later, he leaves her, unsure that he's ready to begin the amble toward the altar that she so thirstily craves. Then, in a move toward more self-involved acquisitions, Big immediately marries a twenty-seven-year-old socialite named Natasha. This relationship dissolves, however, after he walks back into Carrie's life, this time taking her as his mistress, apparently longing for the undivided attention and sense of security Carrie's generally unreciprocated love bestows upon him.

Carrie's freedom with her sexuality, which included her stint as Big's side chick, prompted the actor who played Big, Chris Noth, to label her a "whore."[30] For our purposes, we can reframe his (misogynistic) remark to the more relevant descriptor of Carrie as embodying the working-girl-as-sex-worker mandate popularized by *Playboy* and *Sex and the Single Girl*. Big's playboy-cum-fuckboy turn and Carrie's complicity in his behavior have been explored in other works.[31] I will, however, point toward another element of the Big and Carrie affair that (mis)led many young women to believe she was empowered: the fact that she was the one who pursued the object of her affection.

Carrie's agency in trying to secure Big's affections despite his obvious reticence may have seemed in the early '00s like a feminist statement. Women had historically been told to wait passively to be chosen. Carrie's identification of whom she wanted and her "stop at nothing" attitude toward making the relationship work gave us all false hope that we might be able to manufacture romantic success through grit and determination.

But, of course, this was the outlook on romance prescribed for (insufficiently white) women in the post-movement period. Big puts Carrie in a romantic bind that is, in fact, the social position for women that *Esquire* and *Playboy* had largely engineered—one of prolonged anticipation for commitment in which all but the most attractive, elite white women routinely found themselves. The reasoning of these men's magazines was later validated by more mainstream publications, which argued that women were facing a "man shortage" and had better roll up their sleeves and put in the effort if they wanted the commitment, thus closing the loop on the snare.

In other words, insufficient whiteness plays a role in what happens between Carrie and Big. There are unrecognized ethnic and class prejudices in Big's behavior. He appears as the epitome of white masculinity: tall, handsome, composed, accomplished, and, god help 'im, wealthy. From their first interaction, Carrie feels insecure in his presence. She articulates this as a matter of her being younger, poorer, less accomplished, and lacking the requisite social connections to be a traditional partner for someone of Big's stature. When Big marries Natasha, a twenty-something debutante-cum-clerk at Ralph Lauren, after a perfunctory courtship, Carrie is devasted, believing that age, looks, and family money are the reasons Big chose Natasha.

These factors are indeed relevant to Big's selection of Natasha as a wife. She is an attractive blueblood whose profile is boosted by the unstated if palpable promise of old money. Carrie, by contrast, is a self-made woman. Her path from obscurity to celebrated writer has been marred by debt and insecurity. When she finally makes it, she is still "new money," and in spite of her wealth, she nevertheless lacks the requisite social polish to circulate in high society without incident.

"Old" and "new," particularly as they pertain to wealth and status, have always carried racial connotations. In the US, "old money" is a term reserved for originalist Americans, those deemed well-bred and refined by the "founding" fathers: wealthy Anglo-Saxon Protestants.[32] Indeed, this variation of the term WASP is, according to some scholars, the original meaning behind the acronym. That the terms "wealthy" and "white" might today function interchangeably within the moniker speaks to the contemporary enmeshment of whiteness and riches. For a healthy portion of US history, however, "whiteness" was a necessary but not a sufficient condition for amassing assets and social respectability. Irish, Italians,

Russians, and Jews at various points in US history were all deemed "white-ish," so-called hybrid whites who, while typically considered superior to the colored races, were nevertheless inferior to cultivated Anglos.[33] In other words, folk in these groups were insufficiently white.

There is one group among these historically degraded white persons who have been continuously associated with the gross crime of having (new) money: the Jews. The most memorable narrative exploring how a new-moneyed Jew cannot hope to assimilate within the American mainstream is arguably found in F. Scott Fitzgerald's *The Great Gatsby*. Scholars have debated whether or not Jay Gatsby was actually Jewish, with some people claiming he is never expressly identified as a Jew, while others point to his discarded birth surname, "Gatz," as of possible Hebrew origin.[34] The character's chosen name, "Gatsby," is an Anglo-Saxon name. In the US, when ethnic "new money" whites change their last names, it has largely been in an attempt to pass as or assimilate with Anglo-Saxons.

The creators of *Sex and the City* make no mention of Carrie Bradshaw's ethnicity. However, it is the case that Sarah Jessica Parker is half Jewish. When asked about Carrie's ethnicity point-blank, the show's producer, Darren Star, who is himself Jewish, stated that she "could be considered a Jewish character."[35]

Reading Carrie as Jewish changes the entire game. For if a character like Gatsby can hope to pass as sufficiently Anglo-Saxon by making money (and ultimately be thwarted in this aim), it is undoubtedly the case that for women (historically and in current times) passing is largely achieved through having the looks and behavior that lead to matrimony with a successful WASP. In this sense, Carrie isn't simply pining for Big; she is looking for the WASP acceptance that she has been denied by her ethnically Othered and financially humble beginnings.

These elements of ethnicity and class give us greater purchase on Carrie's disdain for Natasha. Played by Irish American actor Bridget Moynahan, Natasha is not technically a WASP, but she leans more toward sufficiency than Carrie. Described by Carrie as "the idiot stick figure," she is tall and slender, with aquiline features and old money. Save her brown hair and eye color, she represents, aesthetically the epitome of elite white femininity.[36] Natasha doesn't need Big to pass, but if Carrie is Jewish, in addition to being relatively poor, she does.

Carrie even hints at her (unstated) Jewishness by likening herself to Barbra Streisand. In one of her many conversations with her girlfriends about her relationship with Big, she admits to relating to Streisand's character, Katie, in *The Way We Were*:

MIRANDA: What are you, an alien? How could you have not seen it,
   The Way We Were?
SAMANTHA: Chick film.
MIRANDA: Okay. Robert Redford is madly in love with Barbara
   Streisand.
CHARLOTTE: Katie.
CARRIE: K-k-k-Katie.
CHARLOTTE: K-k-k-Katie, right!
MIRANDA: But he can't be with her because she's too compli-
   cated . . . and she has wild, curly hair.
CARRIE: Hello? C-c-c-curly.
MIRANDA: Yeah. So he leaves her and marries this . . . simple girl
   with straight hair.
CARRIE: Ladies, I am having an epiphany. The world is made up of
   two types of women: the simple girls and the Katie girls. I'm a
   Katie girl, and where are our drinks?[37]

None of the characters openly state the obvious—that a "Katie girl" is a complex, accomplished, possibly feminist, insufficiently white woman. Natasha, by contrast, is WASP-adjacent enough to be "simple" or "basic." She is nonthreatening, attractive, and genteel. The producers were even believed to have her wearing white in the majority of her appearances in an effort to portray her as "vanilla."[38]

Seen in this way, *Sex and the City* constitutes a six-season passing narrative. Carrie's lack of old money mixed with her abundant curly hair and other features deemed "irregular" by Anglo-Saxon racial discourse make her not just "complex" but insufficiently white. Her marriage to Big would be the vehicle of upward mobility that would give her, too, access to a simplicity that is overdetermined by whiteness. That is, she is trying to circumnavigate her insufficient whiteness and somehow convert her assets into the form of capital that would give her access to the ultimate prize (for a cishet white woman): a commitment from a peak white male. Funny how this goal remained atop the list for single cishet white women, and—by extending the logic of the racial, gendered, and sexual hierarchy—supposedly for *all* women.

Big's emotional withholding, his fuccboism, needs a target, a Katie type.[39] He has few qualms settling down with a "simple," quiet, wealthy woman who more closely matches the white-racial ideal. Indeed, even though he cheats on Natasha (whose last name suggests a Slavic origin),[40] her high-class standing means that she knows full well she doesn't have to tolerate his infidelity and other fuckboy antics. She has the luxury, because of her infinite social currency, of dropping Big. Big, in his emotional immaturity and self-absorption, then goes back to toying with the affections of the woman who needs him to prove that she has ascended to the upper crust of white society.

Sex and the City is a solid repackaging of Helen Gurley Brown's "working girl" femininity. This renovation of womanhood existed to accommodate the "new man" innovated by *Playboy* and its view of women. It ensured that post-feminism, elite white men would still hold onto the reins of power wherever women were concerned.

■   ■   ■

Philip Wylie's magnum opus on American womanization was not his last treatise in *Playboy* on the problem of women. The author was something of a *Playboy* favorite. He had a particular way of conveying his views on feminism and women's new place in society that was at once literary and venomous. So after excoriating feminism for ruining men's sacred spaces of respite, he turned his attention to the wreckage women's imposition caused in the modern workplace.

In general, the men of *Playboy* wanted women to work and earn enough money to survive—but only just. These men didn't want to be saddled with the burden of being a "provider" and thus responsible for supporting a woman financially, but they also wanted to make sure women maintained a self-regulated cap on their ambition. Women ought to have known that their work—their being working girls—shouldn't place them in the position of competing with men for high-paying, high-powered careers. Many *Playboy* authors, and readers, espoused the belief that if women could earn enough to feed themselves whilst staying slinky (à la Helen Gurley Brown) *that* was hot. But women barging into men's spaces of money, power, and public influence was to be prevented at all costs.

Wylie articulates this much in a 1963 article simply titled "Career Women." Laying characteristic waste, Wylie charges career women with having an "obscene compulsion" to compete with men. This, he argues, threatens to "cripple manhood and masculinity." The problem with these kinds of women is that they are not fighting fair, he says. They use tools not available to men, such as their looks, spying, blackmailing, and "whoring," to reach their career goals. How are men supposed to compete with women willing to hump their way to the top, not in the good earnest way, but in the way of the world's oldest profession?

It wasn't, of course, that men did not want *any* women in the workplace. Just as in the bars, young (white) women with tight bods and come-hither eyes were nice to have around. So long as they were pretty, polite, and unassuming, they were a welcome distraction from both the shrews at home and the hags now populating these same watering holes.

Which is to say that these loathsome career women were certainly not the right types to have around the workplace. So Wylie, after having been invited to do a takedown of these women by a few of the *Playboy* higher ups,[41] issued yet another call to action for all manly men:

> Let us, then who are still masculine, or who wish to become masculine, and those who would undertake to restore a birthright now stolen by the career sisterhood . . . let us unite to celebrate womanhood as feminine, as gorgeous, as titillating and sexy—and let us hoot down with hearty bass guffaws any and all vulgar . . . dames who try to stride in and put a stop to our fun.[42]

Playboy left modern women no possibility for social advancement that did not involve a particular type of sexualized relationship with men. No longer could a woman expect to remain a virgin, meet a gentleman, marry, and start a family—at least not a woman who wanted to hook up with the new man as inspired by the magazine. Neither could the modern woman expect to get an education, start a career, and earn the respect of her male peers. The prototypical partner for the playboy was one willing to be sexy *at* work, without the expectation of any payment for what—for all intents and purposes—constituted sex work. She had to be a hot young (white) thing, swishing her tail for her male counterpart with absolutely no expectation of any compensation. Free sex-based labor. No possibility for promotion.

Between *Esquire, Playboy,* and *Sex and the Single Girl,* most women had been downgraded. Women were now considered by some of the most powerful publications in mass culture to be working girls/sex workers. This of course did not include those most elite of women, sufficient as they were in whiteness.

Still, up to now, the major philosophers of this ideology had been white, and overwhelmingly white men. In the years to follow, Black men would add to the w/horification of women who fell below this standard for partnership. Hip-hop would reveal this too.

CHAPTER 6

SEX TRAFFICKING
(A.K.A. PIMPIN')

The death of the Notorious B.I.G. sent shockwaves throughout the rap world. Laid to rest in March 1997, his death came less than six months after that of his comrade-in-arms turned enemy-in-battle, Tupac Shakur. Being that they were two of the biggest hip-hop acts in the world, many rap fans like myself wondered what would come of the nascent genre.

West coast gangsta rap artists still ruled the airwaves. Westside Connection, featuring Ice Cube, blew the top off the charts with their 1996 album *Bow Down*. Dr. Dre, largely via his protégé Eminem and the release of N.W.A's greatest hits album, was a constant presence that same year. Snoop, who in the mid-to-late 1990s was regularly in collaboration with artists Daz and Kurupt (a.k.a. Tha Dogg Pound), was steadily in the business of releasing bangers.

These weren't the only rapping-ass, hood-ass niggas to contend with. By 1996, the Dirty South—a nickname that fittingly inverts the image of the South as a dancing white Dixieland into one of Black struggle for survival—could no longer be ignored.[1] OutKast, who shot to public notice with their inventive take on a Christmas song, "Player's Ball," in 1993, muscled their way to the top of the rap game in 1996 with the release of their album *ATLiens*. Master P and Geto Boys were among the other movers and shakers of the late '90s.

But no one had counted New York out. New York was the genesis of the thing. Acts like Diddy and Wu-Tang were a force. Many were still on Nas's first studio album *Illmatic* (1994), which critics and fans had pronounced the best rap album ever. And between Missy Elliot, Lil' Kim, and Foxy Brown, women in the game, too, were starting to get their long overdue acclaim.

Yet, it is undeniable that the death of two young rap icons changed the whole tone of the game. A lot of rap in the '90s took relish in thug life. Niggas boasted about loading, toting, and aiming guns at other niggas. That this posture had animated rap's most deadly feud left many artists, including B.I.G.'s right hand, Puffy, to turn from producing songs about shooting and killing to those about love and loss.

But the mournful mien wasn't meant to last. The way forward in a genre built on braggadocio was, well, another form of braggadocio. Recognizing as much was part of Jay-Z's genius.

In the era of Jay, rap music continued to encourage men to kill their feelings of love for women as a means of getting and keeping the upper hand. Cue the accession of the "pimp aesthetic," by which rappers like Jay-Z declared themselves pimps. This metamorphosis reworked the original vision from "we don't love those *hoes*," which carried a specific racial intonation, to a more general "don't catch feelings" admonition against loving any woman. Moreover, pimp rap not only encouraged men to withhold love and money from women—which was also popular in *Playboy* and other men's magazines—but frequently celebrated Black men's ability to make money off the real and metaphorical sale of Black and other insufficiently white women.

In place of love, rappers like Jay-Z promoted the w/horification of women. The pimp aesthetic asserts that men can enjoy their best commodity fetishistic life—the kind also promoted by *Playboy*—when they don't fall in love. For rappers who were not born having access to big bank, the real and imagined sale of Black and IWW bodies was their way to make a come up.

*   *   *

Jay-Z, né Shawn Corey Carter, was born in late '60s Brooklyn. He was the youngest of four children raised by his mother, Gloria, in the infamous Marcy projects.[2] This public housing complex was, according to at least one criminal trial, a base of operations for the distribution of crack rock and heroin throughout the neighborhood.[3]

For many Black men in Reagan's post-industrial America, the presumably underground drug economy was one of the few visible ways to get over. Expectedly then, the constant exposure to illicit drugs and guns—because where there are illegal narcotics so, too, will there be firearms to defend their movement—had a formative impact on the young creative. By the '80s, the height of the crack epidemic in America, Jay was swept up in the business of moving weight and loading clips. In an interview with *The Guardian* in 2010, Jay describes the terror he felt when he decided to pull the trigger on his own brother, a crack addict, after he'd stolen Jay's ring. He was only twelve years old at the time. In a surprise twist, his brother apologized for his behavior, opting not to press charges. Had he done so, one of the world's best-known hip-hop acts might never have had the freedom or opportunity to switch from being a drug hustler to a rap star.[4]

Jay's rise to stardom wasn't foreordained. He entered the rap game in earnest in the late '80s, allying himself with an older artist named Jaz-O—one inspiration for his stage name—to release a track titled "The Originators." It achieved nominal success, earning the pair a spot on the iconic *Yo! MTV Raps*.

That track and the TV appearance it garnered could hardly be considered his big break. Rap in the late '80s, during the golden age of hip-hop, was still teeming with revolutionary possibility. There was a crush of artists rapping about liberation, strife in the ghetto, love in the ghetto, and their beefs with other rappers. Within this evidently political milieu, it wasn't easy for Jay to push his way to the fore. What was arguably the main draw of Jay and Jaz, their style of "speed rap," might have been novel, but the novelty alone didn't make their act a huge draw.[5] It would take Jay years to devise a blueprint with this style that would propel him to the status of rap legend.

By 1995, he'd arrived at fresh formula for success. After a string of rejections from major labels, he teamed up with Dame Dash and Kareem Burke to launch Roc-A-Fella records.[6] Their label, in collaboration with Priority Records, released Jay's first full-length LP, *Reasonable Doubt*, in 1996. Several industry players made an appearance on the album, including Mary J. Blige and the Notorious B.I.G. a matter of months before his demise.

Big's appearance on the album inevitably helped it get spins. Biggie was, after all, at the height of his powers in 1996. Their joint track, "Brooklyn's Finest," was a showcase of MCing reminiscent of the proverb "steel sharpens steel." As they trade bars, you can hear each rapper raising his game in what feels like an effort to edge the other one out.

The competition between the two rappers came from a place of love and mutual respect. They had attended the same high school, George Westinghouse Career and Technical Education High School, in BK. They were reportedly friends. And though Jay was in Big's shadow at the time the track was recorded, Big affiliate Lil' Cease went on the record in 2016 to claim that Biggie thought Jay was "nicer" than him in terms of rap skills.[7] (Not for nothing, another rap legend, Busta Rhymes, could also be counted in that student population—when he deigned to show up to school. Busta and Jay had regular lunchroom speed rap battles that, according to Busta, helped him to up his game dramatically.[8])

Still, it was another track on the album, "Ain't No Nigga" with fellow Brooklynite Foxy Brown, that made the most noise. Besides being featured on *Reasonable Doubt*, it also appeared on the soundtrack to the hit movie *The Nutty Professor,* no doubt boosting its sales and mainstream popularity. The song was certified gold on its release. It is also where we learn about Jay's views of Black women.

On the track, he confesses to sleeping with a mountain of Black women, bragging, "Had more Black chicks between my sheets than *Essence.*" It is on this song that he identifies himself as a player. The player aesthetic, like that of the playboy, relies on having a covey of women parading through a rotating door. The women implicated are frequently kept in line by the false belief that they are either the only or the "main" chick. Usually, the side and main chicks are given gifts that are both tokens of appreciation and inducements to remain in a sexually exploitative situationship.[9]

The player's philosophy is to keep several (insufficiently white) women believing they have found "love." They must also believe that in spite of the love they share with their men, their men (& only men) *must* fuck around. The problem of the roving erection is presented to women as a biological imperative, an uncontrollable fact that is part of cis male bodies. This too reveals itself as a con. Not only do all genders have the capacity to feel and experience the craving to act on sexual desire, but the Romantic Ideal—once advocated for by men but being violated here yet again—posited that when a man was in love, he had eyes and dick for only one woman. There was no element of the ideal that American men treated as received wisdom for much of US history that necessitated a sidepiece for additional humping.

True to form, in the song, Jay describes lavishing gifts on his partner-in-rhyme, Foxy, whom he refers to as "love." Per Jay, he gifts her a beeper and flashy pumps to show he cares. But he still steps out on her: "You know these hoes be makin' me weak." Here, Jay approaches Foxy as if leveling with her. She is his "love," but she needs to accept—and is expected to accept—the fact that he is a known player. So, between the gifts and Jay's boast that "no one can fuck you better," Foxy is wheedled into accepting the nature of the game. Her only option, if she wants a man who is neither cheap, nor broke, nor a terrible lay—which makes a player already three times better than a fuckboy—is to get them gifts, get that good D, and believe that the other Black women on his roster are basic sidepieces who do not have the same place in his heart, although it's not immediately clear how that makes a difference.[10]

Foxy plays the part of a woman who doesn't care if her man is on the prowl, so long as he brought the jewels home to mama. She raps that she was never stressin' the other women, because she is the one with the jewels, and therefore the status. She claims the titles of both "wifey" and "wife" during her verse, neither of which he cops to. Both appear to be self-proclaimed statuses which, having no validation from her male counterpart, represent a woman's attempt to gas herself. Indeed, her otherwise disavowed discomfort with the situation—since she has less freedom to step out than he, which is the entire point of the player plan—is exposed when her friends advise her to leave his cheating self. She coos, "Friends'll tell me I should leave you alone," as if weighing their advice. He laughs this off, and his rejoinder is devasting in its effectiveness: "Tell the freaks to find a man of their own."[11]

As if deploying a Jedi mind trick, he convinces her that jealousy is behind her friends' counsel, not care. This does the job. The reason for its persuasiveness is clear: In the Black community women outnumber men, and since the movement era, men have been less interested in commitment than women. A Black woman who wants a Black male partner may face the expectation that she "share" him, as noted in an earlier chapter. So Jay asserts that women who knock the game aren't in it, that is, they don't have a man in their lives at all. It would have been quite the shameworthy charge for women living in a time when singledom and queerness were subject to ostracism. These "freaks" better get with the program and "find a man of their own."

A man of her own is, of course, precisely what Foxy doesn't have, and is the source of her friends' consternation. But how could she say this to her "love" in a known player economy? No, the final verse is the one that ensnares. There was nearly no such thing as a man of one's own in the world of players that many Black women found themselves in. Any man her friends get will, too, likely be sleeping around. This is the realization Foxy must come to in the end. For Black people during the late '90s, the peak of playeration, a man was held in common, and Black women were The Commons.

"Ain't No Nigga" was one of the most successful tracks on *Reasonable Doubt*, an LP that was met with a spattering of applause from critics, nothing overly.[12] Today it is considered a classic album. But it didn't catapult Jay to the top of the game. This was likely due to the fact that neither this track nor many of the other tracks on the album could be considered innovative in their content. The album existed in the space long occupied by other rappers with more acclaim, like Big and Pac. It was the "I wield guns, I have money, and I fucks plenty of Black chicks" look. Jay hadn't yet found his niche. He didn't come to consistently occupy the spotlight in hip-hop and enter the conversation as one of the greats until he changed his persona. When he remade himself and the profession.

By the late '90s, Jay-Z had transformed. Instead of rapping from the perspective of a pistol-popping, drug-dealing player, he'd elevated himself. Now, his main objective was to stack chips and floss whips. In embodying this new character, rather than spending his bounty of money on the legion of women he'd bedded, he'd learned to withhold it from them. He was now, in his own words, no longer a player but a pimp—and not just any pimp. He was the kind of pimp the rap world hadn't yet seen: a polished pimp. By remixing his persona in this way, he helped move pimping from ghetto side streets to the center of American popular music. And he had been inspired by one of America's most notorious pimps.

▪   ▪   ▪

In his comedy special *The Bird Revelation,* Dave Chappelle puts a pause on the jokes near the end of the set to let the audience settle into a lengthy story. He holds up a copy of Iceberg Slim's most revered work, *Pimp: The Story of My Life*. He uses Slim's breakdown of the pimp game to narrate the paces that led to his shadowy departure from Comedy Central in the middle of filming the third season of his iconic *Chappelle's Show*. To hear Chappelle tell it, he'd left because the relationship between himself and the network wasn't one of mutual respect and understanding. It more resembled that of pimp and ho. In his long metaphor, the network was the pimp, and Chappelle, it seems, had reached his limit of being whored out.

I'd heard the name Iceberg Slim dozens of times. I didn't think to investigate who he was until advised to do so by the comic. (This was before his transphobic remarks made it impossible for me to enjoy his sets, much less take lessons from them.) I picked up my own copy of *Pimp*.

Iceberg Slim's birth name was Robert Moppins Jr. He was born in Chicago in 1918. His father and namesake wanted him to be left on somebody else's doorstep, to make his son some other body's problem.

His mother, Mary, put an end to such talk. But, by her son's own assessment, she was hardly the kind of mother a son could champion. Mary would later marry a doting husband named Henry who helped her open a beauty parlor. But Mary was seduced by the street life. She dropped Henry and the shop, bundling up Junior and following a hustler named Steve into the hardscrabble grift of Black Milwaukee.

In the midst of all this, young Robert found himself living out something of a riches-to-rags story. He was whisked away from a relatively quiet family life complete with a stable home and caring father figure and deposited in a claustrophobic attic in a lean Black neighborhood. He could spy the local whorehouse from his attic window. He watched the decked-out pimps and hustlers. Their swagger gave him a taste for the life that he, ironically, despised his mother for wanting.

A string of grafts kept the young man—who now went by Robert Beck in straight society and Cavanaugh Slim among the hustlers—in a do-si-do with the local lockups. But by the time he was a teen, he knew pimping would be his business. The early years were a struggle. He couldn't maintain control over "his whores." While incarcerated, he asked a more senior pimp for advice who told him, "You gotta back up from them fabulous pussys. You gotta make like you don't have a swipe." A "swipe" is a penis. The old heads in the penitentiary were advising him to get a handle on his member. In order to do so, they cautioned, he should be wary of beautiful women. These pimps concluded their counsel with the following: "You gotta keep your mind on the scratch. Stay cold and brutal."[13]

Recall that up to this time in the US, the Romantic Ideal was the reigning ideology for heterosexual comingling. It had advised men that attractive women—those with enough charms to stir the heart and loins—were to be sought after, pursued, fought over, and won over. This, according to the Romantic Ideal, was how men should (and often did) fall in love.

But this, according to the senior pimps, was the wrong way to lead a life trafficking in women. If a pimp followed the Romantic Ideal, he'd be led around by the wrong head. The way to win as a man who peddles flesh is to "stay cold and brutal." The cold meaning emotionally uninvested. The brutal meaning physically and psychically abusive.

It was routine advice for a pimp hoping to maintain a stable. Out of lockup, another procurer he'd admired counseled him to deaden his emotions: "Pimping ain't no game of love."[14] Slim repeats this to himself, in honor of his mentor. He later avows, "The best pimps keep a steel lid on their emotions and I was one of the iciest."[15]

Icy indeed. Slim and other hustlers lived by this rule, part of a code Slim described as "written in the skulls of proud slick Niggers freed from slavery."[16] The information was memorized, passed down generation after generation by word-of-mouth only to those panderers deemed worthy. After getting his first Black woman to prostitute for him, Slim was judged worthy of getting the full rundown of the code's contents. It was relayed to him by a particularly murderous pimp who went by the ironic name "Sweet."

To hear Sweet tell it, pimping was Black men's original entrepreneurial endeavor. Right after slavery, seeing as how white men's hankering for Black women hadn't abated, Black men devised a plan to make money off of Black women's inability to escape white men's clutches. Rather than advising them to reject white men outright in the early post-slavery days—which was not likely to have been an effective response in any event—Black men advised Black women that rather than giving it up to white men for free, they oughta charge for the experience:

> Those first Nigger pimps started hipping the dumb bitches to the gold mines between their legs. They hipped them to stick their mitts out for the white man's scratch. The first Nigger pimps and sure-shot gamblers was the only Nigger big shots in the country.[17]

Black pimps worked to actively kill their emotions in order to get the jump on women for the original purpose of selling Black women's bodies to white men. Eventually, these pimps would also take on white women as their whores. The women weren't always interested in sex work—some, like Slim's first, had to be brutally strong-armed. Slim's willingness to go the distance, to engage the requisite psychic and physical violence, won Sweet's approval, as he tells Slim he'll make it in the business because he has the requisite "hate" for women needed to be a good pimp.

If the Black men who entered the pimp life were trying to resist their own feelings of love, they were doing it for similar reasons as the men writing in *Esquire* and *Playboy* would decades later. They, too, saw the power of the Romantic Ideal as it hung over sexual relationships. Black pimps may have been among the first men to realize that by quietly disavowing it they occupied a position of power vis à vis women. Women (regardless of race) would have often been unaware of men's rejection of this cultural script for finding heterosexual partners. Even if they had known, it's unclear how they would have responded, since those who did not want to fall into the ignominy of being a gold digger had no other readily available frame for building a sexual partnership. This is why men's—both pimp and civilian—refusal to play along with the nine-centuries-old ideal has been so powerful.

Scholars have noted that, during the early twentieth century, pimping exploded in the American North, owing in part to the Great Migration.[18] This was the period roughly between 1916 and 1970 when scores of Black people left the destitution and segregation of the post-emancipation South to find, in many instances, similarly curtailed opportunities and affronts to their dignity in the North.[19]

This is part of the reason that Black pimps since at least the early twentieth century rejected the reigning cultural ideal surrounding romance, preferring to *make money off* of low-income Black and white women. White men during the same period, and especially those in entertainment, cried gold digger in response to what they saw as white women's routine dereliction of the ideal in an effort to amass the gifts of courtship. These white men thus worked to *keep money from* lower-income white women. Evidence of a relationship between these ideologies in the early twentieth century has proven elusive. But this marriage was realized in mass culture by the late twentieth century.

Black pimps like Slim eventually amassed an army of women. Slim, like many, got his start re-selling Black women's sex to white men who were nostalgic for the old days of unfettered access. The days when rape went without reprisal. Now sex with Black women was payable in full to the (cold) pimp.

If Iceberg was icy, it was partially an effort to follow the handbook to the letter. In one final bit of advice that formed part of the code, Sweet bestowed the following,

> Never get friendly and confide in your whores. You got twenty whores, don't forget your thoughts are secret. . . . You gotta always be a puzzle, a mystery to them. That's how you hold a whore. . . . Tell them something new and confusing every day. You can hold 'em as long as you can do it. Sweet is hipping you to pimp by the book.[20]

The "cold" way of sex trafficking went beyond simply not loving "ho's," to the avoidance of general intimacy. Pimps shouldn't divulge information to women. But the double-standard of the code demanded "strict rules for a whore"[21] who must hand over all the cash and describe all of the day's events. Keeping women in the dark while knowing everything you can about them is the key to pimping.

Iceberg was icy to all the women he trafficked. But he appeared to be particularly vicious toward Black women. When he meets Phyllis, the first Black woman he gets to turn tricks for him, he tells her she is a "bitch" straight off. She rears back, saying, "Goddamnit, call me Phyllis. Be a gentleman and respect me. I'm a lady." To this, Slim replies, "There's no such thing as a lady in our world. You either got to be a bitch or a faggot in drag. Now Bitch, which is it?"[22] To Slim and other Black men in the underground economy, it was impossible to view Black women—who were similarly kept out of white society by Jim Crow—as ladies. Phyllis, and all the women "in our world" that is *all* Black women, could only be bitches or despised homosexual men in drag.

Slim didn't just strike at Phyllis's self-concept. When he comes back from a long night, she asks where he's been, tells him she loves him, and asks him if he missed her. In keeping with the code, Slim describes his response:

> I shuddered and punched the runt with all my might against the left temple. On impact, needles of pain threaded to my elbow. She moaned

and shot backward onto the bed. She bounced like she was on a tram-
poline. There was a crunching, pulpy thud on the second bounce. She'd
crashed face first on the steel edge at the foot of the bed.[23]

Phyllis, who was only eighteen years old, was w/horified. She asks
him why he hit her. He says, "Bitch, if I have you a hundred years don't
ever ask me where I been. Don't ever try to play that bullshit love con
on me."[24] Is it surprising that a pimp would view a woman professing
love as a "con," when getting women to express love and devotion for
him while withholding such was *his* con?

While Iceberg had learned to keep a tight lid on his emotions, his
reaction to white lovelies was quite different. He describes women of
a variety of different races as attractive in the book, but white women
occupy a special place in his esteem. Talking to another Black man on
the corner at the outset of his path to pimping, he gestures to a white
woman who walks by, saying, "That sure is a fine silk girl, huh?" The
man responds, "Yeh Kid, she's fine as a Valentine. Two sights I ain't never
seen and that is a pretty bulldog, and an ugly white woman."[25] Slim and
other Black men routinely refer to white women to as "silk" or "silky,"
terms evoking luxury and comfort. The finer things.

Slim eventually meets a young white woman named Melody. He's
wild about her. She has "big curvy legs" and a "fabulous . . . rear end"
with "silky black hair" and "electric blue eyes." Furthermore, "[h]er even
choppers gleamed like rare china. . . . She was doing a bit that would
have shook up a eunuch."[26]

He hopes to pimp Melody, too, but he cannot deny the pull of her
whiteness, her affluence. He vows instead, "I'll stay outta the pimp role
until I case her. I'll go Sweet William on her." Melody presents Slim with
a rare opportunity to access the high-class white-only spaces denied
Black men. "She lived a long way from the black concentration camp,"
he muses. "I could smell the pungent odors of early April plant life. This
white world was like leaving Hell and riding through Heaven." As they
get to the business of getting it on, Slim realizes that Melody is a trans
woman. He replies, "[Y]ou stinking sissy sonuvabitch! . . . I'm a pimp,

not a faggot."[27] His fear and loathing of trans women carries him out the door. But it isn't enough to keep him from seeking out other white women for the pimp trade. He eventually, according to lore, had more than four hundred women turning tricks, Black and white.

In 1960, Iceberg Slim found himself back in prison for sex trafficking. This time, he spent a year in the hole. That's a lot of time to spend in a tight space where the only thing at one's disposal is reflection. Remorseful, he shelved his pimp cup upon his release. It was, after all, the revolutionary '60s. He got inspired by the likes of Malcolm X to clean up his act. He went headlong into the straight life.

Thereafter, Slim became a writer. He even entered long-term relationships with a few women. One of them, Betty, is credited with giving him the "Iceberg" in his name. Another, Diane, was reportedly his wife at the time of his death in 1992. There is little known about the third, Catherine. Photos of Betty and Diane reveal them both to be white women. When he went square, giving up his disavowal of sexual love to embrace it, he committed to (sufficiently) white women.

■   ■   ■

With *Reasonable Doubt,* Jay-Z had moved from an up-and-comer heating up the block to a lyricist earning applause from other lyricists. His record of claps on the back from other rappers, including Big, the soon-to-be assassinated king of the game, had to have added a swell to his chest. But that wasn't enough to move units.

Commercially, the album didn't strike gold, not at first. It made it onto the *Billboard* 200, cresting at number twenty-three. It sold a respectable 420,000 copies in its first year—a solid showing but well short of an earthquake. It completed its lurch toward platinum status by the early '00s, making its success a slow burn, but it would remain the lowest-charting album of his career.

He would improve upon these specs with his next album, *In My Lifetime, Vol.1*, released in '97. The album had more than a touch of Bad Boy, seeing as how Diddy had joined the production team. Looking at the video for one of the singles, "(Always Be My) Sunshine," the puffy suits, choreo'd breaks, and the fishbowl vision are delightfully reminiscent of B.I.G.'s "Mo Money, Mo' Problems."

We learn on this song something about the kind of woman Jay-Z would cape for. Her skin color isn't mentioned, but she is biracial, or in his words, a "half-Phillipine thing." She's dressed to the nines in Versace. She is dripping in jewels that he apparently gave her. But she's no gold digger, something she says he knew already. In fact, she'd be willing to pawn the jewels at a moment's notice, if he needed to be sprung from the pen. Nor does she bother with other men. The men pressin' up on her are largely doing it, she believes, to hate on Jay. This is something he, too, intuits, declaring, "Cats would love to creep (uh-huh)/Just to say they crept with mine, slept with mine."[28]

The pair aren't married, but it's clear that the possibility of something that resembles married life is one of the things he's holding out as a prospect. First, she must pass muster. She has a leg up, being attractive, stylish, uninterested in sleeping with other men, and lacking in gold-digging pretensions. But there's more to being chose.

In order to get the comfortable life of lovebirds in the suburbs, to live what is played as the halcyon middle-class life often reserved for (sufficiently) white women, his partner must also be properly ride or die. Her looks excepted, she should be a real street-chick, a down-ass chick. That is, she should be a best-of-both-worlds mix: a type of attractive that's only a slight remix on the white beauty ideal while also being a right-hand woman willing to do anything and everything for her man. This includes being willing to turn tricks for him, if and when the money runs low. Testing her devotion, Jay offhandedly enquires about her willingness to sell herself for him, as if he nearly forgot about it, as if it were a small request: "One more thing, if I ever go broke, would you hit the block for me?" Her reply is a swift and unbothered, "Fo' sho.'"[29] While having sex with other men for her own pleasure would have been sufficient grounds for being dumped, she might be tapped to do as much if he needed her to, which is to say if he would benefit from it.

If that logic feels reminiscent of pimp principles, that's because it is. Around the time this album was due to be released, Jay purportedly started calling himself "Iceberg Slim."[30] It's unclear how long this may have gone on, but we do find evidence of this predilection on another track from the same album, titled "Who You Wit II." Here, Jay names himself as the one and only "Iceberg Slim."[31] But unlike Slim's fascination with the (what at the time of his writing were exclusively white) suburbs, Jay announces that he's a regular in tony areas, riding "rims through the suburbs" because he can.[32] That is to say that he presents himself as someone with the heart of a pimp but the burnish of a member of the Wall Street elite.

In My Lifetime, Vol. 1 was to outperform Jay-Z's first LP by leaps and bounds. His sophomore effort debuted on the *Billboard* 200 at number three. It sold over one million copies in its first year of release.[33]

If the acclaim changed, that's because the game changed. Jay-Z was beginning to put away his player persona. He was now firmly a member of the pimp club.

■   ■   ■

Clearly, Jay-Z was not the first rapper to shape his image around sex trafficking. Much has been written, for instance, about the graphic sex depictions in the rhymes and visuals of 2 Live Crew. Less, however, has been said about their relationship with the principle of pimping women. There was even one (Black male) scholar who worked to deny 2 Live Crew's promotion of the pimp lifestyle, claiming individuals like lead artist Luther Campbell were "not so much pimps, but playaz."[34] It's difficult to buy this argument when one of 2 Live Crew's biggest hits, "Me So Horny," begins with a sample from the 1987 hit movie *Full Metal Jacket*.[35] In it, a young Vietnamese woman, played by French-Chinese actor Papillon Soo Soo, propositions two American GIs:

"What'll we get for ten dollars?"

"Everyt'ing you want."

"Everything?"

"Everyt'ing."[36]

The Vietnamese sex worker in question has learned that offering white men "everything" for $15 (and settling for $10) is the best strategy for survival.[37] 2 Live Crew uses this iconic scene of (white) men lowering the price for sex with a woman of color—a fitting metaphor for colonial-cum-post-movement-era sex and race relations—in the song's opening sequence.

The thread of prostitution in its most explicit form—paying for sex— is not taken up on the rest of the track. The group preferred instead to deliver graphic depictions of how they orchestrate sex with "freaks," a term that is often code for sex worker, although they do not specify if they're paying the women. Evidently, pimps make money from sex rather than paying it out. Still, 2 Live Crew's promotion of prostitution here puts them at least in the conversation about sex trafficking women of color, especially since there is at least one potential (white male) john present on the track.

If the opening of the song leaves it uncertain if they'd function as procurers, johns, or men who sometimes have sex with "freaks" without paying them, the remainder of the track gives additional evidence of their investment in pimp principles. The Crew admits that part of the path to getting off for them involves the emotional manipulation and diminution of women: "I leave you fucked and deserted/I'll play with your heart just like it's a game."[38]

Additional evidence of the rappers' proximity to pimping can be found throughout their catalog. In "If You Believe in Having Sex," for instance, the Crew members advise women to say that they will withhold sex from men who cannot pay the price of admission: "Say you ain't gettin' no pus-sy! . . . Cause you ain't got no money!"[39] Whether what they are advising is sex work or a form of *Playboy*-era "working-girl" dating is unclear. What is clear is that they are encouraging women to demand that men at least have the ability to either pay for sex outright or to engage the slightly less obvious pay-to-play practice of "treating." The track even encourages white men to join in on the play-for-play fun, displaying a camaraderie that could be viewed as an attempt at Black male–white male allegiance in the interest of taking advantage of women as sex workers. In this instance, the Crew appears to take on the job of panderers, enlivening white men with the prospect of sex with women mere moments after the women are encouraged to monetize their time: "Okay, okay, I-I-I can't forget about my white-boy friends at the depot (Fuckin' 'ey, dudes, you wanna get yer cock sucked?? Repeat after me!!)" The Crew stops short of actually arranging the transaction. Still, many other elements of the sex trade appear on this and several other of their songs.

We see further pimpish moves on their song "A Fuck Is a Fuck." Here, in the mode of Iceberg Slim, the rappers disavow love. All they claim to care about is money and sex. Brother Marquis raps, "Fuck relationships; motherfuck love (Ha ha!)," adding that the only thing on his mind is the money. Their hatred of the concept of romantic love entwines with their desire for money to make the next (convoluted) step a fantastical notion: a woman offering to pay for oral sex *on him*, purportedly ponying up $500 to provide him with pleasure. He neither offers nor agrees to be her pimp. But in true pimp fashion, he manages to get one-sided sexual gratification and the money she appears to have earned in the underground sex economy. Audaciously, he demands additional perks, crying, "I want the pussy, the pay, and a place to stay!"[40]

2 Live Crew extoll the benefits that accrue to men who procure women in the sex trafficking economy. Still, they are not the most pimp-a-rific of rappers. West coast legend Todd Shaw, a.k.a. Too $hort, has done them one better, as his entire oeuvre is an ode to pimping.

Too $hort was born in South Central LA. It was the revolutionary '60s. His family was staunchly middle-class, with both of his parents working as accountants. As a teen, he moved to Oakland and there became mesmerized by the pimp game that flourished in what was at that time the heavily Black and impoverished sectors of the city. In the early '80s, he started writing his own rhymes about the pimping he witnessed—but did not engage in—on the streets of Oakland. By 1983, he was hustling his first self-made cassettes out of the trunk of his car.[41]

By 1986, with the release of his second album, *Born to Mack*, he'd managed to sell approximately fifty thousand tapes using this business model. He was a local phenom, which was just the amount of swag (and number of units) needed to attract the attention of Jive Records.

The industry behemoth released his third album, *Life Is Too . . . Short*, in 1989. The album is his most successful to date, having gone double platinum, and making it onto *Rolling Stone*'s list "The 200 Greatest Hip Hop Albums of All Time."[42]

Too $hort's take on the underground sexual economy has a sense of humor. Consider his song "Invasion of the Flat Booty Bitches," which nevertheless came out before the height of gentrification. In it, he describes his glee in sexing a light-skinned honey with a big ole booty, before going on a nightmarish bender where every woman he sees has no butt to speak of. Confused because he is in East Oakland, he surmises, "I must need glasses/Where's them bitches with the big brown asses?" But he's willing to forego that most prized asset if the woman is willing to hand over her dough: "Baby right there ain't got no ass/But she's OK if she's got cash."[43]

We'd never have time to enumerate all the songs in which Too $hort revels in the life and times of pimping. But it is worth mentioning that one of his most celebrated songs, "Blow the Whistle," is where he asks an audience in a call-and-response, "What's my favorite word?/BITCH!" It's also the song in which he reminds fans that Dave Chappelle got the catchphrase "I'm rich, bitch!" from him.[44]

The list of pimped-out early players in rap is expansive. Curiously, there is a close relationship between the concepts of "pimp" and "gold digger," the prime separation seeming to be that gold-digging women regularly try to secure the bag through the lighter sex work of flirting and dating, often work with their clothes on. Perhaps that's why so many (Black male) rappers have worked doggedly to affix the label of "gold digger" firmly onto the bodies of Black women, calling themselves pimps for aspiring to do the same thing as women labeled gold-digging whores.

By now the evolution that took place between the early "pimps" in the game and Jay-Z's rise to the throne should become clear. Early spitters of sex trafficking began working the block and stayed there. Not Jay. By the late '90s, he'd worked to elevate pimping Black women from the gutter to the world of glitz and glam.

■   ■   ■

The platinum-selling *In My Lifetime, Vol. I* raised Jay's profile. But his next album, *Vol. 2. . . . Hard Knock Life*, in one body of work, solidified his place as the king of rap. It went quintuple platinum and continues to be the best-selling album of his career. Multiple singles on this album charted. The track that carried the distinction of being, at the time of its release, his highest-charting song was "Can I Get A . . ." The song was released in 1998. It had incredible exposure from the start, being featured on both *Vol 2*. and the soundtrack to the first installment of Chris Tucker and Jackie Chan's sensation *Rush Hour*. The track features the gravelly voiced Ja Rule alongside the lesser-known artist Amil Kahala Whitehead.

Amil Whitehead met Jay in 1997, when she was a young woman rhyming with a girls' group called Major Coins. A relative novice, Amil auditioned for Jay by freestyling. He was impressed. He had been considering another artist, but chose Amil for the song instead, giving her the role of feminine counterpart to the masculine mainline.

From the opening line, we find Jay-Z calling a woman a "bitch" after she has apparently said something he has taken as an affront. This sets the tone. Then the bass drops.

The artist, it seems, was expressing anger about some presumptive rejection and/or demand for dough by an unknown woman. The first verse picks up where the opening crack leaves off. Speaking in low tones as if ruminating over events that have just transpired, he asks what appears to be a rhetorical question: "Can I hit in the mornin' without givin' you half of my dough/And even worse, if I was broke would you want me." The lyrics read, at first glance, like an interrogation of this woman's gold-digging bona fides. However, to the extent that the listener cannot be sure to whom he is speaking, the "you" plays to the universal, serving as an interrogation of the would-be gold-digging pretensions of any woman.

For the remainder of the verse, Jay presents the woman, ultimately identified as Amil—and still by proxy any woman—with a bounty of potential scenarios in which men are either broke or rich. He inquires whether she would be interested in an everyman or if she needs a baller? He concludes that it's the latter, then he enlists any (Black) man in earshot, making them now the interlocutors—to tell women like this one,

"Fuck you." These men don't love hoes, and hoes will not be picking their pockets.

After the men have been riled into a frenzy by the idea of a woman out for the come up, the women are given a chance to chime in. Unlike Lil' Kim on Big's version of a man-woman battle rap, "Get Money," the women in "Can I Get A . . ." are not given space to tell the men to stand down. Instead, the women, represented by Amil, do not reject the idea that they want the cash. Neither do they seem upset about having been called "bitches" and "hoes." Amil leads a tepid and nonthreatening call-and-response for the women: "Can I get a woop woop/To these niggas from all of my bitches/Who don't got love for niggas without dubs."[45]

This part of the chorus is the lead-in to Amil's verse, in which she appears to affirm that she—and by extension, lots of women—are in fact gold diggers. "Can you afford me?" she asks. She admits that no, she cannot have fun with a man without funds: "I'm high maintenance/High class, if you ain't rolling, bypass/If you ain't holding I dash yo."[46]

Alongside Amil's "admission," offered with womanly authority, that women expect a certain amount of richesse, the lyrics and the video evoke images of haute class. Jay here concocts a tale that's not on the low-end, that is not about downtown hustle-hard street life. No, this song-and-video package are tales of a former hustler who got out. Now there is the possibility of "diamond rings" and a sunrise in Thailand, because he is by self-description now an "eight-figure nigga." Amil, too, is no longer about the aspect of hood life that involves dealing with broke men. She "likes a lot of Prada" and wears "Gucci" to cover the "coochie." She's waiting on "the rock" (or diamond ring), and she anticipates finally introducing the man who can deliver it to her parents, since he would be a proper partner.

While Jay-Z boasts about his billfold—and his desire to keep it from the women he's trying to sleep with—he does not outright call himself a pimp in this song. Pimpin' is mentioned as ideal in another song on the album, "Money Ain't a Thang," featuring Jermaine Dupri, in which he brags about spending the equivalent of a square's life earnings in one go: "Platinum, spend your whole life in the day."[47] Yet the vibe of "Can I Get A . . . " does reveal what Slim's mentor identified as the hatred of women needed to pimp. Not only does Jay-Z lead men in a chorus of "fuck you" to women described alternately as avaricious "bitches" and "hoes," but the song doesn't even make space for a genuine rebuttal of the idea of women *as* gold-digging bitches and hoes.

It wasn't just the lyrics that made *In My Lifetime . . . Vol. 2*, his best-selling album, a far cry from the hood hustle of his first album. The optics also got a makeover. According to Jonathan Mannion, the photographer responsible for the first album cover, its mood was mafioso, that of a crime boss running shit. The rapper's image began to evolve with *Vol. 1*, on the cover of which Jay sports a blazer-cut jacket that looks like fur. He pounds his fists together, allowing his gleaming timepiece to peek out from under the sleeve.[48]

But it is the cover art of *Vol. 2* that reflects Jay's pop success and persona as a polished pimp. A lot of rappers at the time were rocking fitted caps and jerseys. On the cover of *Vol. 2*, however, Jay-Z is dressed in an immaculate black suit. His jacket is unbuttoned to reveal a black polo. It's a head-to-toe black business-like affair, with the exception of the white sleeveless tank barely visible under the polo. He's leaning on a shiny black sports car. It's a look that befits a man of taste who has ascended to a new social status but who nevertheless keeps his project origins close to his chest.

This evolution is also visible in the music videos for *Vol. 2*. His diamond earrings, clearly visible on the cover of *Vol. 1*, are showcased in the "Can I Get A . . ." video. The set looks to be a lavish club populated with bouncing women—mostly light-skinned or white—wearing crop tops and short skirts. The women are props, accessories to the luxurious lifestyle of a mogul pimp.

This particular video reflects—or, arguably, initiates—the filtering of the "bottles and models" aesthetic into hip-hop. The aesthetic itself was, fittingly enough, orchestrated largely by wealthy white men. At the tail end of the 1990s, Manhattan was witnessing a major overhaul. In the aftermath of the '70s and '80s, violent crime plummeted, and city investments went up. This, in tandem with the War on Drugs and the War on Crime, which sent scores of Black and Brown men to prison, typically for nonviolent drug charges, meant that the character of New

York's formerly blighted areas was swiftly changing. New cultural venues were popping up everywhere—art galleries, fashion houses, and clubs.[49]

The new clubs weren't like those where folks went to boogie on a Saturday night in the '70s. These modish clubs were upscale, catering to the superrich, since fortunes were, paradoxically, shifting *upward* in the aftermath of the movement era. Luxury and leisure services were cropping up to fête the new VIPs. And whereas clubs in the '70s might have offered small VIP sections, cordoned off with red rope, the new clubs revolved completely around the rich and famous. Which is to say the wealthy developed an entirely new ecosystem for nightlife, one that was centered around the elites consorting with one another. Dancing wasn't the main attraction. Flaunting one's wealth, seeing and being seen while ordering bottle service became the new high-end club experience.[50]

Men who didn't fit the bill couldn't get in. Women's best chance for making the cut was either arriving on the arm of a rich man who did have the cred to be granted entrée or being a fashion model. At the outset of this new nightlife, models were not clamoring to get into these clubs, which had yet to make their affluent aura widely known and respected. The models had to be procured. So men with lesser means—often Black men or other men of color—were hired to be "club promoters," using charm to enlist (overwhelming white) models, bringing them to clubs for the pleasure of high-class (almost exclusively white) men.[51]

Many of these promoters' motives were to make money and to be put on by powerful rich (white) men. But, in fact, they circulated as go-betweens, arranging opportunities for elite white men and women to find one another. That is, they were yet another type of procurer for older white men's sexual reveries. Unlike the pimps who traffic in marginalized women, these club promoters were to find and deliver to powerful rich white men the specific kinds of women they wanted to see. They were supposed to be "girls," meaning young women, of high value who would emanate opulence and compound the VIP feel. These women, according to sociologist Ashley Mears, were "young (typically between 16–25 years old), thin, and tall." Moreover, they were usually "white, owing to the dominant preference for white women among both elite men and the fashion industry."[52] This description highlights the fact that not only are men and women of color overwhelmingly unwelcome in these spaces cultivated for the enjoyment of the world's white and cishet male prime movers, but the most elite white women serve as *everyone's* currency in these spaces.[53] Which is to say they are also being trafficked.

The reality of white men's preferences for thin white women ultimately transformed the consciousnesses of many men of color who procured for these clubs. In Mears's field research within the high-end world of clubbing, she interviewed a thirty-one-year-old Black man named Joe. He described how his time as a club promoter had transformed his preference in women. At first he thought, "You know, some of them in fashion, they look really strange and super-skinny." But after five years as a procurer, he avowed, "My eyesight changed! Now, when I see a super-skinny model, I think that's normal. And when I see normal, I think she's fat!"[54] Being "fat" is such an obvious and palpable violation of the aesthetic tenets of the white gentry that Joe doesn't bother to question or analyze why fatness poses a status risk in the high-end club.

Even though women and men of color who are neither models nor promoters are unwelcome in these spaces, rap music—especially that which w/horifies Black women—is in continuous rotation there. It clearly functions as a reminder of all the hilarious and damning ways the white male elite have contorted these same people in order to gather their prodigious profits. That the music of men like Jay-Z and the "promotion" work of procurers like Joe would be the motor—the labor that is—generating a sexually tantalizing ambience for rich white men is shot through with a staggering amount of colonial residue. Even Jay-Z himself, who helped popularize the models and bottles style in hip-hop, and thereby among a broad swath of both elites and non-elites alike, would ultimately boycott the tony bubbly brand Cristal. He'd toasted and boasted about the product until its managing director showed real, and public, concern about the brand's unsolicited affiliation with the "bling lifestyle."[55] It was an unsubtle reminder that white elites might enjoy Black cultural productions, benefit from Black labor, and even take Black dollars, but they know that the way to remain exclusive is to keep *Black people* out of the equation. Unless they are working as helpmeets to white men's fantasies.

"Models and bottles" became a mantra in rap. It would be impossible to identify all the rappers who promoted this as an ideal. But it is worth mentioning that in 2015, another legendary swift-spitter, Twista, released a song featuring Jeremih titled "Models & Bottles." There was even a magazine featuring mostly the backsides of thick women in a variety of shades titled "Bottles N Modelz," a kind of Black remix to white habit. Regardless of Black peoples' excitement about promoting this lifestyle, in reality, very few Black people have been allowed in this exclusive space (and most others) for the white and moneyed.[56]

Jay-Z wasn't the only rapper to appropriate the idea of the elite club for his videos. But with "Can I Get A . . ." he was one of the first not just to shoot a video in what appears to be a high-end club but also to convert his very (stage) identity into the type of person who belonged there. Well-dressed. Plenty rich. The most obvious hood aspect of his bearing being his speech, which included his verbal whoring of Black women.

There is another thing worth noting here, which is Amil's own views about being a woman in rap in the aftermath of her appearance in "Can I Get A . . ." Shortly after she shot the video, she was dropped from Roc-A-Fella. In an interview with *Hip Hop News Uncensored* in 2018, she provided details about the factors that derailed her career. It seemed that sizeism was at the top of the list: "I heard it was because I got real big and s–t—I got up to 135 lbs, if you want to call that 'big.' . . . I was 110 lbs, if [not] less than that, when I did 'Can I Get A . . .' So, I gained a couple pounds!"[57] It's eye-opening to see a Black woman describe the pressure to be ultra-thin in space that is at least fronted by Black men. But it's an important reminder that within hip-hop, even when the white man isn't the big boss (as with Roc-A-Fella), the almighty dollar is. And no one has more money in America than white men.

White men have been rap's primary consumers since its crossover during the early 1990s,[58] during the golden age of rap, when playful and conscious hip-hop were still getting heavy play. But this period also marked the moment when hardcore rap—the kind about Black men killing one another and/or sexually exploiting Black women—began to dominate the genre through its sheer sales pitch alone.

This shift took place despite the consternation of Black leaders and several hip-hop fans, who saw this as a degradation of a beloved art form, of Black people, and of Black communities. It added insult to injury that such a trend had arrived on the heels of the movement era. Civil rights activist C. Delores Tucker, for instance, went on a mission to de-pimp de-w/horify rap, but her efforts largely drew ire and eye rolls from Black people and many hip-hop fans.[59] Hip-hop activist and cultural critic Kevin Powell provided his own analysis of the destruction caused by this w/horifying turn in rap. In an article that reads as a read, he intones,

> 20 years after the Reagan backlash on civil rights, the influx of crack and guns and the acceleration of a disturbing class divide in black America, hip-hop has come to symbolize a generation fragmented by *integration*, migration, abandonment, alienation and, yes, self-hatred.[60]

If it is astute of Powell to recognize that "integration" is indeed integral to the issue, he has further notes on the problem. Powell tells how hip-hop was "once vibrant, edgy, fresh and def," but today is "as materialistic, hedonistic, misogynistic, shallow and violent as some of the films and TV shows launched from Hollywood." For Powell, like myself and so many young people during the era, the creeping misogyny and anti-Blackness of the genre would not be such a crushing weight were it not a matter of proportion: "In other words, Jay-Z's 'Big Pimpin' would not bother me so much if Dead Prez's 'Mind Sex' received as much notice."[61] All of which is to say that the white male gaze, above and beyond other claimants to the throne, including the notorious Iceberg Slim himself, is the ultimate pimp.

■   ■   ■

Jay-Z's own time reveling in the pimp ideal hadn't yet reached its apex. This, of course, came with one of, if not the single most-discussed song of his career, "Big Pimpin'." On the track he says he'll never give his heart to a woman and will instead be "forever mackin'."[62] A full treatment of its lyrics is not needed here, as a multitude of Black and feminist scholars have already addressed the inescapably dehumanizing nature of this song for (Black) women.[63] What's valuable for our purposes is that Jay's move to embrace his inner pimp that began after *Reasonable Doubt* would not be his final image shift. After his marriage to pop superstar Beyoncé in 2008, his rap persona transformed again. The change in personal style was evident almost immediately, and fans did wonder about his latest remake.

It started with his crown. In a 2009 interview with Hot 97, the radio personalities asked why he was growing his hair. He responded offhandedly, "When I make music, I normally don't cut my hair," adding "I started [working on *Blueprint 3*] last year and it's getting really bad. It's terrible. But I think for the art, I can live with it." Finding it had some appeal with women, he continued, "A lot of girls kind of like . . . So I'm trying to hold onto it."[64] Nearly a decade later, the decision to grow his hair out had clearly become intentional. By 2017, his locks garnered significant media attention. It came with the speculation that he was becoming a "conscious" rapper.[65]

His lyrical content was evolving too. He turned his skills as a philosopher away from ruminating over the nature of relationships between sex traffickers and the women who support them sexually (and thereby financially), to questions of the Black (male) struggle. By *4:44*, he, too, had officially hung up his pimp cup. The album was a critical success and was nominated for eight 2018 Grammys, including Album of the Year. The track "The Story of O.J."—in which Jay denounces ostentatious spending "at the local strip joint" and instead "outlines basic financial principles for the middle class," such as "buying property rather than depreciable assets, like cars with a V12 engine"—was nominated for Song of the Year.[66] He nevertheless failed to clasp the golden calf.[67]

And yet, while *4:44* debuted at number one on the *Billboard* 200, its time at the top was much shorter-lived than albums like *Vol. 2, a.k.a. Hard Knock Life*, which achieved quintuple platinum status. Which is to say that while Jay-Z's appetite for (Black) women's w/horification declined in the later years of his career, believing now that real wealth is found in a loving family[68]—so did his album sales.

■   ■   ■

It's hard to overstate Jay-Z's impact on hip-hop. Generations of hip-hop artists who grabbed mics in the wake of his explosive success have offered homage. He has provided them with insight on how to tell stories, how to live large.[69]

For years in his career, living large involved elevating the brutal practice of pimping into an actionable business model for the upwardly mobile Black man. He took it out of the streets and added a spit shine. As he told it, a pimp was no longer just some low-class hustlin' nigga. He was a debonair and well-appointed man-about-town. And even as artists have praised his lyrical deftness on every album from *Reasonable Doubt* to *4:44*, few (if any) decided to follow the example of his transition from pimping aficionado to "conscious" dude. Rappers young and old continue overwhelmingly to toss their titled brims into the pimp-rap space.

White men, since the advent of Eminem circa 2000, have increasingly stepped out from behind the paywall to spit rhymes of their own. To talk their own shit. The women they demean are often—as in the case of Eminem talking about his impoverished baby mother, Kim—(insufficiently) white. Not for nothing, there are internet conspiracy theories that "Slim Shady" was inspired by a Notorious B.I.G. line about Iceberg Slim: "Iceberg Slim, the Most Shady, Franky Baby,"[70] although Eminem claims the name just came to him while he was sitting on the toilet.[71]

Since 2017, R&B and hip-hop have been the number one musical genres in the United States. That year, a telling number of rappers making the Hot 100 list were white men. Nicki Minaj took some heat for exposing the obviousness of this truth, when she took to IG to post, "It's a great time to be a white rapper in America huh?"[72] The backlash was seemingly wholly unjustifiable, yet she deleted the post and logged on later to clarify that she was simply taking note of this new demographic distribution of success because she hoped to sign a white rapper herself to cash in.

It's beyond the scope of this work to detail the content of white rappers' lyrics. But we can be assured that many of them are rapping about getting money and bedding honeys of diverse ethnic backgrounds. We can also be assured that neither Black uplift nor the love of women features prominently in these songs.

The work of nineteen-year-old Aussie rapper Kid LAROI is indicative. In 2021, he was tapped by none other than Jay-Z to grace the stage at his Made in America festival. Jay selected him on the heels of the teen rapper's unprecedented success with his debut mixtape *F*ck Love*. The album reached number one on the Australian charts, making him the youngest person to ever command the top of the charts in the country.

■ ■ ■

If idealizing sex trafficking had a huge impact on Black male hip-hop artists—and sold big with their mostly white male fans—at the turn of the twenty-first century, it wasn't the only form of sex work informing the genre. Pornography played an outsized role, such that rather than simply being "pimp rap," much of the rap then (and now) could more accurately carry the label "pimp-porn rap."[73] Perhaps not surprisingly, Hugh Hefner himself had much to do with this convergence. Hef appeared to be a fan of artists like Jay-Z, seeing as how the song "Big Pimpin'" apparently featured at parties at the mansion.[74] (Interestingly enough, Jay-Z himself would later regret having made the song.[75])

But the reverse—rappers' admiration of Hefner—is more crucial in connecting porn with rap. Luke Campbell, a.k.a. Uncle Luke of 2 Live Crew took on another alias belatedly: The Black Hugh Hefner.[76] Rappers including French Montana, Future, Joe Budden, the Migos, Nicki Minaj, Wiz Khalifa, Wu-Tang, Eric Sermon, and Jay-Z have all repped the pornographer on their tracks.[77] Which is to say that Hef's influence has spanned—and maybe even helped spawn—many generations of hip-hop artists.

Indeed, while Hugh Hefner and others at *Playboy* were prepared to litigate the accusation by one journalist that Hef was a "pimp," several rappers have called him a pimp as if it were some form of honorific.[78] According to Luke Campbell, "We would probably be in the ages of underground dirty pimps on the streets treating women in a disrespectful way. Hugh brought class with it, and entrepreneurship."[79] Ice-T, himself a former pimp, offered similar praise, "The biggest pimp in the history of the world is Hugh Hefner. . . . He came up with a genius plan where he said, 'I won't sell p**sy; I'll sell the image of p**sy.'"[80]

In reality, the line between pimping and porn is nearly invisible. Porn does more than merely hint at sex trafficking—there is evidence that smut encourages it. A report from NBC News exposed the link between the rise in prominence of both pornography and the trafficking of young girls.[81] It is undeniable, then, that pimp rap builds on the legacy of Iceberg Slim and *Playboy*, and Hugh Hefner specifically. Much of Jay-Z's most successful work—including the songs deconstructed here—were variations of *Playboy's* own kitty entrapment. Jay rhymes about being rich and claims that money is the most important thing—to women. So, he flaunts it. This triggers a hatred of women for wanting the things wealthy men are holding out as a promise, to lure them.

There is, however, a critical distinction between *Playboy* and pimp rap that is worth exposing: Hef was selling the fantasy of access to sufficiently white women to all men, although it was clear from the outset that white men were his target audience. Rappers have been selling the exploitation and denigration of Black (and other insufficiently white) women to a largely white male audience at a profit. If Dave Chappelle's analysis of his own experience is to be taken seriously, when Black men work as intermediaries to meet white male desires, they, too, are pimped. Ice cold.

CHAPTER 7

MASTURBATION GENERATION/S

Joshua David Hawley, Republican senator from Missouri, is known on the left for his regressive posture. His Trump-tenderness blended with his anti-queer, ammosexual politics leads many progressives to view his public statements as a series of airborne toxic events.[1] Regardless, his view on pornography is at least worth considering.

Speaking, appropriately, to a cluster of conservatives on Halloween night in 2021, Hawley dispatched his sentiments on "the future of the American man." He argued that the men of today are becoming "idle men" who would rather watch porn and play video games than start families. Hawley also suggested that attending their porn and other "idle" addictions was a decline in their school success. In making this connection, Hawley referenced a recent article in the *Wall Street Journal* showing that the decline in young men's educational performance is more dramatic than ever before. Helpfully, the article points out that social scientists have identified men's dedication to filling their eyeballs with hardcore porn as among the principal hindrances to their academic achievement.[2]

In Hawley's analysis, men's new idleness has been caused by claims on the Left that masculinity is "toxic." "The Left want to define traditional masculinity as toxic," he offers. "They want to define the traditional masculine virtues—things like courage and independence and assertiveness—as a danger to society." The fallout of this was that American men are "withering."[3]

It's difficult to argue against the charge that American men are shriveling up, especially in terms of educational achievement. Currently, just shy of 60 percent of all persons enrolling in college are women. Women also graduate at a higher rate than men. Since the mid-00s, Americans have read an unending series of articles about purported causes of this so-called boy crisis. According to many of its proponents, the modern educational environment has become so "feminized" in recent decades that boys' supposed natural rambunctious and aggressive behavior is met with punitive measures that hurt their ability to succeed.[4]

If feminism itself is not named outright as a cause of men's dwindling achievement, it is certainly implied. Conservatives since at least the 1980s have argued that feminism has ruined both politics on the Left and our educational system.[5] This conservative move is an under-analyzed aspect of the backlash against feminism.

But let's consider Hawley's (and others') claim that the new Left and the current educational system are launching missives against "traditional" masculinity—labeling it "toxic." While elements of traditional masculinity have been evaluated as toxic for some time, it has never been the case that *all* aspects of masculinity have been met with this epithet.[6] The specific aspects of masculinity deemed toxic all revolve around emotional dysfunction: feigning disinterest, masking distress, investing in "violence as power."[7]

Coincidentally, several of the elements of masculinity deemed toxic are specifically those that fuckboys are likely to deploy against women, hence the dramatic uptick in women making these charges. As it turns out, suppressing emotions can be a useful tool in the latest war of the sexes. Men have learned that feigning disinterest is an incredibly valuable weapon in the degradation and manipulation of women, especially those who are insufficiently white.

Hawley misidentifies the source of boys' and men's current struggles, preferring to view porn as their chosen solution to vituperative claims about masculinity, instead of one of the signal causes of their issues. Owing to porn, a mounting number of men are becoming what the literature calls "autosexuals," people who prefer masturbation to having sex with other real people. I have identified a subset of autosexuals I am terming "cishanded" men. Cishanded men are a brand of fuckboy who might identify as cishet, but his sexuality mostly revolves around consuming pornographic w/horifying images of women and masturbating, or in, some instances, forcing real women to participate in their one-handed w/horifying fantasies. Cishanded fuccboism creates the conditions for men to feel justified in seeking subtle ways to exploit, harass, and violate women. Troublingly, because of the widespread availability of w/horifying porn via the internet, cishandedness may be most prominent among the younger purportedly more socially conscious generations: millennials and Gen Z.

As porn is absorbed into pop culture and becomes mainstream, its creators raise the bar, and it becomes more hardcore—nothing like the *Playboy* images of years ago. The types of sexual relationships being presented to men as justifiable are chilling. These colliding developments have had serious consequences for many women and men who might have otherwise wanted to form loving and sexual relationships.

*   *   *

Playboy, at its inception, was an entirely novel vehicle for peddling information about (hetero)sexuality and what it means to be a man. Evidently, that scores of presumptively heterosexual men relied on a magazine curated by (older white) men for their shared sexual arousal is not without a certain homoerotic irony. And, despite the fact that many of us thought men were just shitting us when they, like the affable Jim Gaffigan in one of his specials claimed that the magazine had "good articles," it turns out that men were, in fact, reading the magazine, many seeking advice on how to behave toward women in the wake of feminism.

Playboy's anti-feminist messaging was immensely popular in the period spanning the 1950s to the 1970s, but not all of *Playboy*'s readers thought it wise to put its suggestions into practice. Some men could sense the problems associated with adopting the magazine's view of heterosexual men as commodity fetishists in a constant state of artificially induced arousal, gay men as a pestilence, and women as sex workers.

By the 1970s, men against the degradation of women and men in this manner were talking back. One young man offers a rousing narrative exploration of the harms to himself and others caused by his stint as a *Playboy* connoisseur. He had a few early sexual experiences with other young men—a common trajectory for white men in America.[8] Feeling shame for these homo-dalliances, the author writes that he turned to pornography to find the appropriate "sex objects" (read: women) that might help him properly reorient his sexuality. After masturbating every single day to the images of spare alabaster forms that were routine *Playboy* fare, he finds himself terrified at the prospect of having sex with someone other than himself:

> I was scared shitless. . . . What if I can't get an erection? What if she gets pregnant? What if I can only come if I masturbate? What if her body doesn't meet the standards according to *Playboy*? . . . For the first time, here was a real woman, a sensitive, thinking person, whom I had somehow to communicate with when we made love. Before, it was just me . . . my body and *Playboy*.[9]

Many things are compelling in this first-person account. First, there is the fear that he won't be able to climax when having sex with a woman. While many men worry that they will not be able bring a woman to climax, this man dreads the real possibility that his solo sexual conduct could prevent him, too, from being able to climax. In this way, his porn-fueled behavior is working counter to his identity as a heterosexual by wreaking havoc on his ability to savor sex with women.

There are other ways in which porn disrupts the author's heterosexuality. There is considerable gravity to his concern that the women he likes will be in bodies that don't meet "the standards according to *Playboy*." Porn is often represented as a space of imagination and fantasy. Rarely do the people who revel in it admit that this so-called fantasy, as it pertains to women, is being generated for them by someone else, usually older white men. As described by his narrative, the fantasy about women can quickly come to tyrannize men, serving less as a form of imaginative play and more like a dictate (or *dick-tate*) rooted in the white supremacist idea that only (sufficiently) white women should be deemed worthy of something other than fleeting interest. Choosing a woman outside those chosen for you via white men's authority may contribute to a young man's sense of shame, to the extent that now neither she nor, by extension, *he* meets the demands of white heteropatriarchy.

This young man's nostalgia for the ease of a masturbatory sexuality is heartrending. During his time as a porn adherent, there was no fear that porn might disappoint him or that he might disappoint it. There was no accountability to any woman. It is clear that this porn-generated behavior, far from being a solo or hetero act, constitutes a curious three-way between a man's hand, his penis, and the sexual fantasies created by white men.

In awakening to this sober reality, this young man was not alone. He attests to having met several men who feel similarly, as an activist in the budding men's liberation movement—a movement filled with men who hope, among other things, to liberate themselves from what would, decades later, be popularized as "toxic masculinity." Based on this compilation of experiences, he concludes that men "must . . . recognize ourselves as warm, sensitive, vulnerable human beings, not shadows of the images that . . . Hugh Heffner . . . [has] created for us.'"[10] Many readers, just like this anonymous author, long considered *Playboy* to be an expert "masturbatory aid."[11] And yet this reformed pornography enthusiast articulates the downside to porn's easily manufactured self-gratification. That is, when overdone, it can diminish these same men's interest in and capacity to perform in real-life sexual situations with women. Said differently, it undermines these men's status as "heterosexual."

The pornography that lived in the pages of *Playboy* and other magazines constituted a creed. They presented women as docile bodies—compliant creatures who never say no (unless teasingly). These were women who did not expect men to provide for them in any way; satisfaction and reciprocity weren't on the table. They were the hollowed-out receptacles of (white) men's reveries.

By the turn of the twenty-first century, pornography had become something else—something more insidious. In the heyday of *Playboy*, only men aged eighteen or older could buy or subscribe to the magazine. Younger boys had to find an older male accomplice to hand one over, or they had to discover their fathers' or other older male relatives' stashes. With the advent of the internet, however, anyone of any age could log on to jack off. This new platform took porn from a sexist and racist genre to one that peddled violent dreams and w/horific taboos.

▪   ▪   ▪

Porn wasn't exactly difficult to find during the analog era. *Playboy* and, by the mid-'70s, *Hustler* reigned over what was, before and during the movement era, a multimillion-dollar industry.[12] The '70s–'80s saw the explosion of full-length pornographic feature films released in theaters, earning the period between 1969 and the 1980s the moniker the "Golden Age of Porn."[13] But few could have anticipated how a new technology would push an already profitable industry from a seven-figure enterprise to an eleven-figure juggernaut.

There are those who argue that pornography helped create the internet.[14] In fact, before the internet existed as we know it, there was a popular computer application known as Bulletin Board Systems, or BBS for short. Launched in 1978, BBS was used by people with computers and modems to share information and play games with others in the same area code.[15] Not surprisingly, men quickly realized they could use it to share pornographic snapshots. Before long, porn was one of the major forms of information shared on BBS.

Some of the earliest forms of porn on this platform were scanned images from *Playboy* and *Penthouse*.[16] Recognizing the super cash windfall BBS operators were making from its content, the *Playboy* company decided to sue one of the BBS member organizations to the tune of $500,000.[17] The judgment in *Playboy*'s favor was heard like a sonic boom around the BBS community.

The BBS boards diversified. By the late '80s, they offered more than just smutty photos. So, too, could users talk dirty to one another through phone sex and chat forums using the pioneering technology of Internet Relay Chat (IRC) and, later, AOL.[18]

All of this allowed for text, voice, and low-res photos that helped heterosexual and autosexual men get off. But it was in the possibility of salivating over high-res shots of men rutting women that the internet held real promise. Much of the earliest online porn came from BBS entrepreneurs who simply moved their product to the World Wide Web. In an effort to safeguard their content, porn providers were among the innovators of websites that required registration,[19] complete with usernames, passwords, and, ultimately, credit cards on file to pay providers—as one might a pimp—to gain access to sexed-up women.

Purportedly, streaming, too, was a porn permutation. In 1994, Red Light District, a company headquartered in the Netherlands, developed one of the earliest systems for video streaming. Three years later, Ron Levi, founder of the website Cybererotica and a current principal at the diversified media company Voice Media, generated what many have described as the first live video feeds.[20] Levi is also credited with innovating double opt-in emails, a ubiquitous internet safeguard against an unknown person or bot signing you up for content you do not want.[21]

But the true game-changing mutation came in the early '00s.

≡   ≡   ≡

When the legendary pop star Janet Jackson teamed up with aged teenybopper-cum-sex symbol Justin Timberlake for the 2004 Super Bowl, the world was treated to an unforgettable show. The duo crooned a duet to Justin's smash single "Rock Your Body" from his multiplatinum first solo album, *Justified*. At the insistence of the line, "Bet I'll have you naked by the end of this song," Justin tore off a piece of Ms. Jackson's bustier, leaving one of her breasts exposed. Her nipple was accented by a star-shaped jewel. The spectacle was christened "Nipplegate."

Both Jackson and Timberlake have long averred that the exposure was an accident. Looking at photos of the event, his movements appear to be orchestrated—timed to match the lyrics. And yet, once the fabric covering Jackson's breast is snatched off, both parties look surprised at the result.

It's hard to separate fact from fiction as it pertains to what is now deemed a moment in US history. But I will mention that singer Lizzo went on Hannibal Burress's *Handsome Rambler* podcast in 2018 and, among other things, intimated that she may have witnessed what could be described as a rehearsal of the "wardrobe malfunction."[22]

Purposeful or not, many Americans were outraged by this blatant intrusion of obscenity into their enjoyment of organized violence. Republicans foamed over the singers' indecent performance. Republican Tom DeLay, then the House Majority Leader, cried, "They knew that this was beneath the standards, including CBS running some lewd and crude commercials during the Super Bowl."[23]

In no time, the FCC gathered its forces. It fined CBS and Jackson over half a million dollars for nine-sixteenths of a second of naked tit. The fine was disputed in court and voided in 2008. Later that same year, the Supreme Court of the United States vacated *that* ruling, sending the case back to a Philadelphia court of appeals. It was finally decided in 2011, many years after the split-second during which Jackson's nipple was free, that the FCC's fine could not be enforced, seeing as how it was both arbitrary and capricious.[24] The final decision marked the end of a years-long saga in one respect. But the 2004 event has widely been credited with creating something else: YouTube.

In 2005, three twenty-something tech mangenues working at PayPal were discussing the world's most notorious nip slip. They were frustrated that they could not find any coverage of it online. They decided to create a site where people could share videos, such as the clip of the portion of Jackson and Timberlake's performance that featured the unabridged glimpse of her partially denuded upper torso. Within a year, YouTube .com had an untold number of videos with millions of views.[25]

This included video of the breakaway bustier that exposed Janet in more ways than one. For after her breast slid out, Les Moonves, the CEO of CBS, purportedly set his sights on destroying her career. Moonves ordered all Viacom stations—including VH1 and MTV—to stop playing Jackson's videos, striking a crushing blow to the potential popularity of her recently released album.[26] It was a move broadly condemned as anti-Black and sexist, since no similar action was taken against Timberlake, the person responsible for tearing the garment.[27]

YouTube's own beginnings, then, are arguably pornographic. But its real effect on the porn industry is that it has served since its creation as a kind of inspiration for pornographers trying to figure out how to get more smut in front of (overwhelmingly men's) eyeballs. One year after the launch of YouTube, porn "tube" sites appeared that followed the same model of allowing users to share video content. Next-generation BBS had arrived. But the new tube porn sites compounded the BBS problem of pilfering, as users frequently poached content from other porn sites and posted them to the tube sites scot-free. Two years after YouTube got its start, PornHub followed its business model to the tune of millions of viewers and sponsorship dollars. In 2022, PornHub was the eighth most visited website in the world, getting more digital visitors than Walmart.[28]

This had the effect of exploding the amount of porn available online. It also removed the price, and, critically, age controls. When the industry relied on upfront credit card payments, age controls were easier to enforce. But with tube sites, all anyone has to do is "verify" that they are eighteen or older (by clicking a button), and they can have an all-access pass to porn town. The result is that younger and younger kids are exposed to explicit material. The estimated age of exposure to internet pornography is eleven to twelve for girls and ten for boys.[29]

Evidently, in some instances, kids are looking for live sex videos due to their own curiosity. But in many cases, they inadvertently stumble upon it while searching for something else. According to the nonpartisan nonprofit organization Enough Is Enough, which compiles research on the effects of pornography on children, 62 percent of eleven-to-thirteen-year-olds surveyed claimed to have first run across porn unintentionally. Porn purveyors have learned to use popular terms for kids, like "Selena Gomez" in their searchable content, leading unsuspecting preteens down a skin-flick rabbit hole.

Inculcating children with images conveying the message that women are for ramming, harrowing as that is, may not even be the worst of it. Ironically, as early as the 1950s, the incipient era of porn going mainstream, a few men writing in *Playboy* intuited the problems with the dissolution of the Romantic Ideal in favor of porn's own "women-as-sex-workers" model. It was none other than the infamous Philip Wylie, one of *Playboy*'s favored mouthpieces, sounding the alarm.

Philip Wylie had a reputation for wielding his pen to eviscerate feminist interlocutors. And yet, years before this became his schtick, he'd offered a sobering look at the ramifications of men's inching rejection of the Romantic Ideal. Before Wylie became an expert in anti-feminism, he'd fashioned himself as an expert in another aspect of the politics of womanhood: mothering.

In 1943, Wylie penned what *Playboy* deemed his "magnum opus,"[30] a book of essays titled *Generation of Vipers*. In "Common Women," Wylie warned men of the slow creep of what he called "Momism." The book took off like gangbusters, running through several editions by the mid-1950s. And it was the 1955 edition that tickled the fancy of a *Playboy* panel convened to discuss Wylie's earth-rattling 1958 *Playboy* treatise on the "Womanization of America." The moderator, listed only as a representative of the magazine, sums up Wylie's portentous take on how undercutting the Romantic Ideal has contributed to the shambling cult of mom:

> When we agreed upon the American Ideal Woman, the Dream Girl of National Adolescence . . . the Pin-Up, the Glamour Puss—we insulted women and *disenfranchised millions from love*. The hen-harpy, the Cinderella chick come home to roost: the taloned, cackling residue of burnt-out puberty in a land that has no use for mature men or women. Mom still commands. While she exists, she will exploit the little 'sacredness' we have given motherhood as a cheap-holy compensation for our degradation of women. . . . She will act the tyrant—because she is a slave. . . . We are deep in the predicted nightmare now, and mom sits on its decaying throne.[31]

Wylie can hardly be considered a useful figure for the goals of women's lib. And yet here, he illuminates the steps American men took that undermined the Romantic Ideal to the, in his own words, "degradation of women." The first step in this process was the creation of a series of (sufficiently white) ideal women—the women worthy of love, the women to whom men clamor to reveal their affections. American beauty ideals scarcely diverged from those inaugurated with race science; the primary difference being that in America there was a heightened focus on being tall and thin.[32]

Under the ideal of romance, when a man finds a woman to *his* liking—which required no panel of men to validate—he places her on a pedestal and sees himself as beneath her. He fights for her, wages a war in her honor the same as he might do for king and country.[33] This was the view of romance before the instatement of the racio-aesthetic hierarchy under slavery and colonization. And it was propagated by some of the most storied male authors ever to put pen to paper.[34]

The installation of a beauty hierarchy hobbled the Romantic Ideal and debased all women. Further refinements, including those depicted by Wylie, undercut the intensity of courtly love, making *white men's ideas* the true object of men's affections. The irony is palpable: the heteronormative white-fetishistic ranking of women that diminishes them is an inherently homoerotic enterprise. It is also a numbers game; a woman's beauty (and thereby loveworthiness) is to be determined by the sheer number of (white) men who would openly admit to getting stiff just thinking about her.

For all of Wylie's bluster, his analysis here is spot-on. It represents in one paragraph what the demand for white sufficiency has done to sexual relationships, revealing with searing clarity what the foregoing chapters have taken hundreds of pages to illustrate. Moreover, by Wylie's reasoning, men's beguilement of the Romantic Ideal may just have been the reason that (white) women needed feminism in the first place. When women were removed from their traditionally vaunted place in the culture, he argues, it led them to look for power elsewhere, in the territory of men's rights. This book is not attempting to confirm or deny that theory. But it is a devastating angle to entertain.

To Wylie, there is an even more insidious problem undermining women's loveworthiness. The women who have been, in his own words, "disenfranchised" from love by the betrayal of the courtly love contract have two options: become so-called cackling harpies, those very feminist women the men of *Playboy* describe with dripping condescension, and/or hole up in the last corner of respectable womanhood, motherhood, and fortify the position. Motherhood, is, in Wylie's estimation, the only cage afforded women post-feminism that men haven't attempted to rattle.

Mothers, he reminds us, are still treated as sacred. Mothers are still deemed worthy of love, regardless of their behavior or appearance. By the basic fact of having given birth, they are given the "cheap-holy" compensation of men's remaining respect—Momism—whereas respect for other women (*all* other women) began to deteriorate when men started to make themselves the reference point for other men's sexual desires.

To be sure, this polemic, like all of Wylie's work, has plenty of detractors. I didn't find any of them in *Playboy*. But at least one writer in the *Washington Post*, a man who had once been an admirer of *Generation of Vipers* in his youth, concluded upon reading it in the sobering light of middle age that Wylie's views of moms, wives, and women in general are "nutty fruitcake."[35]

Tellingly though, the post-'60s revisionist reception of Wylie's work is largely centered on his denunciation of Momism. In retrospective reviews of *Generations of Vipers*, the *New York Times*, the *LA Review of Books*, and *Lapham's Quarterly* have all printed pieces asking, more or less, "What was with Wylie's hatred of mothers?"[36] Outside the one piece in the *Washington Post*, I have not seen nearly as much interest in addressing his generally sexist views. Perhaps critics' continued confusion speaks to men's continued desires to keep mom on the pedestal long since burned to the ground for other women. So it was that at least one prominent man frequently writing for the industry that worked to turn all women into sex workers made the bold—and accurate—proclamation that men had in fact been working *for decades* to deprive women of love. Motherhood now stood alone as the sole respectable role for cis women.[37] This meant that "mother" became an aggrandized title, worthy of an esteem regularly denied other women. But their esteem in men's hearts wasn't the only thing swelling.

■   ■   ■

I first heard the term MILF in graduate school. It was around 2010. There was some Brody going around bragging about how much he'd love to fuck the mothers he'd seen around his son's school. I knew immediately there was something funky afoot. I said to this Brody, "Soo . . . this is about your moth . . ."

"No!" he interrupted me. "Not *my* mother. Other women who are mothers. Some of these mothers are *soo* hot!" he attempted to clarify.

"But," I continued, "why would you focus on the fact that they are mothers? Like why not just call them wom—"

"Because *they are* mothers! That's the thing! They are the Mothers I'd Like to Fuck." He let the term linger, his wide-open mouth fixed in a toothy, conspiratorial smile.

I didn't want to continue this conversation for obvious reasons, so I didn't. Because his rationale made no sense—like much of the logic of white male domination—my mind started doing the work of trying to fill in the gaps. *Well*, I thought, *maybe this is men's way of saying that just because you popped out a pup or two doesn't mean you're outta the game. Men want you to know even if you've got kids, they'd still tap it.*

We've all heard tales of men who are uninterested in single women with children. Now, men were openly salivating over women with children, regardless of their marital status. They'd be DTF *because of* the baggage. Viewing the situation through my rose-tinteds, it almost seemed feminist.

Almost. The acronym wasn't MILD (with D for "date") or something else potentially humanizing. They were sexualizing women specifically because they were mothers. And in spite of the mental gymnastics I had been trying to work on myself, the glaring obviousness of its Oedipal implications did not leave me. But I was sick of thinking about it, so I suppressed the alarm bells this term and its creed sounded. It would be another decade before I was forced to confront the implications of men's MILF fantasies.

·   ·   ·

It was the dawn of the age of COVID-19. None of us really knew what to do yet. In the absence of any real medical knowledge, we were given the cautionary information to stay indoors and wear a mask in public but to try not to find yourself in public. I tried to take a middling approach—following the rules but not becoming a grocery-skeptical, package-washing convert.

One of my associates at the time was a feminist and an artist, Jane. We weren't particularly close, but I enjoyed talking with her about art and politics. Sometime around June 2020, she called me to see if I wanted to go on a walk. After twelve weeks indoors, I guessed we were ready to see the outside world again.

She picked me up, and we headed to a familiar nearby trail. Jane started talking to me about her son. She almost never mentioned him. Because he was away at college, I'd only seen him a couple of times.

"My son wants to talk to you!" she relayed in a high-pitched voice.

"What?" I said.

"My son. He wants to talk to you," she repeated, slightly less anxiously.

"Huh?"

"My son!" she screeched. "He's a sociology major. He says he wants to learn more about sociology."

"Oh!" I replied. "I'll talk to him. I talk to students across the country—really around the world—all the time. A lot of the time they want to speak to a person of color about being in the academy." This is true, but in hindsight I can see how I was filling in the blanks. She appeared to be relieved that I had agreed to talk to him. The conversation moved on.

I didn't hear anything else from her for another several months. She finally turned up again in September. By now, everyone we knew had turned into a hiking fiend. This time, we'd taken our Live March to the nearby shore.

I was emotional that day. For years, since shortly after I was raped, I had realized that a lot of men were garbage and I didn't want to be bothered. I'd started calling myself "queer." What I thought I meant was that I was a conscientious objector to men's horribility. I believed that I'd eventually be done with men altogether or meet a man who was not despicable or meet one of the rare women who interested me.

But, in 2018, something happened to open my eyes to who I really am. That summer, I watched the show *Pose* and cried nonstop. The show was *so* good. I felt such a powerful connection and attraction to so many of the characters. I wished I could know queers like those on the show, wished I could spend time with people like them for love and companionship.

Still, it was when I saw the show *The Politician* that I was finally able to make sense of my own sexual identity. The storyline is heavily queer—which is such a delight. But I was riveted by one character: James, a transman played by Theo Germaine. I was like, "OMG! James is *soo* fine! Why aren't more people talking about this? He a thirst-trap and a half!" I googled him. I would rewatch episodes to see more James.

In the middle of this odyssey, I remembered something else that had gotten me going years before. *The Rocky Horror Picture Show,* which stars Tim Curry as the omnisexual trans character Dr. Frank-N-Furter. I had seen the movie in 2001 and thought, "Oh! This is what I want. How can I get this?" The word "transgender" was not in common parlance at that time. We called people like Frank-N-Furter "cross-dressers." I would tell people I was attracted to men who wore dresses—an expression that I would not use today but used at the time because I didn't know the proper term. *Everyone* tried to convince me I was simply gay and afraid to admit it. I knew that wasn't true. But there wasn't any way at that time to understand my sexuality.

Next thing I knew, I was crying on the phone to my sister. I'm the oldest, but in many ways I find her to be the wise one. I was sobbing like, "Desi! I don't know what I am! There isn't a word for people who like trans people! There's no word!" I cried. I added, "I do like cis people sometimes."

My sister, with her characteristic calm, replied, "You're a pansexual." She was being sympathetic. But to my sister, who is a deep-cut millennial, being pan didn't seem like a big deal. I'm a xennial. I was terrified.

"Des!" I cried, "I'm a forty-year-old virgin!"

I wasn't a true virgin, just a virgin in this new identity. What's funny is that I remember one of my wonderful UG students from like 2017 trying to tell me I was pan. We were walking back to my office after class one day, and she asked how successful pan women navigate the consummate demand that *all* women get married. I said I didn't know. I was confused about why she'd asked me; I thought maybe she was trying to say she was pan and was looking for a life coach. I realized later that she'd probably asked me because she intuited that I was.

My acceptance of this new identity was slow-going. I just wanted to be gay or straight, not something almost no one understood. And by no one, I mean no one. I searched for support groups for pan people. I wanted to know exactly how common it was to be pan, and within our group, how many of us were trans lovers by another name? I couldn't find anything. I contacted the local LGBT centers. They had support groups for gay and trans people. Not pan people.

So it was that on the September day when I saw Jane again for the first time in three months, I decided to come out to her. I had told my sister and a handful of close friends. Jane and I weren't especially close, but I was trying to feel normal again, and didn't want to be ashamed to tell people who asked what I was up to during the COVID lockdown about this plot shift in my character development.

"Jane," I began. "I realized I am a pansexual." I said it with the solemnity I thought it deserved.

"Oh, really?" she replied, nonplussed. "My son is pan."

"Oh, wow!" I said. He was one of the only other pan people I'd ever had some personal connection to, however loose. I had another friend, a woman, who had admitted to me she was pan. But she'd dated—as far as I could tell—cis men exclusively. Jane's son was the first and only male pan person I'd ever known.

"Yes. He's had girlfriends and boyfriends. I thought I told you that." True, I knew he dated different (cis)genders. But if we could be so different sexually and both still pan, what united us? I still didn't know.

"My son wants to talk to you," she continued. Her anxiety had returned.

"I know," I said. "You told me that the last time. He can just call me. I talk to students from all over all the time." I saw her relax. By now, though, I was becoming suspicious of her. *Why does she keep telling me her son wants to talk to me, and then not giving him my number? What is she afraid I'm gonna do?*

She still didn't give him my number.

About five months later, she reached out again. We went for another walk, and this time, she wanted to give me the rundown on her son.

"My son is struggling with mental health issues," she disclosed. "He had to leave school and move back in with us because he had an episode." She explained that unrequited love had triggered his break. He had fallen for a woman who'd rejected him, and he didn't know how to deal. I felt sorry for what their entire family had gone through.

She laid in with another request for me to talk to her son.

"So," she sighed, "my son wants to talk to you."

"You keep telling me that," I replied. "Aren't there people at his university he can talk to? Are there no faculty of color or . . ."

"He says he doesn't feel comfortable talking with them."

I nodded. It can be difficult posing questions that seem simple or vulnerable if you think people will be dismissive. "OK," I began, "but what specifically does he want to discuss?"

"I don't know." She shrugged.

That confirmed for me her sense that her son's repeated requests were just a ruse to get to me, his mother's much younger friend. She went on to describe how he had been active in Black Lives Matter protests. She described him as smart but also as struggling mightily with adulting.

Before we parted ways, she informed me that her son, having nothing else to do under COVID and on meds in the suburbs, was probably going to ask me to walk and talk, the way she and I had been doing. That had me feeling a bit tense, but I didn't object. She affirmed that she was, at long last, going to put me in touch with him.

I'd expected that he'd simply call or text me, but instead she opened a three-way text. She introduced us, and he immediately asked, "Would you like to go on a walk?"

That was a cause of further tension for me. I took the long road to explaining why, on a weekday, I'd prefer to talk on the phone. We set the day and time.

On the day of, I was suddenly nervous. I took a huge anxiety dump right before the call that made me late. Turns out he was high as a kite and didn't really care. On the phone, he proceeded to ask me some pretty basic questions.

"So what do you want to know about sociology?" I had flattered myself that he'd actually wanted to be in touch with me in part because I was a known author. But he didn't have any specific questions about my book or other research.

He was so quiet throughout most of our conversation, I wondered if we had a faulty connection. I kept going, "Hello?" midstream. He was always still there on the line, just nearly completely silent, except for a little bit of heavy breathing now and then. A few times, though, after I'd completed a thought, he'd make a joke that made me laugh. It seemed he mostly just wanted to have me on the phone. To keep me talking. I feared he was just lonely. But none of this explained why he'd spent months trying to get to me specifically.

My mind changed when the subject shifted to questions of how people of color, and especially women of color, get by in the academy. I was probably the person who took us there—since he didn't seem to care what I talked about so long as I kept talking.

After I mentioned how the academy overworks and underpays women of color, he said, "Oh yeah?"

I added, "Well your mother is in the academy. Surely your mom—"

When I started talking about his mother, he was suddenly agitated. He started yelling in a deeper voice, "YEAH YEAH YEAH YEAH YEAH." The aggressiveness of his effort to shut down this strand of the conversation surprised me.

This didn't make any sense. Surely if you ask your mother's friend to talk to you on the phone, she is bound to bring up your mother?

The conversation didn't last long after that. He didn't ask many new questions. In fact, shortly after I'd mentioned his mom, he seemed to be trying to rush me off the phone. Before we hung up, I wanted to ask him about being pan, but it somehow seemed inappropriate, so I didn't. The call ended abruptly, after only about fifteen minutes.

I realized shortly after we'd hung up that he had been masturbating during the call.

It seemed like such a strange thing to do; I didn't have a framework for understanding it. My first thought was, *Maybe this is a thing pan men do?* That didn't really make sense, but what did I know about pan men? I felt strange about it, but I figured there was a gaping hole in my understanding of sexuality that perhaps a young person could help me get a handle on. Even though I was certain he'd been masturbating during our talk about "sociology," I still hoped to talk to him about pansexuality.

Presently, Jane reached out to thank me for talking to him. I offered an empty paean like "Glad to help!" But I didn't elaborate. For weeks after that, she'd suddenly become very interested in texting me. She texted me about a bunch of things she'd read or seen in the news—behavior that was utterly brand-new. I thought it was clear evidence that she was suspicious of something being in the works between me and her son that she was trying to insert herself into.

I didn't reach out to either one of them for weeks. I kept weighing the pros and cons. On the one hand, she and I had been like friends, when she found the time which wasn't often. And it was clear that she did not want him and me to continue this correspondence. On the other hand, he and I were full grown, and I wanted someone to talk to about this pan business.

After two months of deliberation, I decided to reach out. To him. I sent him the text "Hi. Let me know if you'd like to take that walk sometime."

He didn't reply.

A couple of weeks later, he sent me a message. It said, "Hi, I lost all my contacts. So Idk who this is . . . due to a mental health concern . . ."

I started to say something, anything. Then I thought it was a weirdly divulgent message to send a presumptive stranger—after two weeks of sitting on the message.

He'd spent nearly a year trying to get to me through his mom. He had written in the text that he'd lost all his contacts *before* he returned to his parents' home. So you finally get the number of the woman you've been pursuing for months and you lose it? Can't search the message list for other times that number has appeared? I was puzzled for about a week. I thought surely he knew the message was from me. I couldn't shake the feeling that it was a ploy for sympathy—the kind of sympathy a fuckboy expects from an older woman.

The answer came from the least likely place: comedian Bill Burr. I had been a regular listener to his *Monday Morning Podcast*. On one episode, a man wrote in to say that masturbating alone had become unfulfilling, so he'd begun surreptitiously "using" women he talked to online for phone sex—his way of still being able to get off through masturbation. This man also had a girlfriend he was hoping to marry. Which meant he was engaging in nonconsensual phone sex and lying to and cheating on his girlfriend.

Bill Burr's response was compassionate—but only to the man who wrote in and not the women he was lying to and misusing for nonconsensual sex:

> Yeah, talk to a therapist. One of the problems that has developed in this age of technology—yeah, you're addicted to phone sex. And yeah, ya know I had a porn addiction. I finally realized I'm fucking doing this all the time. This is how you know you're addicted to porn: if you try to jerk off with just your thoughts and you can't make it happen, you've got a fucking problem that needs to be addressed.[38]

I knew in that moment that this was what this young man had done to me. This young man of color who had been active in Black Lives Matter. He had committed phone sex assault using me, a Black woman, after maneuvering to make it happen for months. Here I was trying to give him the benefit of the doubt. Trying to understand his behavior as some "pan thing." All the while he'd been a cishanded fuckboy using me as a mom-adjacent masturbatory aid. The minute he got was he was looking for in me, someone older, someone who knew his mother, someone who reminded him of her, and *even someone who would talk to him about her*, he feigned surprise and disinterest in what ultimately had gotten him off, then ended the conversation.

In the police report, I implicated him and his mother. She had been grooming me for months. She had told me he'd left school due to "unrequited love" which seemed awfully suspicious in retrospect. I explained to the police that I thought he'd probably left school due to, well, some form of similar assault. I thought *no way a young man tries this ruse for the first time on a professor.* The police asked why I thought he chose me for this. Then I remembered.

We'd actually talked briefly once before. Or I did. I went to Jane's house when her son was a college freshman to pick her up for an art-house film. Jane's husband, Jason, answered the door, and he'd grown this beard. I was like, "Oh! Jason, don't you look . . . you're not Jason!" It was actually the son. He was home from school that week. He didn't say anything but stood there, a wry smile playing on his lips.

In my mortification, I pushed past him and encountered Jane coming down the stairs. I blurted, "Uhh, sorry, I almost complimented your son on his beard because I thought he was Jason, which shouldn't he be at school and since when do eighteen-year-olds have beards . . .?"

She interrupted my logorrhea to explain that yes, her son looks like her husband, and, yes, he looks older than his age. She was so nonchalant about it, I let go the terror gripping me. But in hindsight, I remember that he was wearing socks (no shoes) when he opened the door. The minute I pushed past him to confess to his mother, I saw him out of the corner of my eye, sliding *Risky Business*–style toward his bedroom. After the phone-sex assault, I understood why.

⁙   ⁙   ⁙

Internet pornography has revealed, and shaped, the sexual fantasies and practices of these cishanded fuckboys. A good deal of their fantasies involve mom. Other top categories? Queer women and Black women. In 2017, PornHub released its annual statistics. It showed that of the six most-searched for terms worldwide, *half* of them involved mothers. "Milf" came in at number three, "stepmom," number four, and w/horifyingly enough, just the word "mom" was number six. If we include other intrafamilial sex, "stepsister" ranked fifth, making incest quite popular among the top global porn search terms.

It would appear that American men are leading the incest charge. In 2017, the US was far and away the most prolific porn-consuming nation.[39] It had approximately *triple* the PornHub traffic of the nearest competitors, the UK and India. And when each nation was considered separately, most did *not* have incest among their top searches. In an analysis of what Americans alone were masturbating to, three of the top seven searches involved "mom": "milf" (number two), "stepmom" (number five), and "mom" (number seven). Also noteworthy on the US-specific search lists are "lesbians" at number one and "ebony" at number four. It would seem that in pursuing me for assault (while I am not a lesbian, I am often mistaken for as much), the Gen Z cishanded fuckboy was attempting a grand slam.

These data were updated for 2021,[40] and the findings were similar, but the order had shifted. "Ebony" has been rising in the ratings, up to number four on the "most-searched" list of terms worldwide. In the US, "Ebony" was the single most viewed porn category. For many men— estimates suggest that over two-thirds of all porn viewers are men, but the overall *share of total porn consumed* that is filtering through men's eyeballs is likely to be much higher—masturbation is their primary sexual activity. A number of cishands have long been addicted to porn and frequently can only get off by violating unsuspecting women with less easily detectable forms of assault. For if traditional fuckboys hope to use feelings to take advantage of (insufficiently white) women, the cishanded version uses feelings (e.g., sympathy) to furtively assault women. And many of them are learning this from porn.

As I processed these events with a therapist, I decided to google "unsuspecting phone sex." Sure enough, there is a prolific amount of porn available to men who want to cum to the idea of covertly assaulting a woman. Turns out nonconsensual phone sex is an entire genre of porn. It's called "sneaky" or "noncon" phone sex. It either gives men the idea to do this or sanctions it as a fun and funny way of defiling women.

We are living under a tsunami of male sexual dysfunction. It was frothed up by pornography during the 1950s. It was further pushed to the fore by "pimp" rap. And at the center of it all, the women men fantasize about sexing are mothers. Incest is the most prodigious male sex fantasy in America. And of course, when it comes to graphic porn and violating sex in RL, Black women are still the preferred group. Treating Black and other insufficiently white women like beasts to be used and discarded has a long history in this country. There is ample evidence that Black and white men have been keeping this tradition alive for their sexual and financial benefit.

Among many men across race, there's still the hope that "Ebony" women will forever be The Commons.

▪   ▪   ▪

In 2022, A&E released a ten-part docuseries on life at the *Playboy* mansion. Many of the women who'd lived there described it as a sex cult.[41] They claimed Hugh Hefner was a "predatory" man who dominated and raped them, and allowed his friends (e.g., Bill Cosby) to do the same. They even attested to "miserable mass orgies" and his craving for bestiality. One of the things that struck me from the Playmates' recollections was their claim that the longer Hef pursued his own porn-fueled predilections—that regularly involved violent and nonconsensual contortions of women's bodies—the more "he needed crazier kinks to get himself excited." In other words, to many of his former Playmates, his own w/horification of women led him to constantly seek new, more degrading ways of treating women to get off.[42] Clearly, Hefner's porn obsession was a slippery slope to hell, replete with flights of sex with four-legged animals and sad orgies, but more than anything else, according to many of the women who knew him, the violent sexual abuse of women.

If the *Playboy* mansion was indeed the location of a sex cult, I would argue that the cult extended far beyond the mansion. The cult included all the men who praised Hugh Hefner, who hoped to be like him. Hefner has been treated by many as a godlike figure. He created an ideal of masculinity that many other men have tried to emulate. Hef (perhaps inadvertently) made himself the figurehead of a masculine sex cult.

Male cult leaders in particular are fond of using "physical violence to sexually exploit" women.[43] There are also other elements of the Hefner legacy that align with cultish behavior. The men who consumed *Playboy* were given sacrosanct images (i.e., those of women with the "approved" look) and encouraged to perform ritual sex acts to these images (i.e., consummate masturbation). Perhaps most importantly, the cult of the *Playboy* mansion created an ideology about women and relationships that was meant to unseat the preexisting ideology (the Romantic Ideal) for men. Indeed, these are just about all the elements needed to establish a cult.[44]

Until Hugh Hefner's death there was an air of secrecy about what took place in the mansion. There has also been an air of secrecy about what porn really is. Men, for decades, have acted as if porn is just looking at images of naked women or people having sex. But the Greek origin of the word *pornography* is "writing about whores." The bold feminist Andrea Dworkin debunked the idea that porn could be benign in the '70s. As she wrote in *Last Days at Hot Slit*, "Pornography is the fundamentalism of male dominance," wherein "women are consigned to rape and prostitution."[45] In other words, pornography throughout history—and certainly mainstream non-queer and non-feminist porn today—has always been about consolidating male power and turning women into whores.

WE ARE LOVE

A s I was finishing this book, I found a new hair salon. It's owned by a vivacious Black woman and filled with other laughing, joyous, loving, and kind Black women. Going in there felt like coming home.

Once, though, while I was getting my locs tightened, I was subjected to a reality TV series I had never seen before. It's called *Nellyville*, and it chronicles a two-year stretch, 2014–2015, in the life of rap-cum-pop-superstar Nelly, whose government name is Cornell Iral Haynes Jr.

In the episodes I was forced to sit through, we see Nelly's adopted son, a rapper whose birth name is Shawn Thomas Jr. and whose stage name is Lil Shxwn, in the studio working on a song in which he rhymes about never falling in love with a "ho." We have no indication that Nelly has any problem with these lyrics. Later, we catch the infamous "Tip Drill" creator in another episode on the beach in the Bahamas, spitting some of his most well-known rhymes—not a few of which degrade Black women—before an almost entirely white crowd.

The weight of colonialism taints this scene and many others in the show. But what capped it for me was a conversation Nelly has with his adopted daughter, the younger sister of Lil Shxwn, Sidney Thomas, a.k.a. Stink. Stink is eighteen and looking to work as a model. Nelly nearly collapses when he sees some of the outfits she is asked to wear: barely-there jeans and thigh-high boots. He doesn't want a sweet girl like his daughter to be viewed in this manner. To be, as it were, w/horified.

One of the young Black women in the salon was thoughtful and smart in ways that a college education often can't simulate. She summed up Nelly's actions in that scene more succinctly than I could: "You want to destroy us. You want to destroy whole Black communities. But you still want respect for you and your family."

In spite of it all, I do have compassion for what many Black men are going through. The civil rights movement witnessed the assassinations and attempted spirit murders of some of our most important Black and male leaders. Besides the most known folks, there was John Huggins and Mumia Abu-Jamal and too many others to name all at once. What did it do to those men who saw these events and were asked to take up the mantle? It must have been a confusing time. Here was the prospect of integration and getting what white people had been keeping from Black people. That felt like a better plan to many, it seemed, than continuing the fight for our collective liberation. So instead of remaining in the struggle, they took on the goal of a financial and penile freedom, the kind articulated in *Playboy*, which was a multivalent booby trap.

Imagine a conversation with the ancestors about where we've been heading since the second wave of feminism:

Women: "We have greater access to education, are working in record numbers, are creating new movements for radical social change . . ."

Men: "We got all the masturbation we can get hands on."

The latter poses a serious problem for men's sexual functioning. Indeed, alongside the troubles described by men in the previous chapter, men (often cis and straight-identifying) have sought the counsel of sex advice columnist Dan Savage for masturbation-induced sexual dysfunction. In a 2020 post of his column *Savage Love* titled "Belly Up," a twenty-something man details his distress: "I can easily orgasm when I masturbate. I've had sex four times in my life and I'm worried because I wasn't able to orgasm by someone else's hand, through oral or during penetration."[1]

With characteristic compassion, Savage includes advice to help this young man enjoy sex with women, including, "cutting back on porn and using your imagination." He also advises the young man that the goal of every instance of sexual stimulation shouldn't be the most immediate ejaculation conceivable. Instead, this man (and others like him) should try to retrain their penises to enjoy subtler forms of sexual arousal and let go the idea that cumming is a necessity. If more subtle forms of sex can't get the man off, he advises, "put your dick away and go to bed or work or school."[2]

Men reared under the dicktates of porn, the Pornographic Ideal as it were, have in many instances lost perspective about the many RL possibilities of sex. Arousal does not have to be the signal to get yourself to climax as quickly as possible. Having the pornographic principle of swift ejaculation as the model can lead to sexual dysfunction when attempting sex with someone other than oneself.

*   *   *

The reason fuckboys are multiplying and ruining your sex life is that porn and popular rap have upended gender relations by conquering the Romantic Ideal. The ideal of romance is not completely gone, but the proportions have shifted. The RI was always an elite ideal that left peasant women, slave women, and prostitutes out of the equation and open to con games and assault. But with the arrival of the Pornographic Ideal inspired by *Playboy*, millions more women were dragged under the proverbial bus as unsuspecting sex workers.

This was done largely by white men in an effort to put women back in their place after the (limited) feminist gains of the early-to-mid-twentieth century that led to greater gender integration. Black men added to the cause post-CRM, using rap as a vehicle to distance themselves from Black women, to keep us as The Commons, as they worked to align their gendered aims and sexual desires with those of white men.

It might be hard for people to reconcile themselves to the idea that many men (although not all men) have willingly (although unwittingly) entered a masturbatory sex cult (MSC). It is a cult centered around the notion that older white men can tell them who to lust after and who to love. It tells them not to love or marry women who are insufficiently white in looks or behavior. It tells them to try to fuck as many women—especially Black and other insufficiently white women—as possible. It gives them masturbatory rituals that simultaneously remind them of what kind of women they should want and lower their sexual confidence in their identity as "straight." The cult makes many men fear real women—especially consensual sex with real women—while encouraging them to feel justified in violating us. It's hard to argue that this, the origin story for fuccboism, is not also the origin story for a (homoerotic) masturbatory sex cult.

I may be the first writer to describe an entire branch of masculinity as an MSC, but I am far from the first person to describe masculinity as a cult. One of the foremost American feminists, Gloria Steinem, cowrote a piece with Lauren Wolfe for *The Guardian* titled "Sexual Violence Against Women Is the Result of the Cult of Masculinity." In it, they state,

> The use of sexualised violence on the streets of Britain or America is the result of the cult of masculinity——some men become addicted to it and feel they have no identity without it. . . . We can only uncover and cure this wound to humanity—especially to the female half of humanity, whose control and subjugation is the most basic requirement of the cult of masculinity—if we report on and pay attention to the victimiser, not just the victim.[3]

In this book, I have tried to reveal the cost to women—especially Black women—and men of this latest evolution of masculinity. Especially since, like Steinem and Wolfe, I, too, believe that "boys who are raised in nonviolent environments that foster empathy don't grow up to fuse sex with violence or become rapists."[4] We need to understand "nonviolent environments" as encompassing more than the home and the neighborhood. They must also include the media.

It is clear that the spread of newer forms of assault—like the phone sex assault I endured—are the result of pornography addiction. They are facilitated by smartphones, which are porn-delivery devices for many people. Forms of assault that attach to B/IWW are aided by dating apps. These apps not only commoditize anti-Blackness and give white fetishism free rein,[5] but they have created a new hunting ground for men so addicted to self-fondling that they are bored by it if they cannot violate a woman in the process. I have revealed here only one of the many occasions in which a porn-fed assault affected me. Yet, I was also cyber-stalked by a porn-addict neighbor while I lived in the faculty housing for the University of British Columbia. Neither the property management, RCMP, nor the university administration could bring themselves to figure out how to interrupt this harrowing and traumatizing crime perpetrated against me for months. Ultimately, my only recourse was to quit.

■   ■   ■

The alignment of men across race, and especially Black and white men, for the diminution of Black women and the elevation of sufficiently white women is sad and frightening. But all is not lost. There is cause for hope. Indeed, I have saved the deepest insight of this book for last. And I owe it, at least in part, to The Carters.

When Beyoncé's *Lemonade* dropped, it shook me. Like many other Black women, I could see myself in Beyoncé's struggle for love and recognition as a member of a degraded segment of America. There were arresting portions of the visual album where she reveals the relationship between her desire to be loved and respected, and the unending cycle of Black women's dishonor in this place. We see the mothers of so many young Black people who have been summarily executed. We hear the words of Malcolm X describing the unique position of inhumanity afforded Black women. I cried, and sang, and felt.

But it was while listening to the follow-up album by The Carters, *Everything Is Love*, that I began to understand the nature of Black and other IW women's suffering. The album hit iTunes, and just like everyone else, I couldn't wait to consume it. I've always liked singing and rapping along with my favorite hip-hop and R&B jams, but I used to do it quietly, meekly. *Everything Is Love* inspired me to lift my voice and sing loud enough for others to hear it.

While I was in the middle of feeling myself and the album, I enrolled in a racial justice workshop led by a well-known queer Black woman. I didn't know her before I was invited by a colleague to participate, but I was thrilled to meet her and the other (mostly Black) folx leading the training. The event was held in Detroit, and every day during a break in the proceedings I would walk around the mostly Black neighborhood surrounding the training center, singing "Black Effect" as loud as possible. I would be soaring, buzzing when I returned to the hall.

One day it dawned on me: the two albums, *Lemonade* and *Everything Is Love*, didn't actually go together. We were sitting in a multiracial group. I tried to explain my position. I said something to the effect of, "The first album took us through a centuries-long tour of the malevolent treatment of Black women in America. But the second album was just her and Jay's private marital reconciliation. I'm happy for them if they're happy. But the second album does not address Black women's collective wounding, that which was exposed as an explanation of her pain. The salvation she realized did not include the rest of us."

There was a thoughtful anti-racist white woman sitting next to me. She nodded her head, and her eyes widened. "I never thought of it that way," she said. Others nodded too. There was a South Asian woman in her late fifties who was very upset by this take. She kept explaining how she'd been married and divorced and now she wanted to get married again. She kept trying to convince me, all of us, that there was nothing wrong with wanting to get and stay married. Her argument elided mine, but she would have none of it. I was not arguing that no one should get married—although there are plenty of feminists who have made this argument. Indeed, marriage is a patriarchal institution; there is no greater evidence of this to me than the reality that marriage is not deemed necessary and therefore is rare to nonexistent and in many matriarchal societies.[6]

I was pointing out that in America—and possibly in other Western nations—we swim in a sea of beliefs about romance that are all rooted in the now largely defunct Romantic Ideal. It tells women that a handsome, charming, courageous prince will come to liberate us by loving us and then marrying us, thus filling our lives with meaning and purpose. We have all been taught that romantic love *is our salvation*. I realized in hearing the disconnect between *Lemonade* and *Everything is Love* that the opposite is true. The Romantic Ideal has been the main force oppressing women by demanding that we do everything in our power to cultivate and keep sexual relationships with men.

Within the Romantic Ideal, women must be quiet and passive. We must wait on a man to love us. If a man feels us worthy of love, and ultimately marriage, we will be "saved." We will receive the social sanction of having lived our lives the right way as women. If we don't want men, or don't end up getting or staying married to one, for almost all of US history, we have been seen as fallen women.

Which brings us to perhaps the most important lesson of this book: *The Romantic Ideal itself has been integral to the creation and maintenance of gender roles, and, critically, women's domination.* It is the font of heteronormativity. Indeed, while the origins of the (now discredited) gender binary prove nebulous, we find their constant (re)presentation and repackaging in TV shows, films, and of course in music about romantic love. It is complete with courtship rites that show men and women behaving in particular ways to find love, get married, and supposedly "live happily ever after." What percent of all of the aforenamed entertainment vehicles are being used to remind (mostly) women of the importance of falling in love with (mostly) men? Prior to the explosion of porn, men too were inculcated with this ideal. But that is not so much the case today. That is why rom-coms are often called "chick flicks."

The Romantic Ideal has existed for hundreds of years, but it truly began to conquer women with the advent of dating. Prior to the invention of dating in the early twentieth century, families were responsible for matchmaking. Men and women each had roles to live by and responsibilities to each other that were socially regulated. But, with dating, relationships became a free-for-all. Many women (especially the self-described "gold diggers") and men (especially later adherents to porn) began trying to get as much as possible from the other party for nothing at all. Modern technologies have largely added to the problems of exploitation introduced by dating. This is a particular problem for Black and other IW women, since in addition to the dating hierarchy I explored in the introduction, there is also research showing that dating apps and other intimate platforms make a killing by monetizing anti-Blackness.[7]

Dating was originally seen as a way for women and men to find "true love," rather than having their relationships arranged. But the notion of how men and women should behave in order to find love was underwritten by the patriarchal Romantic Ideal. Indeed, it is my estimation that the Romantic Ideal has long been one of the most powerful tools in the patriarchal arsenal. To the extent that women are encouraged to make themselves small for a big man to save us by loving us—not unconditionally, of course, because we must be attractive to him, we must look and act a particular way to keep his love—then, too, many women have been willing to go to sleep and let the male domination wash over us in the name of freedom Guinevere style.

The Romantic Ideal worked for centuries to turn women into docile, desperate creatures dependent on men for social sanction. Which is to say that the Romantic Ideal issues a tyrannical view of love and marriage by by holding it out as the ultimate hope for liberation *for women*, whereas it actually traps us. It makes us dependent on sexual love, usually with a man, to feel whole or, ironically, "free" in our dependency.

The Pornographic Ideal, by contrast, is turning many men into low, conniving, cishanded fuckboys. They think it has freed them from the tyranny of romance, but it has ensnared them in another way, by making them, too, desperate to choose the "right" kind of women for loving, which is supposed to be different from the "right" kind of women for fucking, both as judged by generations of white men. Yes, it was not women's whiteness that was insufficient all along, but men's own. And as a growing number of men of color align themselves with this ideal, we all sink deeper into the clutches of white supremacy.

The Romantic Ideal of which women are so fond oppresses women. And, from its inception, romance has been a white endeavor. Its institutionalization as a courtship rite *always already* excluded women not deemed white enough for the effort. Indeed, there is some evidence that the earliest epic poems to celebrate what we now call romance suggested that only prized European women should be "saved" through heroic acts that prove a man's love. Several also claimed European Christian knights should fight for the valor of "their" most vaunted women in an effort to save them from the Saracens, or Arab Muslims.[8]

The Porno ideal of which men are so fond oppresses women *and* men. The trick of white supremacy has been in getting us to desire so badly the tools of our own annihilation. Coming to this realization is the beginning of getting free.

·   ·   ·

There is a precedent to the complete misalignment of sexual values on the part of men and women that we are witnessing today. It was articulated by the icon Silvia Federici, in her landmark text *Caliban and the Witch: Women, the Body and Primitive Accumulation*. In this work, she explains that during the transition to capitalism, one way in which the population ironically named "nobles" were able to disrupt the revolutionary peasant movements was by turning poor men against poor women. How was this achieved? By decriminalizing the rape of poor women. The parallels between the elite tools used for population management in medieval Europe and those deployed by elite white men with the founding of America (i.e., slavery) are not to be misunderstood.

Again and again, male elites have given oppressed male upstarts a ready source of women to violate. They remind these other men that they, too, can be oppressors without having to overtake the men who are actually in charge. Then they wait for their liberation movements to dissolve. If all men, including Black men, have historically been given free rein to rape and pillage among Black women, is there any wonder that keeping a multigendered Black liberation movement alive has proven difficult?

This book has shown that although ready exploitability has been the condition for Black women in America since its founding, a growing group of other insufficiently white women are seeing their respectability fall off a cliff in the wake of the movement era. It's arguably never been clearer to men *across* race that sufficiently white women are to be loved and respected. The rest of us are considered violable.

If you need one final illustration, take a look at the women many of the men in the media marry. How many rappers and other entertainers have wives that are darker-skinned than they? How many of them are Black? Not many.

■ ■ ■

But there is hope for us. More hope now than ever. The Pornographic Ideal has revealed to all of us that the gender roles articulated in the Romantic Ideal have always been a lie. Men are not wealthy charming warriors, and women are not passive wives and babymakers. And nonbinary and trans people are not anomalies. We are all people with complex stories, emotions, and gender displays.

We are not "naturally" heterosexual, because "opposite" sexes do not exist. Once we recognize that *both* of these ideals (Romantic and Pornographic) deliver a false understanding of sexuality—largely through the mangling of so-called heterosexuality (a meaningless term in the wake of the queer revolution we are undergoing)—we can answer the call for all of us to embrace queerness. Being queer is not the same as being gay. It articulates a rejection of cis heteronormative values in love and family formation. It can, and I think should, involve a rejection of white-centric romantic scripts. We do not need romance to thrive. We do not need to invent a new form of sexual love in its place to reinstate nuclear families headed by a patriarch as an archetypal family unit.

Romantic love is not the height of our expressions of love. It is, in fact, the only form of love that has a history. Unlike love of self, family, community, or even natural forms of sexual love, romantic love is simply a Eurocentric story. It has been foisted on us, and it is ruining our lives.

Romance is not the only (or best) way in which sexual love can manifest. All of the nonromantic forms of love are equally valid ways to express that *we are all inherently love.* And when we fill our lives with the needless partner drama of "couple goals," we expend tremendous energy doing something that at best will make our home lives more companionable but at worst is exhausting, traumatic, bitter, and sorrowful. It steals time that we could put into building communities and movements to actually get free.

We are all love. But many of us are consumed with petty and narcissistic romantic dramas that our non-white forebears could not have even fathomed. How much more can we achieve in a world where we do not foreground white fetishizing romances?

ACKNOWLEDGMENTS

This book would not have been possible without an entire community of Black women supporting the work. Some of them have been family members or friends who encouraged me, others have been scholars, activists, artists, and bad mama jamas who I've known only through the bounty they've brought into the world. Here's an incomplete list of the incredible women who've added to my journey:

Tanya McKinnon, Carol Taylor, Maya Fernandez, Bennetta Jules-Rosette, Belinda Robnett, T. Denean Sharpley-Whiting, Angela Davis, Maggie Hunter, Sandra Smith, Amani Allen, Tressie McMillan Cottom, Roxane Gay, Octavia Baker, Kelli Moore, Irene Headen, Tiffany Willoughby-Herard, Ronda Carson, Patricia Helms, Linda Helms, Samantha Warwick Brown, Shanyce Campbell, JoAnna Hardy, Zenju Earthlyn Manuel, and Leslie Booker.

Alma Green, Alma

Green, Alma Green.

Tammy Green, Tammy

Green, Tammy Green, Tammy Green, Tammy Green, Tammy Green, Tammy Green, Tammy Green, Tammy Green, Tammy Green, Tammy Green, Tammy Green, Tammy Green, Tammy Green, Tammy Green.

Betty Ann Allen, Shirley Strings, Lesley Strings, Brandy Strings, Tiffany Strings, Cathy Strings, Vanessa Strings, Joyce Strings, Monique Strings, Cynthia Strings, Dianna Strings, Desiree Strings, LaRita Strings, Sharon Cole, Sami Kirkewood, Kendall Eberheart, Tami Eberheart, Briyonna Ingraham, Ashley Roberts, and, finally, my mother, Joan Strings.

This is by no means an exhaustive list.

NOTES

INTRODUCTION

1. This conversation took place before I'd done significant research on sizeism. There is no way I would remotely entertain a response even this generous to this question today.

2. This phenomenon is now known to some as "Foxitis." See Paul LeBlanc, "Man Who Claimed 'Foxitis' Prompted Him to Rush Capitol Says He Believed 'America Was Being Robbed of a President,'" CNN, May 10, 2021, https://www.cnn.com/2021/05/10/politics/foxitis-us-capitol-riot-cnntv/index.html.

3. Jacob Sutherland, "Remembering the Compton Cookout: Analyzing Our Coverage," *UCSD Guardian*, January 5, 2020, https://ucsdguardian.org/2020/01/05/remembering-the-compton-cookout-analyzing-our-coverage.

4. To see an image revealing the size and scope of the protests against the Compton Cookout, go to Ana Tintocalis, "UCSD Students Demand Swift Actions," KPBS, February 25, 2010, https://www.kpbs.org/news/2010/feb/25/ucsd-students-demand-swift-actions.

5. Angela Carone, "The Compton Cookout and Pop Culture," KPBS, February 23, 2010, https://www.kpbs.org/news/2010/feb/23/Compton-Cookout-And-Pop-Culture.

6. Anna Brown, "Nearly Half of U.S. Adults Say Dating Has Gotten Harder for Most People in the Last 10 Years," *Pew Research Center's Social & Demographic Trends Project*, August 20, 2020, https://www.pewresearch.org/social-trends/2020/08/20/nearly-half-of-u-s-adults-say-dating-has-gotten-harder-for-most-people-in-the-last-10-years.

7. Janet Adamy, "U.S. Marriage Rate Plunges to Lowest Level on Record," *Wall Street Journal*, April 29, 2020, https://www.wsj.com/articles/u-s-marriage-rate-plunges-to-lowest-level-on-record-11588132860.

8. Aziz Ansari and Eric Klinenberg, *Modern Romance* (New York: Penguin Books, 2015).

9. R. Kelly Raley, Megan M. Sweeney, and Danielle Wondra, "The Growing Racial and Ethnic Divide in U.S. Marriage Patterns," *Future Child* 25, no. 2 (Fall 2015): 89–109, https://www.ncbi.nlm.nih.gov/pmc/articles/PMC4850739.

10. Elisabeth M. Caucutt, Nezih Guner, and Christopher Rauh, "What Is Driving the Racial Marriage Gap in the United States?" BSE Focus, Barcelona School of Economics, March 9, 2022, https://focus.bse.eu/what-is-driving-the-racial-marriage -gap-in-the-united-states.

11. Annabel Iwegbue, "I've Had It Up to HERE with Black Women Dating Horror Stories on TikTok," *Cosmopolitan*, April 29, 2022, https://www.cosmopolitan .com/sex-love/a39676615/tik-tok-black-women-dating.

12. Ansari and Klinenberg, *Modern Romance*; The Betches, *I Had a Nice Time and Other Lies . . .: How to Find Love & Sh*t Like That* (New York: Gallery Books, 2016).

13. Ben Stuart, *Single, Dating, Engaged, Married: Navigating Life and Love in the Modern Age* (Atlanta, GA: Passion Publishing, 2017).

14. Kevin Fredericks and Melissa Fredericks, *Marriage Be Hard: 12 Conversations to Keep You Laughing, Loving, and Learning with Your Partner* (New York: Convergent Books, 2022).

15. "Arthurian Legend," *Encyclopaedia Britannica*, December 12, 2022, https:// www.britannica.com/topic/Arthurian-legend; Joshua J. Mark, "Lancelot," *World History Encyclopedia,* April 25, 2019, https://www.worldhistory.org/Lancelot.

16. Mark, "Lancelot."

17. Kimberly Ellis, "Lancelot and Guinevere's Affair Through the Ages," Hanover College Vault, December 12, 2000, https://vault.hanover.edu/~battles/arthur /affair.

18. Andreas Capellanus, *The Art of Courtly Love*, trans. John Jay Parry (New York: Columbia University Press, 1990), 149.

19. Capellanus, *The Art of Courtly Love*, 149–50.

20. Capellanus, *The Art of Courtly Love*, 150.

21. Capellanus, *The Art of Courtly Love*, 148–50.

22. Amanda Serrano, "T. H. White's Defence of Guenever: Portrait of a 'Real' Person," *Mythlore* 21, no. 1 (Summer 1995): 9.

23. Serrano, "T. H. White's Defence of Guenever."

24. Norma Lorre Goodrich, *Guinevere* (New York: HarperCollins, 1991).

25. Miriam Eliav-Feldon, Benjamin Isaac, and Joseph Ziegler, *The Origins of Racism in the West* (Cambridge: Cambridge University Press, 2009); Irven M. Resnick, "Figuring Racism in Medieval Christianity by M. Lindsay Kaplan (Review)," *Antisemitism Studies* 5, no. 2 (Fall 2021): 416–23, https://muse.jhu.edu/pub/3 /article/835793.

26. One of the people credited with popularizing blond hair and blue eyes was Eleanor of Aquitaine herself. See Resnick, "Figuring Racism in Medieval Christianity by M. Lindsay Kaplan (Review)"; "Eleanor of Aquitaine," EHISTORY, https:// ehistory.osu.edu/biographies/eleanor-aquitaine, accessed February 15, 2023.

27. Capellanus, *The Art of Courtly Love.*

28. Capellanus, *The Art of Courtly Love.*

29. Capellanus, *The Art of Courtly Love*; Régine Pernoud, "Eleanor of Aquitaine," *Encyclopaedia Britannica*, November 18, 2022, https://www.britannica.com /biography/Eleanor-of-Aquitaine.

30. Capellanus, *The Art of Courtly Love.*

31. Meg Bogin, *The Women Troubadours* (New York: W. W. Norton, 1980).

32. Bogin, *The Women Troubadours*; Laura Ashe, "Love and Chivalry in the Middle Ages," Discovering Literature: Medieval, British Library, January 31, 2018, https://www.bl.uk/medieval-literature/articles/love-and-chivalry-in-the-middle-ages.

33. Emilie Amt, ed., *Women's Lives in Medieval Europe: A Sourcebook*, 2nd ed. (New York: Routledge, 2010).

34. "The History of Romance," National Women's History Museum, February 13, 2017, https://www.womenshistory.org/articles/history-romance, accessed April 19, 2021.

35. Frances Kendall, *Understanding White Privilege: Creating Pathways to Authentic Relationships Across Race* (New York: Routledge, 2012).

36. François Bernier, *Travels in the Mogul Empire, A.D. 1656–1668*, trans. Archibald Constable (London: Oxford University Press, 1916).

37. Bernier, *Travels in the Mogul Empire*, 404.

38. Bernier, *Travels in the Mogul Empire*, 404.

39. François Bernier, "A New Division of the Earth," *History Workshop Journal*, no. 51 (Spring, 2001): 249, https://doi.org/10.2307/4289731.

40. Bernier, "A New Division of the Earth," 249–50.

41. Bernier, "A New Division of the Earth," 249.

42. Londa Schiebinger, "The Anatomy of Difference: Race and Sex in Eighteenth-Century Science," *Eighteenth-Century Studies* 23, no. 4 (July 1, 1990): 387–405, https://doi.org/10.2307/2739176.

43. Caren M. Holmes, "The Colonial Roots of the Racial Fetishization of Black Women," *Black & Gold* 2, no. 1 (2016): 2.

44. Sabrina Strings, *Fearing the Black Body: The Racial Origins of Fat Phobia* (New York: New York University Press, 2019).

45. Bernier, *Travels in the Mogul Empire*; Edward W. Said, *Orientalism* (New York: Pantheon Books, 1978); Robin Zheng, "Why Yellow Fever Isn't Flattering: A Case Against Racial Fetishes," *Journal of the American Philosophical Association* 2, no. 3 (Fall 2016): 400–419, https://doi.org/10.1017/apa.2016.25.

46. Roderick A. Ferguson, *Aberrations in Black: Toward a Queer of Color Critique*, Critical American Studies Series (Minneapolis: University of Minnesota Press, 2004); Sabrina Strings, "Women (Re)Making Whiteness: The Sexual Exclusion of the Fat 'Black' Irish," *Ethnic and Racial Studies* 43, no. 4 (2020): 1–18.

47. "The History of Romance," National Women's History Museum.

48. Mary Wollstonecraft, *A Vindication of the Rights of Woman: With Strictures on Political and Moral Subjects*, new edition (London: T. F. Unwin, 1891), 82.

49. bell hooks, *Ain't I a Woman: Black Women and Feminism*, orig. 1981 (New York: Routledge, 2014).

50. Dewey D. Wallace, *The Spirituality of the Later English Puritans: An Anthology* (Macon, GA: Mercer University Press, 1987); hooks, *Ain't I a Woman.*

51. Eduardo Bonilla-Silva, "'New Racism': Color-Blind Racism, and the Future of Whiteness in America," in *White Out: The Continuing Significance of Racism*, ed. Ashley W. Doane and Eduardo Bonilla-Silva (New York: Routledge, 2003), 278.

52. Karen Brodkin, *How Jews Became White Folks and What That Says About Race in America* (New Brunswick, NJ: Rutgers University Press, 1998).

53. Sandra G. Harding, *Feminism and Methodology: Social Science Issues* (Bloomington: Indiana University Press, 1987).

54. It would have been possible to use an alternate method, say interviews, to reveal how cishet men commonly approach relationships or to describe cishet women's experiences in the situationships that are ubiquitous in hookup culture. However, I chose an exploration of media narratives in conversation with my own personal narratives for the express purpose of burrowing into the kinds of messages mass culture delivers regarding what should constitute cis-male values and priorities in choosing a partner and how the women one (de)values should be treated and, relatedly, how these women actually are chosen and treated. In this respect, the renegade methods I am using work to sidestep self-reporting—how men (or women) believe they are behaving and what they say they value.

55. bell hooks, "Theory as Liberatory Practice," *Yale Journal of Law and Feminism* 4, no. 1 (1991), http://digitalcommons.law.yale.edu/yjlf.

56. Sandra Cisneros, "Sandra Cisneros: A House of Her Own," *On Being with Krista Tippett*, podcast, 52:17, February 13, 2020, https://onbeing.org/programs/sandra -cisneros-a-house-of-her-own.

CHAPTER 1: BLACK IS THE COMMONS

1. *"Friends* Star Aisha Tyler Reveals If She'd Date Ross or Joey in Real Life," March 1, 2020, YouTube video, 1:16, https://www.youtube.com/watch?v=i6U0fiwPp5Q, accessed June 22, 2020.

2. For reference, see "Aisha Tyler Looks Back at the 'Colorblind Casting' That Got Her on Friends," *InStyle*, July 24, 2022, https://www.instyle.com/aisha-tyler -friends-colorblind-casting; Aisha Tyler, "Aisha Tyler Made History on the Show 'Friends,'" *The Late Show with Stephen Colbert*, YouTube video, 2:52, May 6, 2018, https://www.youtube.com/watch?v=7wXbk7uFAHk, accessed June 18, 2020; Maitri Suhas, "Aisha Tyler Always Knew Being Cast on 'Friends' Was a Big Deal & Here's Why," *Bustle*, February 6, 2019, https://www.bustle.com/p/friends -guest-star-aisha-tyler-revealed-what-it-was-really-like-being-the-first-recurring -black-woman-on-the-show-15931070; "Aisha Tyler Reveals What It Was Like to Work on FRIENDS," MSN, accessed June 18, 2020, https://www.msn.com/en -au/entertainment/tv/aisha-tyler-reveals-what-it-was-like-to-work-on-friends /ar-AAIovEj.

3. Harriet A. Washington, *Medical Apartheid: The Dark History of Medical Experimentation on Black Americans from Colonial Times to the Present* (New York: Anchor, 2008); Rachel A. Feinstein, *When Rape Was Legal: The Untold History of Sexual Violence During Slavery* (New York: Routledge, 2018).

4. Washington, *Medical Apartheid*; Stephanie E. Jones-Rogers, *They Were Her Property: White Women as Slave Owners in the American South* (New Haven, CT: Yale University Press, 2019).

5. Darlene Clark Hine, "Rape and the Inner Lives of Black Women in the Middle West," *Signs: Journal of Women in Culture and Society* 14, no. 4 (Summer 1989), https://doi.org/10.1086/494552; Feinstein, *When Rape Was Legal.*

6. Black women becoming The Commons was to be only one of the social ramifications of white male rule. Others, those affecting the relationships between Black women and men, and Black and white women will be discussed elsewhere. Suffice it to say for now that the communal appropriation of Black women's bodies had negative effects on Black women's connections with each of these groups.

7. Jeffrey J. Pokorak, "Rape as a Badge of Slavery: The Legal History of, and Remedies for, Prosecutorial Race-of-Victim Charging Disparities," *Nevada Law Journal* 7, no. 1 (2006): 1–54.

8. Feinstein, *When Rape Was Legal.*

9. Soraya Nadia McDonald, "'The Rape of Recy Taylor' Explores the Little-Known Terror Campaign Against Black Women," *Andscape*, December 14, 2017, https://andscape.com/features/the-rape-of-recy-taylor-explores-the-little-known-terror-campaign-against-black-women/; Rosalind Bentley, "Four White Men Raped a Black Coed and Her Case Became a Landmark," *Atlanta Journal-Constitution*, February 25, 2018.

10. *The Rape of Recy Taylor*, documentary, dir. Nancy Buirski, Artemis Rising Productions, 2018.

11. Buirski, *The Rape of Recy Taylor.*

12. Danielle L. McGuire, *At the Dark End of the Street: Black Women, Rape, and Resistance—A New History of the Civil Rights Movement from Rosa Parks to the Rise of Black Power* (New York: Knopf, 2010); Buirski, *The Rape of Recy Taylor.*

13. Buirski, *The Rape of Recy Taylor.*

14. McGuire, *At the Dark End of the Street*; "Montgomery Improvement Association (MIA)," Martin Luther King, Jr., Research and Education Institute, Stanford University, accessed June 5, 2017, https://kinginstitute.stanford.edu/encyclopedia/montgomery-improvement-association-mia.

15. Sewell Chan, "Recy Taylor, Who Fought for Justice After a 1944 Rape, Dies at 97," *New York Times*, December 29, 2017, https://www.nytimes.com/2017/12/29/obituaries/recy-taylor-alabama-rape-victim-dead.html.

16. Danielle L. McGuire, "'It Was Like All of Us Had Been Raped': Sexual Violence, Community Mobilization, and the African American Freedom Struggle," in *The Best American History Essays 2006*, ed. Joyce Appleby (New York: Palgrave Macmillan, 2006), 123–50.

17. Gloria Wekker, *White Innocence: Paradoxes of Colonialism and Race* (Durham, NC: Duke University Press, 2016).

18. Barbara Ransby, *Ella Baker and the Black Freedom Movement: A Radical Democratic Vision* (Chapel Hill: University of North Carolina Press, 2003).

19. Michael Eric Dyson and David L. Jagerman, *I May Not Get There with You: The True Martin Luther King, Jr.* (New York: Simon and Schuster, 2000).

20. Rhoda Lois Blumberg, "Women in the Civil Rights Movement: Reform or Revolution?" in *Women and Revolution: Global Expressions*, ed. M. J. Diamond (Berlin: Springer Science & Business Media, 1998), 86.

21. Roderick A. Ferguson, *Aberrations in Black: Toward a Queer of Color Critique*, Critical American Studies Series (Minneapolis: University of Minnesota Press, 2004).

22. Joe Johnson, "Books," *The Crisis*, March 1985.

23. Rosalind Miles, *The Women's History of the Modern World: How Radicals, Rebels, and Everywomen Revolutionized the Last 200 Years* (New York: HarperCollins, 2021).

24. Feminista Jones, "Malcolm X Stood Up for Black Women When Few Others Would," *Medium*, August 7, 2020, https://zora.medium.com/malcolm-x-stood -up-for-black-women-when-few-others-would-68e8b2ea2747.

25. Nancy Bercaw and Ted Ownby, eds., *The New Encyclopedia of Southern Culture, Volume 13: Gender* (Chapel Hill: University of North Carolina Press, 2014), 231.

26. Ted Conover, "The Strike That Brought MLK to Memphis," *Smithsonian Magazine*, January 2018, https://www.smithsonianmag.com/history/revisiting -sanitation-workers-strike-180967512/.

27. Assata Shakur, *Assata: An Autobiography* (Chicago: Lawrence Hill Books, 2020), 93.

28. Shakur, *Assata*.

29. "Racism and Rape," National Alliance to End Sexual Violence, https://end sexualviolence.org/where_we_stand/racism-and-rape, accessed March 2, 2023.

30. Brooke Flagler, "A Brief History of Rape Law," The Feminist Poetry Movement, December 13, 2019, https://sites.williams.edu/engl113-f18/flagler/a-brief-history -of-rape-law, accessed January 3, 2022.

31. Kyla Bishop, "A Reflection on the History of Sexual Assault Laws in the United States," *Arkansas Journal of Social Change and Public Service* (April 15, 2018), https://ualr.edu/socialchange/2018/04/15/reflection-history-sexual-assault-laws -united-states.

32. Kim Fox, David O. Dowling, and Kyle Miller, "A Curriculum for Blackness: Podcasts as Discursive Cultural Guides, 2010–2020," *Journal of Radio & Audio Media* 27, no. 2 (2020): 298–318, https://doi.org/10.1080/19376529.2020.1801687.

33. Danielle Page, "Are You in a 'Situationship'? What It Is and How to Get Out of It," *NBC News*, October 3, 2019, https://www.nbcnews.com/better/lifestyle/are -you-situationship-what-it-how-get-out-it-ncna1057141.

34. Emphasis mine. bell hooks, "Eating the Other: Desire and Resistance," in *Black Looks: Race and Representation* (Boston: South End Press, 1992), 23.

35. Christian Rudder, *Dataclysm: Love, Sex, Race, and Identity—What Our Online Lives Tell Us About Our Offline Selves* (New York: Broadway Books, 2015), 110–16.

36. Celeste Vaughan Curington, Jennifer Hickes Lundquist, and Ken-Hou Lin, *The Dating Divide: Race and Desire in the Era of Online Romance* (Oakland: University of California Press, 2021), 105.

37. Wendy Wang, "Interracial Marriage: Who Is 'Marrying Out'?" Pew Research Center, June 12, 2015, http://www.pewresearch.org/fact-tank/2015/06/12/interracial-marriage-who-is-marrying-out.

38. David Smith, "David Schwimmer: 'I'm Very Aware of My Privilege as a Heterosexual White Male,'" *The Guardian*, January 27, 2020, https://www.theguardian.com/culture/2020/jan/27/david-schwimmer-im-very-aware-of-my-privilege-as-a-heterosexual-white-male.

39. Devon Ivie, "David Schwimmer Says He Fought for More Diverse *Friends* Casting," *Vulture*, January 28, 2020, https://www.vulture.com/2020/01/david-schwimmer-friends-diversity.html; Keyaira Boone, "David Schwimmer Reveals He Pushed for His Character Ross to Date Black Women on 'Friends,'" *Essence*, December 6, 2020, https://www.essence.com/entertainment/david-schwimmer-friends-black-women.

CHAPTER 2: THE BLACKER THE BERRY . . . THE LESS LOVEWORTHY

1. *The Original Kings of Comedy*, documentary, dir. Spike Lee, written and performed by Cedric the Entertainer, Steve Harvey, D. L. Hughley, and Bernie Mac, Paramount, 2000.

2. Brian Boyd, "Motown Magic Broke Racial Barriers—but at a Price," *Irish Times*, January 30, 2009, https://www.irishtimes.com/culture/motown-magic-broke-racial-barriers-but-at-a-price-1.1238093.

3. "Mamie Smith and the Birth of the Blues Market," *All Things Considered*, NPR, November 11, 2006, https://www.npr.org/2006/11/11/6473116/mamie-smith-and-the-birth-of-the-blues-market.

4. "Fats Waller," *Biography*, https://www.biography.com/musician/fats-waller, accessed July 30, 2019.

5. "Dinah Washington—Am I Asking Too Much[?]" YouTube video, 2:48, recorded 1948, posted May 27, 2014, https://www.youtube.com/watch?v=7Qf6yFL-ZVk.

6. "Nat King Cole—Unforgettable," YouTube video, 2:31, posted August 20, 2012, https://www.youtube.com/watch?v=JFyuOEovTOE.

7. Johnny Otis, "Turtle Dove," Spotify audio, 2:30, 2020, https://open.spotify.com/track/4B9Kwo8Ze24KgQJ24ixvHg.

8. Lois Wilson, "Life and Soul," *The Telegraph*, May 25, 2018, https://www.telegraph.co.uk/travel/discover-america/evolution-of-music/soul/.

9. It is worth mentioning that despite the power and positive valence of his music, Marvin Gaye's personal life was rife with troubles of the domestic sort. His second wife, Janis Hunter, accused him of various forms of cruelty. His father notoriously shot and killed him one day before his forty-fifth birthday. See Larry Getlen, "Marvin Gaye's Wife Reveals How He Tortured Her," *New York Post*, May 3, 2015, https://nypost.com/2015/05/03/marvin-gayes-wife-revealed-how-he-tortured-her; "Marvin Gaye," *Biography*, April 27, 2017, https://www.biography.com/musician/marvin-gaye.

10. James Brown, "Brother Rapp," *Sex Machine*, 1970, Genius, https://genius.com/James-brown-brother-rapp-lyrics, accessed January 20, 2023.

11. Matt Brennan, "Funky Drummer: How a James Brown Jam Session Gave Us the 'Greatest Drum Break of Them All,'" *The Conversation*, March 26, 2020, http://theconversation.com/funky-drummer-how-a-james-brown-jam-session-gave-us-the-greatest-drum-break-of-them-all-134493.

12. Tera W. Hunter, *Bound in Wedlock: Slave and Free Black Marriage in the Nineteenth Century* (Cambridge, MA: Belknap Press of Harvard University Press, 2017); Dianne M. Stewart, *Black Women, Black Love: America's War on African American Marriage* (New York: Seal Press, 2020).

13. Tera Hunter, "Married Slaves Faced Wrenching Separations, or Even Choosing Family Over Freedom," *History*, September 20, 2019, https://www.history.com/news/african-american-slavery-marriage-family-separation.

14. Thomas A. Foster, "The Sexual Abuse of Black Men Under American Slavery," *Journal of the History of Sexuality* 20, no. 3 (September 2011): 445–64, https://www.jstor.org/stable/41305880.

15. Lydia Maria Child and Lewis Clarke, "Leaves from a Slave's Journal of Life," *Anti-Slavery Standard* (1842): 78–79; Foster, "The Sexual Abuse of Black Men Under American Slavery."

16. Daina Ramey Berry and Leslie M. Harris, eds., *Sexuality and Slavery: Reclaiming Intimate Histories in America* (Athens: University of Georgia Press, 2018).

17. Libra R. Hilde, *Slavery, Fatherhood, and Paternal Duty in African American Communities over the Long Nineteenth Century* (Chapel Hill: University of North Carolina Press, 2020).

18. David Doddington, "Manhood, Sex, and Power in Antebellum Slave Communities," in *Sexuality and Slavery: Reclaiming Intimate Histories in America*, ed. Daina Ramey Berry and Leslie M. Harris (Athens: University of Georgia Press, 2018), 146.

19. Doddington, "Manhood, Sex, and Power, 146.

20. Kathy Russell, Midge Wilson, and Ronald Hall, *The Color Complex: The Politics of Skin Color Among African Americans* (New York: Anchor, 1993); Margaret L. Hunter, *Race, Gender, and the Politics of Skin Tone* (New York: Routledge, 2013).

21. Russell, Wilson, and Hall, *The Color Complex*, 57.

22. Russell, Wilson, and Hall, *The Color Complex*, 57.

23. Ayana D. Byrd and Lori L. Tharps, *Hair Story: Untangling the Roots of Black Hair in America* (New York: St. Martin's Griffin, 2002).

24. Ekeoma E. Uzogara et al., "A Comparison of Skin Tone Discrimination Among African American Men: 1995 and 2003," *Psychology of Men & Masculinities* 15, no. 2 (April 2014): 201–12, https://doi.org/10.1037/a0033479.

25. "Cotton Club," Colorism During the New Negro Movement, 2023, https://colorism.commons.gc.cuny.edu/cotton-club.

26. Brenda E. Stevenson, "What's Love Got to Do with It? Concubinage and Enslaved Women and Girls in the American South," *Journal of African American History* 98, no. 1 (2013): 102, https://doi.org/10.5323/jafriamerhist.98.1.0099.

27. Russell, Wilson, and Hall, *The Color Complex*.

28. Maxine Leeds Craig, *Ain't I a Beauty Queen? Black Women, Beauty, and the Politics of Race* (Oxford: Oxford University Press, 2002).

29. Keisha Blain, "These Overlooked Black Women Shaped Malcolm X's Life," *Time*, February 24, 2020, https://time.com/5789057/malcolm-x-women/.

30. Craig, *Ain't I a Beauty Queen?*

31. Craig, *Ain't I a Beauty Queen?*

32. Elizabeth I. Mullins and Paul Sites, "The Origins of Contemporary Eminent Black Americans: A Three-Generation Analysis of Social Origin," *American Sociological Review* 49, no. 5 (1984): 672–85, https://doi.org/10.2307/2095424; Russell, Wilson, and Hall, *The Color Complex.*

33. *Rubble Kings*, dir. Shan Nicholson, Saboteur Digital, 2010, https://rubblekings .com.

34. Robert Hilburn, "Ice Cube Keeps Cool . . . Chills Clash," *Los Angeles Times*, March 25, 1989, https://www.latimes.com/archives/la-xpm-1989-03-25-ca-441 -story.html.

35. De La Soul, "Stakes Is High," *Stakes Is High*, July 2, 1996, Genius, https://genius .com/De-la-soul-stakes-is-high-lyrics, accessed January 6, 2023.

36. Kathleen Knight Abowitz, "Horatio Alger and Hip Hop," *Review of Education, Pedagogy, and Cultural Studies* 19, no. 4 (1997): 409–25, doi: 10.1080 /1071441970190405.

37. Polly Dunbar, "A Look Inside Sexism in the Music Industry," *Marie Claire*, September 16, 2019, https://www.marieclaire.co.uk/reports/music-industry-sexism -426585.

38. Master P, "Bitches & Money," featuring Tru, *Get Away Clean*, February 12, 1991, Genius, https://genius.com/Master-p-bitches-and-money-lyrics.

39. I could find no evidence of Big having any relationships with women who were not Black. Based on this observation and the street-relevant context clues, the "women" in the narrative are Black by implication.

40. Yet another rap mantra, credited to rapper YG.

41. Snoop Dogg, "Ain't No Fun (If the Homies Can't Have None)," featuring Nate Dogg, Kurupt, and Warren G, *Doggystyle*, November 23, 1993, Genius, https:// genius.com/Snoop-dogg-aint-no-fun-if-the-homies-cant-have-none-lyrics.

42. C. Vernon Coleman, "20 'Light Skin' and 'Dark Skin' References in Rap Lyrics," *VIBE*, June 24, 2013, https://www.vibe.com/gallery/20-light-skin-dark-skin -references-rap/.

43. Coleman, "20 'Light Skin' and 'Dark Skin' References in Rap Lyrics."

44. Coleman, "20 'Light Skin' and 'Dark Skin' References in Rap Lyrics."

45. Julia Pimentel, "Kodak Black Says He Doesn't Like Dark-Skinned Women Because They're 'Too Gutter,'" *Complex*, June 30, 2017, https://www.complex .com/music/2017/06/kodak-black-doesnt-like-dark-skinned-women-too -gutter.

46. Jamilah King, "J. Cole Talks About Colorism in Hip-Hop and the White House," *Colorlines*, August 22, 2013, https://colorlines.com/article/j-cole-talks-about -colorism-hip-hop-and-white-house.

CHAPTER 3: BLACK WOMEN ARE NOT TO BE TRUSTED

1. Elisa Kreisinger with Sesali Bowen, "Strong Opinions Loosely Held: Debunking the Black Woman Gold Digger Myth," *Refinery 29*, October 17, 2018, https://www.refinery29.com/en-us/2018/10/214340/black-women-gold-digger-myth-gets-debunked.

2. Brian Donovan, *American Gold Digger: Marriage, Money, and the Law from the Ziegfeld Follies to Anna Nicole Smith*, Gender and American Culture (Chapel Hill: University of North Carolina Press, 2020).

3. Donovan, *American Gold Digger*.

4. US Women's Bureau and Mary Veronica Dempsey, *The Occupational Progress of Women: An Interpretation of Census Statistics of Women in Gainful Occupations* (Washington, DC: US Government Printing Office, 1922).

5. C. E. Persons, "Women's Work and Wages in the United States," *Quarterly Journal of Economics* 29, no. 2 (February 1915): 201–34, https://doi.org/10.2307/1884958.

6. Betty Friedan, *The Feminine Mystique* (New York: W. W. Norton, 1963).

7. Celeste Vaughan Curington, Jennifer Hickes Lundquist, and Ken-Hou Lin, *The Dating Divide: Race and Desire in the Era of Online Romance* (Oakland: University of California Press, 2021).

8. Susannah Miller, "The Overturning of Michael M.: Statutory Rape Law Becomes Gender-Neutral in California," *UCLA Journal of Gender and Law* 5, no. 1 (1994), http://dx.doi.org/10.5070/L351017619; Estelle B. Freedman, *Redefining Rape: Sexual Violence in the Era of Suffrage and Segregation* (Cambridge, MA: Harvard University Press, 2013).

9. Donovan, *American Gold Digger*.

10. US Women's Bureau and Mary Veronica Dempsey, *The Occupational Progress of Women*.

11. Donovan, *American Gold Digger*.

12. "Gold Diggers of 1933 (1933)," Hollywood's Golden Age, http://www.hollywoodsgoldenage.com/movies/golddiggers-of-1933.html, accessed March 2, 2023.

13. Donovan, *American Gold Digger*, 23.

14. Donovan, *American Gold Digger*.

15. Donovan, *American Gold Digger*, 30.

16. Donovan, *American Gold Digger*.

17. *Gentlemen Prefer Blondes*, dir. Howard Hawks, 20th Century Fox, 1953, IMDb, https://www.imdb.com/title/tt0045810/, accessed March 2, 2023.

18. Editors, "The Negro Question," *New York Times*, April 25, 1903, https://archive.nytimes.com/www.nytimes.com/books/00/11/05/specials/dubois-souls.html.

19. Malcolm X, "Racial Separation," 1963, BlackPast, January 23, 2013, https://www.blackpast.org/african-american-history/speeches-african-american-history/1963-malcolm-x-racial-separation.

20. Fred Hampton, "Fred Hampton— It's a Class Struggle Goddammit!, November, 1969," text, Jean Michel Bruyère, January 21, 2015, https://www.lfks.net/en/content/fred-hampton-its-class-struggle-goddammit-november-1969.

21. "The Kennedys and the Civil Rights Movement," John Fitzgerald Kennedy National Historic Site, National Park Service, September 12, 2021, https://www.nps.gov/articles/000/the-kennedys-and-civil-rights.htm.

22. Malcolm X and Imam Benjamin Karim, *The End of White World Supremacy: Four Speeches* (New York: Arcade, 2020).

23. W. Gardener Selby, "Lyndon Johnson Opposed Every Civil Rights Proposal Considered in His First 20 Years as Lawmaker," PolitiFact, April 14, 2014, https://www.politifact.com/factchecks/2014/apr/14/barack-obama/lyndon-johnson-opposed-every-civil-rights-proposal/.

24. Joshua Zeitz, "What Everyone Gets Wrong About LBJ's Great Society," *Politico*, January 28, 2018, http://politi.co/2ngIVV6.

25. Michael O'Donnell, "How LBJ Saved the Civil Rights Act," *The Atlantic*, March 20, 2014, https://www.theatlantic.com/magazine/archive/2014/04/what-the-hells-the-presidency-for/358630/.

26. David Smith, "Half-Century of US Civil Rights Gains Have Stalled or Reversed, Report Finds," *The Guardian*, February 27, 2018, https://www.theguardian.com/us-news/2018/feb/27/us-civil-rights-report-kerner-commission.

27. Elizabeth Hinton, "Why We Should Reconsider the War on Crime," *Time*, March 20, 2015, https://time.com/3746059/war-on-crime-history/.

28. Elahe Izadi, "Black Lives Matter and America's Long History of Resisting Civil Rights Protesters," *Washington Post*, April 19, 2016, https://www.washingtonpost.com/news/the-fix/wp/2016/04/19/black-lives-matters-and-americas-long-history-of-resisting-civil-rights-protesters/.

29. Terence McArdle, "The 'Law and Order' Campaign That Won Richard Nixon the White House 50 Years Ago," *Washington Post*, November 5, 2018, https://www.washingtonpost.com/history/2018/11/05/law-order-campaign-that-won-richard-nixon-white-house-years-ago/.

30. "Poverty and Prejudice," EDGE (Ethics of Development in a Global Environment) Seminar Series, Stanford University, 1999, https://web.stanford.edu/class/e297c/poverty_prejudice/paradox/htele.html, accessed March 2, 2023.

31. Benjamin T. Smith, "New Documents Reveal the Bloody Origins of America's Long War On Drugs," *Time*, August 24, 2021, https://time.com/6090016/us-war-on-drugs-origins/.

32. McArdle, "The 'Law and Order' Campaign That Won Richard Nixon the White House 50 Years Ago."

33. Jeremy Lybarger, "The Ugly Myth of the Welfare Queen," *The Nation*, July 2, 2019, https://www.thenation.com/article/archive/josh-levin-the-queen-book-review/.

34. Gene Demby, "The Truth Behind the Lies of the Original 'Welfare Queen,'" NPR, December 20, 2013, https://www.npr.org/sections/codeswitch/2013/12/20/255819681/the-truth-behind-the-lies-of-the-original-welfare-queen.

35. Ange-Marie Hancock, *The Politics of Disgust: The Public Identity of the Welfare Queen* (New York: NYU Press, 2004).

36. Josh Levin, "The Real Story of Linda Taylor, America's Original Welfare Queen," *Slate*, December 19, 2013, http://www.slate.com/articles/news_and_politics

/history/2013/12/linda_taylor_welfare_queen_ronald_reagan_made_her_a
_notorious_american_villain.html.

37. Gillian Brockell, "She Was Stereotyped as 'The Welfare Queen.' The Truth Was
More Disturbing, a New Book Says," *Washington Post*, May 21, 2019, https://
www.washingtonpost.com/history/2019/05/21/she-was-stereotyped-welfare
-queen-truth-was-more-disturbing-new-book-says/.

38. Brockell, "She Was Stereotyped as 'The Welfare Queen.'"

39. Brockell, "She Was Stereotyped as 'The Welfare Queen.'"

40. Tricia Rose, *Black Noise: Rap Music and Black Culture in Contemporary America* (Middletown, CT: Wesleyan University Press, 1994); Lisa Jones, *Bulletproof
Diva: Tales of Race, Sex, and Hair* (New York: Knopf Doubleday, 2010).

41. Daniel Hautzinger, "The Many Pioneering Lives of Etta Moten Barnett," WTTW
Chicago, February 12, 2019, https://interactive.wttw.com/playlist/2019/02/12
/etta-moten-barnett.

42. Dionne P. Stephens and Layli D. Phillips, "Freaks, Gold Diggers, Divas, and
Dykes: The Sociohistorical Development of Adolescent African American Wom-
en's Sexual Scripts," *Sexuality & Culture* 7, no. 1 (Winter 2003): 3–49, http://
dx.doi.org/10.1007/BF03159848.

43. According to the amazing text *Ain't I a Beauty Queen*, by Maxine Leeds-Craig,
beauty standards in Black spaces are very similar to those found in white communities. Differences often include a greater appreciation of big butts and
thighs and facial features linked to Blackness. The preference for light skin, as
previously explored, is the same. It has to be said that Black women called out
for being gold diggers in the popular press are frequently darker than a paper
bag, perhaps a holdover from the terror surrounding the welfare queen. Presumably, lighter skinned women are seen as less threatening when it comes to
the (charged) intersection of love and money.

44. Aldore Collier, "Robin Givens Leaves Harvard Med School for Hollywood," *Jet*,
June 29, 1987.

45. "Robin Took Best Punch, Tyson Says in Biography,'" *Los Angeles Times*, June 23,
1989, https://www.latimes.com/archives/la-xpm-1989-06-23-sp-2706-story.html.

46. "Robin Took Best Punch, Tyson Says in Biography."

47. "Robin Took Best Punch, Tyson Says in Biography."

48. Howard Kurtz, "Givens Files $125 Million Libel Suit Against Tyson," *Washing-
ton Post*, November 17, 1988, https://www.washingtonpost.com/archive/life
style/1988/11/17/givens-files-125-million-libel-suit-against-tyson/06f4f09e
-2fb8-4d8e-84ba-23e4a0e95437/.

49. Ionerlogan, "Mike Tyson Goes in on Gold Digging Ex-Robin Givens in Memoir,"
NewsOne, October 29, 2013, https://newsone.com/2747720/mike-tyson-robin
-givens.

50. Laura Randolph, "Robin Givens: Life After Tyson," *Ebony*, March 1990.

51. A ProQuest search for "Robin Givens and Mike Tyson" on March 18, 2022,
yielded 20,233 results. I reviewed the first 1,020 and found them to be relevant.

52. Kool Moe Dee, "They Want Money," *Knowledge Is King*, May 30, 1989, Genius,
https://genius.com/Kool-moe-dee-they-want-money-lyrics.

53. Even though Kid Rock is clearly not a Black man, I put his name on this list to illustrate the conversation verging on collusion between mainstream Black cishet and white cishet masculinities. See the search results for "Robin Givens Lyrics" at Lyrics.cat, https://www.lyrics.cat/lyrics+robin+givens.

54. Keith Murphy, "Full Clip: Erick Sermon Runs Down His Catalogue Ft. EPMD, Rakim & More," *VIBE*, June 4, 2012, https://www.vibe.com/music/music-news /full-clip-erick-sermon-runs-down-his-catalogue-ft-epmd-rakim-more-0-100507/.

55. EPMD, *Gold Digger*, 1990, Genius, https://genius.com/Epmd-gold-digger-lyrics.

56. J. Douglas Barics, "Maintenance in New York: An Introduction to Spousal Support in NY Matrimonial Actions," August 2019, https://jdbar.com/articles /introduction-spousal-maintenance-support/.

57. Irwin Garfinkel, "The Evolution of Child Support Policy," *Focus* 11, no. 1 (1988): 11–16.

58. Barry Pearson, "History of Child Support in the USA," International History of Child Support, 2003, http://www.childsupportanalysis.co.uk/information _and_explanation/world/history_usa.htm, accessed March 2, 2023.

59. Pearson, "History of Child Support in the USA."

60. Emily Kirkpatrick, "Halle Berry Compares Paying Child Support to Her Ex Gabriel Aubry to 'Extortion,'" *Vanity Fair*, February 12, 2021, https://www .vanityfair.com/style/2021/02/halle-berry-child-support-gabriel-aubry-extortion -nahla-divorce-instagram.

61. Libby Torres, "Britney Spears' Ex-Husband Kevin Federline Is Reportedly Receiving 70% Custody of the Couple's Children in New Agreement," *Insider*, September 3, 2019, https://www.insider.com/britney-spears-kevin-federline -custody-agreement-2019-9; Jason Pham, "Kevin Federline Net Worth 2021: How Much Britney Spears' Ex-Husband Makes," *Stylecaster*, September 27, 2021, https://stylecaster.com/kevin-federline-net-worth/.

62. Darlena Cunha, "The Divorce Gap," *The Atlantic*, April 28, 2016, https://www .theatlantic.com/business/archive/2016/04/the-divorce-gap/480333/.

63. Jeanne Boydston, "The Cult of True Womanhood," *Not for Ourselves Alone* website, PBS, https://www.pbs.org/kenburns/not-for-ourselves-alone/cult-of-true -womanhood, accessed March 22, 2022.

64. Natalia Kolesnikova, and Yang Liu, "Economic Progress Slim for Black Men from 1970 to 2000," St. Louis Fed, July 1, 2010, https://www.stlouisfed.org /publications/regional-economist/july-2010/a-bleak-30-years-for-black-men -economic-progress-was-slim-in-urban-america.

65. "Usual Weekly Earnings of Wage and Salary Workers," Economic News Release, US Bureau of Labor Statistics, January 19, 2023, https://www.bls.gov/news .release/wkyeng.htm.

66. Christian Rudder, *Dataclysm: Love, Sex, Race, and Identity—What Our Online Lives Tell Us About Our Offline Selves* (New York: Broadway Books, 2015).

67. Kanye West, 2005, *Gold Digger*, https://genius.com/Kanye-west-gold-digger-lyrics.

68. In his song "Money Trees," Lamar describes staking out a potential robbery before committing it. It seems you do not go in for a job until you are sure the conditions are favorable, or in his words, persuasive.

69. Shawn Setaro, "How Artists Make Money on YouTube," *Complex*, November 24, 2017, https://www.complex.com/music/2017/11/how-artists-make-money-on -youtube.

70. Emphasis mine. Ray Charles, "I Got a Woman," *I Got a Woman*, 1957, AZLyrics .com, 2019, https://www.azlyrics.com/lyrics/raycharles/igotawoman.html.

71. Ray Charles, "'I Got a Woman' by Ray Charles," 1954, SongFacts, https://www .songfacts.com/facts/ray-charles/i-got-a-woman, accessed March 2, 2023.

72. Denroy Morgan, "I'll Do Anything for You," *I'll Do Anything for You*, 1981, Genius, https://genius.com/Denroy-morgan-ill-do-anything-for-you-lyrics.

73. Jessica Bennett, "Kanye West's Ex-Girlfriends and Dating History," Page Six, *New York Post*, January 3, 2022, https://pagesix.com/article/kanye-wests-ex -girlfriends-and-dating-history/.

74. Bennett, "Kanye West's Ex-Girlfriends and Dating History."

CHAPTER 4: ENTER THE FUCKBOYS

1. Ron Alexander, "Singles Ask Why a Good Man Now Is Hard to Find," *New York Times*, July 15, 1983, http://timesmachine.nytimes.com/timesmachine/1983/07 /15/035321.html.

2. Alexander, "Singles Ask Why a Good Man Is Hard to Find."

3. Alexander, "Singles Ask Why a Good Man Is Hard to Find."

4. Kenneth B. Noble, "One Approach to the Shortage of Men Is Sharing," *New York Times*, September 9, 1983, https://www.nytimes.com/1983/09/09/us/one -approach-to-the-shortage-of-men-is-sharing.html.

5. Noble, "One Approach to the Shortage of Men Is Sharing."

6. "How Black Women Can Deal with the Black Male Shortage," *Ebony*, May 1986, 29–32+; Brenda Gray, "The Black Male Shortage," letter to the editor, *Ebony*, August 1986, 25.

7. Janeese Myra Bland, "The Black Male Shortage," letter to the editor, *Ebony*, July 1987, 13, 16; Letter to the editor, *Ebony*, December 1992; "U.S. Census Figures Say the Odds Favor Black Women in Some Surprising Places," *Ebony*, July 1993; Lynn Norment, "Black Men, White Women: What's Behind the New Furor?" *Ebony*, November 1994; Letter to the editor, *Ebony*, June 2007.

8. Michelle Alexander, *The New Jim Crow: Mass Incarceration in the Age of Color-blindness* (New York: New Press, 2012).

9. Robert E. Staples, "Sex and the Black Middle Class," *Ebony*, August 1973.

10. R. Kelly Raley, Megan M. Sweeney, and Danielle Wondra, "The Growing Racial and Ethnic Divide in U.S. Marriage Patterns," *Future Child*, Center for the Future of Children, the David and Lucile Packard Foundation, vol. 25, no. 2 (Fall 2015): 89–109, https://www.ncbi.nlm.nih.gov/pmc/articles/PMC4850739.

11. M. Belinda Tucker and Claudia Mitchell-Kernan, "New Trends in Black American Interracial Marriage: The Social Structural Context," *Journal of Marriage and Family* 52, no. 1 (1990): 209–18, https://doi.org/10.2307/352851.

12. In Foucault's *The History of Sexuality*, vol. 1, he describes how in the Victorian era, the bourgeoisie set about talking ceaselessly about sexual taboos and restrictions. And yet, he argues, rather than all this talk being evidence of re-

straint, the proliferating conversation served as proof in itself of a certain type of openness and sexual exploration. Michel Foucault, *The History of Sexuality: Vol. 1: An Introduction* (New York: Vintage Books, 1990).

13. Joyce Sunila, "Hollywood and the New Men," *Los Angeles Times*, August 5, 1979.

14. Tressie McMillan Cottom, *Thick: And Other Essays* (New York: New Press, 2019).

15. For this list of qualities, I am deeply indebted to a host of folx writing think pieces on the interweb. These folx, tiring of fuccboy, and the less talked about but nevertheless also problematic fuckgirl behavior, helped me to clarify the at once dizzying and confusing batch of behaviors that are both emotionally stunted and emotionally demanding. Miss Ameribetch, "15 Signs You're Dating a Fuckboy," *Betches* (blog), November 3, 2017, https://betches.com/15-signs -youre-dating-a-fuckboy; Carina Hsieh and Mel Evans, "Why You Can't Let That F*ckboy Go," *Cosmopolitan*, September 18, 2019, https://www.cosmopolitan .com/sex-love/confessions/a22740083/relationships-fuckboy-cosmo-september -2018; 101adultingblog, "7 Signs That He's a F*ckboy—Adulting 101," https:// www.adulting-101.org/2019/07/09/7-signs-that-hes-a-fuckboy; Selma June, "How to Spot a Fuckboy (And How to Deal with Him)," *Her Way* (blog), January 23, 2020, https://herway.net/life/how-to-spot-a-fuckboy-and-how-to-deal-with-him; Brendan Wetmore, "Meet the Comedian Curing Fuckboys," *PAPER*, February 26, 2020, https://www.papermag.com/mary-beth-barone-2645266295.html.

16. OIP Staff, "On This Gay Day: Merle Miller Declared What It Means to Be a Homosexual," *OUTinPerth*, January 17, 2023, https://www.outinperth.com/on-this -gay-day-merle-miller-declared-what-it-means-to-be-a-homosexual.

17. Merle Miller, "What It Means to Be a Homosexual," *New York Times*, January 17, 1971, https://www.nytimes.com/1971/01/17/archives/what-it-means-to-be-a -homosexual-a-fag-is-a-homosexual-gentleman.html.

18. Merle Miller, "The Suicide of the Sexes: The Wife Who Works," *Esquire*, April 1, 1954, https://classic.esquire.com/article/1954/4/1/the-suicide-of-the-sexes-the -wife-who-works.

19. Maggie Smith, "The Suicide of the Sexes: The Well-Kept Husband," *Esquire*, April 1, 1954, https://classic.esquire.com/article/1954/4/1/the-suicide-of-the-sexes -the-well-kept-husband.

20. S. F. X. Szabados, "U.S. Sexlings," letter to the editor, *Esquire*, October 1954.

21. Morris Ploscowe, *The Truth About Divorce* (New York: Hawthorn Books, 1955), as quoted in S. Jay Lasser, "Cupid on Capitol Hill: A New Tax-Maneuver for the Alimony-Stricken Ex-Husband," *Esquire*, May 1, 1956, 77, https://classic.esquire .com/article/1956/5/1/cupid-on-capitol-hill.

22. Dan Wakefield, "The Outriders," *Esquire*, July 1, 1962, https://classic.esquire.com /article/1962/7/1/the-outriders.

23. Robert Alan Aurthur, "Women of America, Now Is the Time to Arise: 'No'!" *Esquire*, July 1, 1962, https://classic.esquire.com/article/1962/7/1/women-of -america-now-is-the-time-to-arise-no.

24. Sally Kempton, "Cutting Loose," *Esquire*, October 1, 1973, https://classic.esquire .com/article/1973/10/1/cutting-loose; Stephen Koch, "The Guilty Sex," *Esquire*, July 1, 1975, https://classic.esquire.com/article/1975/7/1/the-guilty-sex.

CHAPTER 5: WOMEN AS SEX WORKERS

1. Elizabeth Fraterrigo, *Playboy and the Making of the Good Life in Modern America* (Oxford: Oxford University Press, 2011).
2. Fraterrigo, *Playboy and the Making of the Good Life in Modern America*.
3. "Playboy Inspired James Bond—Hugh Hefner," *News24*, May 16, 2011, https://www.news24.com/channel/playboy-inspired-james-bond-hugh-hefner-20110516, accessed June 6, 2022.
4. Fraterrigo, *Playboy and the Making of the Good Life in Modern America*, 20.
5. Fraterrigo, *Playboy and the Making of the Good Life in Modern America*.
6. William Iversen, "Love, Death & the Hubby Image," *Playboy*, September 1963.
7. Fraterrigo, *Playboy and the Making of the Good Life in Modern America*, 138.
8. Fraterrigo, *Playboy and the Making of the Good Life in Modern America*, 138.
9. Fraterrigo, *Playboy and the Making of the Good Life in Modern America*, 143.
10. Fraterrigo, *Playboy and the Making of the Good Life in Modern America*, 146.
11. "The Girls of the Orient," *Playboy*, December 1968, https://ipb-reader.playboy.com/19681201/index.html.
12. "The Girls of the Orient."
13. "The Girls of the Orient."
14. Fraterrigo, *Playboy and the Making of the Good Life in Modern America*.
15. Peg Bundy, the iconic non-working housewife from the hit '80s TV series *Married with Children*.
16. Iversen, "Love, Death & the Hubby Image."
17. Fraterrigo, *Playboy and the Making of the Good Life in Modern America*.
18. Philip Wylie, "The Womanization of America," *Playboy*, September 1958.
19. Suzanne Pharr, *Homophobia: A Weapon of Sexism* (Berkeley, CA: Chardon Press, 1988).
20. "The Playboy Panel: The Womanization of America," *Playboy*, June 1962.
21. Fraterrigo, *Playboy and the Making of the Good Life in Modern America*, 105.
22. "Fuckboy" and "playboy" may be overlapping ideas, but they are not the same thing. The major difference is that playboys do not necessarily try to manipulate a woman by explaining their own emotional baggage. One of the main weapons in the fuckboy arsenal is a self-serving emotional disclosure. The faux-sensitivity of the fuckboy represents a manipulative attempt to meet post-feminist societal expectations around greater emotional openness. Sam De Boise and Jeff Hearn, "Are Men Getting More Emotional? Critical Sociological Perspectives on Men, Masculinities and Emotions," *Sociological Review* 65, no. 4 (2017): 779–96.
23. Quoted in Fraterrigo, *Playboy and the Making of the Good Life in Modern America*, 111.
24. Fraterrigo, *Playboy and the Making of the Good Life in Modern America*, 111.
25. "The Roach Powder in the Maple Walnut," *Playboy*, May 1966, https://ipb-reader.playboy.com/19660501/index.html#p=222.
26. Fraterrigo, *Playboy and the Making of the Good Life in Modern America*, 112.
27. Fraterrigo, *Playboy and the Making of the Good Life in Modern America*.

28. Jen Doll, "Sex and the Single Girl: The Legacy of Helen Gurley Brown," *The Atlantic*, August 13, 2012, https://www.theatlantic.com/international/archive/2012/08/sex-and-single-girl-legacy-helen-gurley-brown/322898; Jocelyn Noveck, "Helen Gurley Brown, the Original Carrie Bradshaw," *San Diego Union-Tribune*, August 14, 2012, https://www.sandiegouniontribune.com/sdut-helen-gurley-brown-the-original-carrie-bradshaw-2012aug14-story.html.

29. Emphasis mine: *Sex and the City*, season 2, episode 10, n.d., 10.

30. Breeanna Hare, "What Was That About Carrie, Chris Noth?" CNN, October 16, 2014, https://www.cnn.com/2014/10/16/showbiz/celebrity-news-gossip/chris-noth-carrie-bradshaw-whore/index.html; Kevin O'Keeffe, "No, Carrie Bradshaw Was Not 'Such a Whore,'" *The Atlantic*, October 15, 2014, https://www.theatlantic.com/entertainment/archive/2014/10/no-chris-noth-carrie-bradshaw-was-not-such-a-whore/381482.

31. Colette Bernheim, "Cracking the Enigma of Carrie's Obsession with Mr. Big," *Lithium Magazine*, August 6, 2020, https://lithiummagazine.com/2020/08/06/cracking-the-enigma-of-carries-obsession-with-mr-big.

32. Andrew Hacker, "Liberal Democracy and Social Control," *American Political Science Review* 51, no. 4 (1957): 1009–26.

33. Sabrina Strings, *Fearing the Black Body: The Racial Origins of Fat Phobia* (New York: New York University Press, 2019).

34. "The Name GATZ," Museum of the Jewish People—Beit Hatfutsot, BH Open Databases, https://dbs.bh.org.il/familyname/gatz, accessed August 5, 2020.

35. Lisa Klug, "Is Sarah Jessica Parker Just a Tease?" *Times of Israel*, July 7, 2015, http://www.timesofisrael.com/is-sarah-jessica-parker-just-a-tease.

36. Sabrina Strings, "Women (Re) Making Whiteness: The Sexual Exclusion of the Fat 'Black' Irish," *Ethnic and Racial Studies* (2019): 1–18.

37. "SATC, Season 2, Episode 18, The Way We Were," *Sex and the City* Archives, YouTube video, 4:58, https://www.youtube.com/watch?v=4et_yCrrhN0.

38. Sarah Wasilak, "Big's Ex-Wife Natasha Only Wore White," *POPSUGAR* Fashion, June 6, 2018, https://www.popsugar.com/node/42041125.

39. This is not to suggest that anti-Semitism is rooted in anti-Blackness. Anti-Semitism precedes this form of racism, historically. However, in the United States it was interpellated by anti-Blackness. As I have articulated elsewhere, the racial discourse in the US claimed that so-called "hybrid whites" were part "negroid." For the Jews and other "white-ish" populations, the so-called racial proximity to Blackness formed a critical part of the Aryan/Anglo-Saxon rhetoric of the US and the resistance to integrating with Jewish people. See Strings, *Fearing the Black Body*.

40. The racial rhetoric surrounding Slavs in the US is complex. Whereas they were treated as racial Others during the nineteenth century, there was also a debate surrounding whether the Slavs were historically Nordic or Viking—ancestors also claimed by Anglo-Saxons. In this way, anti-Slavic sentiment was sometimes tempered by the view that the early Slavs were related to early Anglo-Saxons. See the *Universal Review* 1 (March–June 1859), London: Wm. H. Allen & Co.; Strings, *Fearing the Black Body*.

41. Fraterrigo, *Playboy and the Making of the Good Life in Modern America*, 124.
42. Quoted in Fraterrigo, *Playboy and the Making of the Good Life in Modern America*, 126.

CHAPTER 6: SEX TRAFFICKING (A.K.A. PIMPIN')

1. "Dirty South," Urban Dictionary, https://www.urbandictionary.com, accessed July 8, 2022.
2. "Jay-Z," *Biography*, May 12, 2021, https://www.biography.com/musician/jay-z.
3. United States v. Burrell, 289 F.3d 220 (2nd Cir. 2002).
4. Alexandra Topping, "Jay-Z: I Shot My Brother When I Was 12," *The Guardian*, November 19, 2010, https://www.theguardian.com/music/2010/nov/19/jayz -brother-shooting-interview.
5. Jacqueline Edmondson, *Music in American Life: An Encyclopedia of the Songs, Styles, Stars, and Stories That Shaped Our Culture*, 4 vols. (Santa Barbara, CA: Greenwood, 2013), 599.
6. Jake Brown, *Jay-Z and the Roc-A-Fella Records Dynasty* (Phoenix: Amber Books, 2005); Mickey Hess, ed., *Icons of Hip Hop: An Encyclopedia of the Movement, Music, and Culture*, 2 vols. (Santa Barbara, CA: Greenwood, 2007).
7. Chris Malone, "The Notorious B.I.G. Thought Jay-Z Was a Better Rapper Than Him," *Showbiz Cheat Sheet*, August 1, 2021, https://www.cheatsheet.com /entertainment/notorious-big-thought-jay-z-was-a-better-rapper-than-him.html.
8. Ryan Reed, "Jay Z Talks High School Rap Battle with Busta on 'Kimmel,'" *Rolling Stone*, October 21, 2015, https://www.rollingstone.com/tv-movies/tv -movie-news/jay-z-talks-high-school-rap-battle-with-busta-rhymes-on-kimmel -194181.
9. Sonya Schwartz, "How to Spot a Player: Don't Fall Victim to His Game," *Her Norm*, August 23, 2018, https://hernorm.com/how-to-spot-a-player.
10. It should go without saying that it's common for a player to tell several women that they are the only one for whom he feels any real affection.
11. Jay-Z, "Ain't No Nigga," featuring Foxy Brown, *Reasonable Doubt*, March 26, 1996, Genius, https://genius.com/Jay-z-aint-no-nigga-lyrics, accessed July 13, 2022.
12. Jayson Greene, "Jay-Z: Reasonable Doubt, 1996" *Pitchfork*, May 14, 2017, https://pitchfork.com/reviews/albums/23194-reasonable-doubt.
13. Iceberg Slim, *Pimp: The Story of My Life* (1969; repr., New York: Cash Money Content, 2011), 65.
14. Slim, *Pimp*, 198.
15. Slim, *Pimp*, 258.
16. Slim, *Pimp*, 176.
17. Slim, *Pimp*, 177.
18. Justin Gifford, "Street Poison: The Biography of Iceberg Slim: New Excerpt," *Criminal Element*, August 4, 2015, https://www.criminalelement.com/street -poison-the-biography-of-iceberg-slim-new-excerpt-justin-gifford-robert-beck -black-culture.
19. Isabel Wilkerson, *The Warmth of Other Suns: The Epic Story of America's Great Migration* (New York: Knopf Doubleday, 2010).

20. Slim, *Pimp*, 179.

21. Slim, *Pimp*, 178.

22. Slim, *Pimp*, 62.

23. Slim, *Pimp*, 92.

24. Slim, *Pimp*, 92.

25. Slim, *Pimp*, 17.

26. Slim, *Pimp*, 126.

27. Slim, *Pimp*, 132.

28. Jay-Z, "(Always Be My) Sunshine," featuring Babyface and Foxy Brown, *In My Lifetime, Vol. 1*, November 4, 1997, Genius, https://genius.com/Jay-z-always-be -my-sunshine-lyrics, accessed July 19, 2022.

29. Jay-Z, "(Always Be My) Sunshine."

30. "Why Does Jay-Z Call Himself Hov, Hova & Jigga?" DailyRapFacts, April 6, 2020, https://dailyrapfacts.com/12338/why-does-jay-z-call-himself-hov-hova -jigga.

31. This was not exactly a first among rappers. Both Ice-T and Ice Cube reportedly got the "ice" in their names from the notorious pimp.

32. "Who You Wit II," Musixmatch, https://www.google.com/search?q=who+ya +wit+II+lyrics&rlz=1C5CHFA_enUS904US904&oq=who+ya+wit+II+lyrics&aqs =chrome.0.69i59.1355j0j4&sourceid=chrome&ie=UTF-8, accessed July 19, 2022.

33. Sha Be Allah, "Jay-Z Regrets Making 'Big Pimpin': 'I Can't Believe I Said That,'" *The Source*, May 3, 2021, https://thesource.com/2021/05/03/jay-z-regrets-making -big-pimpin-i-cant-believe-i-said-that; https://thesource.com/2022/11/04/today -in-hip-hop-history-jay-zs-in-my-lifetime-vol-1-lp-turns-25-years-old/.

34. Kermit Ernest Campbell, *Gettin' Our Groove On: Rhetoric, Language, and Literacy for the Hip Hop Generation* (Detroit: Wayne State University Press, 2005), 116.

35. 2 Live Crew, "Me So Horny," Last.fm, https://www.last.fm/music/2+Live+Crew /_/Me+So+Horny/+wiki, accessed July 25, 2022.

36. *Full Metal Jacket*, dir. Stanley Kubrick, Warner Bros., Stanley Kubrick Prods., 1987.

37. Yutian Wong, *Choreographing Asian America* (Middletown, CT: Wesleyan University Press, 2011), 74.

38. To be clear, this is not a polemic against sex workers who choose of their free will to trade in sex for which they feel well compensated. I am trying to show that the pimp ideal in hip hop either encourages or coerces women into an underground sex economy. A heavy weight of literature shows this work is usually violent and preys on marginalized women, helping to crush the possibility of a fair wage for these women.

39. 2 Live Crew, "If You Believe in Having Sex," *As Nasty as They Wanna Be*, February 7, 1989, Genius, https://genius.com/2-live-crew-if-you-believe-in-having -sex-lyrics, accessed July 20, 2022.

40. 2 Live Crew, "A Fuck Is a Fuck," *Sports Weekend (As Nasty as They Wanna Be, Part II)*, 1991, Genius, https://genius.com/2-live-crew-a-fuck-is-a-fuck-lyrics, accessed July 20, 2022.

41. "Too $hort Digital Biography," *Hip Hop Scriptures*, https://www.hiphopscriptures.com/too-short, accessed July 21, 2022.

42. Charles Aaron et al., "The 200 Greatest Hip-Hop Albums of All Time," *Rolling Stone*, June 7, 2022, https://www.rollingstone.com/music/music-lists/best-hip-hop-albums-1323916.

43. Too $hort, "Invasion of Flat Booty Bitches," *Raw, Uncut and X-Rated*, November 5, 1986, Genius, https://genius.com/Too-short-invasion-of-flat-booty-bitches-lyrics, accessed July 21, 2022.

44. Too $hort, "Blow the Whistle," *Blow the Whistle*, 2006, AZLyrics, https://www.azlyrics.com/lyrics/toohort/blowthewhistle.html, accessed July 21, 2022.

45. Jay-Z, "Can I Get A . . . ," *Vol. 2 . . . Hard Knock Life*, 1998, AZLyrics, https://www.azlyrics.com/lyrics/jayz/canigeta.html, accessed July 22, 2022.

46. Jay-Z, "Can I Get A . . ."

47. Jermaine Dupri, "Money Ain't a Thang," *Life in 1472*, 1998, Genius, https://genius.com/Jermaine-dupri-money-aint-a-thang-lyrics.

48. Justin Block, "The Evolution of Jay Z's Cover Art, From 'Reasonable Doubt' to '4:44,'" *Complex*, June 30, 2017, https://www.complex.com/music/2017/06/evolution-of-jay-z-cover-art-from-reasonable-doubt-444.

49. Ashley Mears, *Very Important People: Status and Beauty in the Global Party Circuit*, illustrated ed. (Princeton, NJ: Princeton University Press, 2020).

50. Mears, *Very Important People*.

51. Mears, *Very Important People*.

52. Mears, *Very Important People*, 16.

53. Mears, *Very Important People*.

54. Mears, *Very Important People*, 44.

55. Mears, *Very Important People*, 14.

56. Mears, *Very Important People*.

57. Jessica Bennett, "Amil Never Got Closure Following Exit from Jay-Z's Roc-a-Fella Records," *Page Six*, December 4, 2019, https://pagesix.com/2019/12/04/amil-never-got-closure-following-exit-from-jay-zs-roc-a-fella-records.

58. Martha Bayles, "Attacks on Rap Now Come from Within," *Wall Street Journal*, April 28, 2005, https://www.wsj.com/articles/SB111464272332918867; Derek Thompson, "1991: The Most Important Year in Pop-Music History," *The Atlantic*, May 8, 2015, https://www.theatlantic.com/culture/archive/2015/05/1991-the-most-important-year-in-music/392642.

59. Chuck Philips, "Anti-Rap Crusader Under Fire," *Los Angeles Times*, March 20, 1996, https://www.latimes.com/local/la-fi-tupacdelores20march2096-story.html.

60. Kevin Powell, "My Culture at the Crossroads," *Newsweek*, October 9, 2000, 66. Emphasis mine.

61. Powell, "My Culture at the Crossroads."

62. Jay-Z, "Big Pimpin'," featuring UGK, *Vol. 3 . . . Life and Times of S. Carter*, December 28, 1999, Genius, https://genius.com/Jay-z-big-pimpin-lyrics, accessed July 12, 2022.

63. Tricia Rose, *Black Noise: Rap Music and Black Culture in Contemporary America* (Middletown, CT: Wesleyan University Press, 1994); Margaret Hunter and

Kathleen Soto, "Women of Color in Hip Hop: The Pornographic Gaze," *Race, Gender & Class* 16, nos. 1–2 (2009): 170–91, https://www.proquest.com/docview/218811590/abstract/A982B0FEB9A64153PQ/1; Randa Simpson Hovater and D. Nicole Farris, "Back That Sexism Up: An Analysis of the Representation of Women's Bodies in Music Videos," in *Gender, Sexuality and Race in the Digital Age*, ed. D. Nicole Farris, D'Lane R. Compton, and Andrea P. Herrera (Cham, Switzerland: Springer Cham, 2020), 75–97; Margherita Angelucci and Wissal Houbabi, "From Pimpology to Pimpologia: A Comparative Analysis of Pimp Rap in the United States and Italy," in *Misogyny, Toxic Masculinity, and Heteronormativity in Post-2000 Popular Music*, ed. Glenn Fosbraey and Nicola Puckey (Cham, Switzerland: Palgrave Macmillan, 2021), 73–93.

64. MTV News Staff, "Jay-Z Explains Why He's Growing His Hair," MTV, June 8, 2009, https://www.mtv.com/news/4k7dg5/jay-zs-grows-hair-for-art-mystery-women.

65. Shirvan Williams, "Jay-Z Shares How Long His Dreadlocks Is & Turns to Conscious Rap on Nipsey Hussle Collab," *Urban Islandz*, February 12, 2021, https://urbanislandz.com/2021/02/12/jay-z-shares-how-long-his-dreadlocks-is-turns-to-conscious-rap-on-nipsey-hussle-collab.

66. Ogden Payne, "A Year Later: The Impact of Jay Z's '4:44' by the Numbers," *Forbes*, July 1, 2018, https://www.forbes.com/sites/ogdenpayne/2018/07/01/1-year-later-the-impact-of-jay-zs-444-by-the-numbers.

67. The Carters, "Apeshit," *Everything Is Love*, June 16, 2018, Genius, https://genius.com/The-carters-apeshit-lyrics, accessed July 27, 2022.

68. Jay-Z, "Family Feud," featuring Beyoncé, released June 30, 2017, Genius, https://genius.com/Jay-z-family-feud-lyrics, accessed July 27, 2022.

69. Desire Thompson, "44 Artists & Industry Elite on the Legacy of Jay-Z & His Discography," *Vibe*, January 27, 2018, https://www.vibe.com/features/editorial/jay-z-legacy-44-interviews-cover-story-561779; "Australian Rappers on the Impact and Influence of Jay-Z," *Double J*, February 18, 2021, https://www.abc.net.au/doublej/music-reads/features/jay-z-illy-okenyo-b-wise-sophiegrophy-nfa-queen-p-adrian-eagle/13164944.

70. "Theory—Eminem Thought of the Name 'Slim Shady' Due to a Biggie Smalls Song," Reddit post, R/Eminem, May 30, 2022, www.reddit.com/r/Eminem/comments/v17v5w/theory_eminem_thought_of_the_name_slim_shady_due.

71. "Eminem Created His Alter Ego Slim Shady While Sitting on the Toilet," *DailyRapFacts*, October 9, 2019, https://dailyrapfacts.com/5835/eminem-created-his-alter-ego-slim-shady-while-sitting-on-the-toilet.

72. Lauren Rearick, "Nicki Minaj Sparked a Huge Internet Debate with Her 'White Rappers' Post," *Teen Vogue*, December 18, 2017, https://www.teenvogue.com/story/nicki-minaj-white-rappers-post.

73. Hunter and Soto, "Women of Color in Hip Hop."

74. Nancy Jo Sales, "Hugh Hefner's Roaring 70s," *Vanity Fair*, March 30, 2011, https://www.vanityfair.com/news/2001/03/hugh-hefner-200103.

75. "Hot Spot: 'I Can't Believe I Said That', Jay-Z Regrets Making Big Pimpin' Song," *The Rickey Smiley Morning Show*, May 4, 2021, https://rickeysmileymorningshow.com/2548265/jay-z-regrets-big-pimpin.

76. Kiana Fitzgerald, "Uncle Luke, 'The Black Hugh Hefner,' on the Legacy of His Namesake," *Complex*, September 28, 2017, https://www.complex.com/music /2017/09/uncle-luke-black-hugh-hefner-interview.

77. Preezy, "20 Hip-Hop Lyrics Showing Love to Hugh Hefner," *XXL Mag*, September 29, 2017, https://www.xxlmag.com/hip-hop-lyrics-hugh-hefner.

78. Suzanne Moore, "I Called Hugh Hefner a Pimp, He Threatened to Sue. But That's What He Was," *The Guardian*, September 28, 2017, https://www.theguardian .com/commentisfree/2017/sep/28/hugh-hefner-pimp-sue-playboy-mansion.

79. Fitzgerald, "Uncle Luke, 'The Black Hugh Hefner.'"

80. Courtney Garcia, "Ice-T Reflects on Past as Pimp and Gun Control: 'I Want a Gun,'" *TheGrio*, July 10, 2013, https://thegrio.com/2013/07/10/ice-t-reflects-on -past-as-pimp-and-gun-control-i-want-a-gun.

81. Katherine Hamilton, "Here's How Your Porn Habit Could Be Helping Human Sex Traffickers," *NBC2 News*, June 7, 2021, https://nbc-2.com/news/2021/01 /12/heres-how-your-porn-habit-could-be-helping-human-sex-traffickers.

CHAPTER 7: MASTURBATION GENERATION/S

1. In *Buffy the Vampire Slayer*, season 2, episode 9, November 16, 1997, Principal Snyder refers to Xander Harris's speech as an "airborne toxic event." Just Buffy fangirling.

2. Douglas Belkin, "A Generation of American Men Give Up on College: 'I Just Feel Lost,'" *Wall Street Journal*, September 6, 2021, https://www.wsj.com/articles /college-university-fall-higher-education-men-women-enrollment-admissions -back-to-school-11630948233; Jonathan Edwards, "Sen. Josh Hawley Says Liberals' Attacks on Manhood Are Driving Men to Pornography and Video Games," *Washington Post*, November 2, 2021, https://www.washingtonpost.com/nation /2021/11/02/josh-hawley-pornography-video-games.

3. Edwards, "Sen. Josh Hawley Says Liberals' Attacks on Manhood Are Driving Men to Pornography and Video Games."

4. Caryl Rivers and Rosalind Chait Barnett, "The Myth of 'The Boy Crisis," *Washington Post*, April 9, 2006, https://www.washingtonpost.com/archive/opinions /2006/04/09/the-myth-of-the-boy-crisis/6e0e8e97-4365-4ce5-aff6-6b5d90a19bd5; Cara Okopny, "Why Jimmy Isn't Failing: The Myth of the Boy Crisis," *Feminist Teacher* 18, no. 3 (2008): 216–28, https://www.jstor.org/stable/40535485.

5. James Nuechterlein, "The Feminization of the American Left," *Commentary Magazine*, November 1987, https://www.commentary.org/articles/james-nuechterlein /the-feminization-of-the-american-left; Okopny, "Why Jimmy Isn't Failing."

6. Maya Salam, "What Is Toxic Masculinity?" *New York Times*, January 22, 2019, https://www.nytimes.com/2019/01/22/us/toxic-masculinity.html.

7. Salam, "What Is Toxic Masculinity?"

8. Jane Ward, *Not Gay: Sex Between Straight White Men* (New York: New York University Press, 2015).

9. "Masturbation," *Brother* (Summer 1971): 5, 18. Quoted in Elizabeth Fraterrigo, *Playboy and the Making of the Good Life in Modern America* (Oxford: Oxford University Press, 2009), 184.

10. "Masturbation," *Brother.*

11. Fraterrigo, *Playboy and the Making of the Good Life in Modern America*, 43.

12. Rebecca Whisnant and Christine Stark, *Not for Sale: Feminists Resisting Prostitution and Pornography* (North Melbourne, Australia: Spinifex Press, 2005).

13. Brooks Jeffrey, "The Surprising History and Ultimate Downfall of the Once Popular Adult Movie Theater," Attic Theatre, July 11, 2019, https://attictheatre.org/the-surprising-history-and-ultimate-downfall-of-the-once-popular-adult-movie-theater, accessed June 29, 2022.

14. Brian McCullough, "Chapter 6: A History of Internet Porn," *Internet History Podcast*, January 4, 2015, https://www.internethistorypodcast.com/2015/01/history-of-internet-porn; Bernadette Barton, *The Pornification of America: How Raunch Culture Is Ruining Our Society* (New York: New York University Press, 2021).

15. Benj Edwards, "The Lost Civilization of Dial-Up Bulletin Board Systems," *The Atlantic*, November 4, 2016, https://www.theatlantic.com/technology/archive/2016/11/the-lost-civilization-of-dial-up-bulletin-board-systems/506465.

16. McCullough, "A History of Internet Porn."

17. McCullough, "A History of Internet Porn."

18. McCullough, "A History of Internet Porn."

19. McCullough, "A History of Internet Porn."

20. Edward Cone, "The Naked Truth," *Wired*, February 1, 2002, https://www.wired.com/2002/02/sex; McCullough, "A History of Internet Porn."

21. McCullough, "A History of Internet Porn."

22. Hannibal Buress, "The Lizzo Episode," *Hannibal Buress: Handsome Rambler*, podcast, season 1, ep. 53, May 2, 2018.

23. "Congress Eyes Dirty TV," *CBS News*, February 11, 2004, https://www.cbsnews.com/news/congress-eyes-dirty-tv.

24. Matthew Perpetua, "FCC Loses Janet Jackson Super Bowl Case," *Rolling Stone*, November 3, 2011, https://www.rollingstone.com/music/music-news/fcc-loses-janet-jackson-super-bowl-case-244545.

25. Rob Sheffield, "How Nipplegate Created YouTube," *Rolling Stone*, February 11, 2020, https://www.rollingstone.com/culture/culture-features/youtube-origin-nipplegate-janet-jackson-justin-timberlake-949019.

26. Luke Darby, "The CEO of CBS Tried to Destroy Janet Jackson's Career After Her Super Bowl Show," *GQ*, September 8, 2018, https://www.gq.com/story/cbs-ceo-janet-jackson.

27. Amy Ta and Danielle Chiriguayo, "'Malfunction' at Super Bowl Halftime: Gender Inequity and Media Derailed Janet Jackson, Fans Saved Her," KCRW, November 22, 2021, https://www.kcrw.com/news/shows/press-play-with-madeleine-brand/race-vigilantism-super-bowl-thanksgiving/malfunction-dressing-down-janet-jackson.

28. Anna Iovine, "How Pornhub Changed the World," *Mashable*, May 30, 2022, https://mashable.com/article/how-pornhub-changed-the-world.

29. Kathryn Robinson, "Silent Pandemic: More Children Are Being Exposed to Online Pornography at an Earlier Age," *WKRC Local 12*, February 28, 2022,

https://local12.com/news/local/silent-pandemic-more-children-are-being
-exposed-to-online-pornography-at-an-earlier-age. (Unfortunately, they did
not provide statistics for trans or gender nonbinary children.)

30. "The Playboy Panel: The Womanization of America," *Playboy*, June 1962.

31. Philip Wylie, *Generation of Vipers* (1942; London: Frederick Muller, 1955).
Quoted in "The Playboy Panel: The Womanization of America." Emphasis mine.

32. Sabrina Strings, *Fearing the Black Body: The Racial Origins of Fat Phobia* (New
York: New York University Press, 2019).

33. Meg Bogin, *The Women Troubadours* (New York: W. W. Norton, 1980).

34. This list includes Walter Scott, Edmund Spenser, Geoffrey Chaucer, Alfred Ten-
nyson, and Miguel de Cervantes, author of *Don Quixote*. Although it must be
noted that Cervantes pokes fun at this tradition in *Don Quixote*.

35. Jonathan Yardley, "'Generation of Vipers' Loses Its Bite," *Washington Post*, July
30, 2005, http://www.washingtonpost.com/wp-dyn/content/article/2005/07/29
/AR2005072902124.html.

36. Stephanie Coontz, "When We Hated Mom," op-ed, *New York Times*, May 7,
2011, https://www.nytimes.com/2011/05/08/opinion/08coontz.html; Emily
Harnett, "Married to the Momism," *Lapham's Quarterly*, July 23, 2020, https://
www.laphamsquarterly.org/roundtable/married-momism; Peter L. Winkler, "The
Man Who Hated Moms: Looking Back on Philip Wylie's 'Generation of Vipers,'"
Los Angeles Review of Books, August 13, 2021, https://lareviewofbooks.org
/article/the-man-who-hated-moms-looking-back-on-philip-wylies-generation
-of-vipers.

37. Transwomen here being largely excluded from consideration at all historically,
apart from the routine dread by the likes of Iceberg Slim that they are "faggots"
working a double-cross on men and thus interrupting the con that men have
been working on women.

38. Bill Burr, *Monday Morning Podcast*, April 12, 2021. I am in no way suggesting
that Bill Burr is an expert on matters of porn addiction. Only that this segment
helped me to process my own experience.

39. PornHub Insights, "2017 Year in Review," January 9, 2018, www.pornhub.com.

40. PornHub Insights, "2021 Year in Review," December 14, 2021, www.pornhub
.com.

41. Jade Biggs, "Former Playmates Say Life with Hugh Hefner at Playboy Mansion
Was 'Cult-Like,'" *Cosmopolitan*, January 19, 2022, https://www.cosmopolitan
.com/uk/reports/a38813101/playmates-life-with-hugh-hefner-playboy-mansion
-cult.

42. Nick Schager, "'Secrets of Playboy' Paints Hugh Hefner as a Rapist Monster
Who Was into Snuff Films and Bestiality," *Daily Beast*, January 24, 2022,
https://www.thedailybeast.com/secrets-of-playboy-paints-hugh-hefner-as-a
-rapist-monster-who-was-into-snuff-films-and-bestiality.

43. Zoë Heller, "What Makes a Cult a Cult?," *New Yorker*, July 5, 2021, https://www
.newyorker.com/magazine/2021/07/12/what-makes-a-cult-a-cult.

44. Holly Meyer, "News," *The Tennessean*, September 15, 2016, https://www
.tennessean.com/story/news/religion/2016/09/15/what-makes-cult-cult/90377532/.

45. Andrea Dworkin, *Last Days at Hot Slit: The Radical Feminism of Andrea Dworkin*, ed. Johanna Fateman and Amy Scholder (South Pasadena, CA: Semiotext, 2019), 133–34.

CODA: WE ARE LOVE

1. Dan Savage, "Savage Love: Did My Masturbation Style Wreck My Sex Life?" *NOW Magazine*, February 20, 2020, https://nowtoronto.com/lifestyle/advice/savage-love-february-20.

2. Savage, "Savage Love: Did My Masturbation Style Wreck My Sex Life?"

3. Gloria Steinem and Lauren Wolfe, "Sexual Violence Against Women Is the Result of the Cult of Masculinity," Women's Media Center, February 24, 2012, https://womensmediacenter.com/women-under-siege/sexual-violence-against-women-is-the-result-of-the-cult-of-masculinity, accessed July 25, 2022.

4. Steinem and Wolfe, "Sexual Violence Against Women Is the Result of the Cult of Masculinity."

5. Celeste Vaughan Curington, Jennifer Hickes Lundquist, and Ken-Hou Lin, *The Dating Divide: Race and Desire in the Era of Online Romance* (Oakland: University of California Press, 2021).

6. "Rough Cut: The Women's Kingdom," *Frontline*, https://www.pbs.org/frontlineworld/rough/2005/07/introduction_tolinks.html, accessed September 8, 2022; Caroline Zielinski, "First Comes Love, Then Comes Marriage. Not for Me, Thanks," *Daily Telegraph*, April 15, 2015, https://dailytelegraph.com.au/rendezview/first-comes-love-then-comes-marriage-not-for-me-thanks/news-story/d53ae485a9015c0562b3f054427796f4; Hannah Booth, "The Kingdom of Women: The Society Where a Man Is Never the Boss," *The Guardian*, April 1, 2017, https://www.theguardian.com/lifeandstyle/2017/apr/01/the-kingdom-of-women-the-tibetan-tribe-where-a-man-is-never-the-boss.

7. Benedict Salazar Olgado, Lucy Pei, and Roderic Crooks, "Determining the Extractive Casting Mold of Intimate Platforms through Document Theory," *Proceedings of the 2020 CHI Conference on Human Factors in Computing Systems* (April 2020): 1–10.

8. *The Song of Roland*, trans. Glyn Burgess (New York: Penguin, 1990); Melissa Furrow, "*Chanson de Geste* as Romance in England," in *The Exploitations of Medieval Romance*, ed. Laura Ashe, Ivana Djordjevic, and Judith Weiss (Suffolk, UK: Boydell & Brewer, 2010), 57–72, https://www.cambridge.org/core/books/exploitations-of-medieval-romance/chanson-de-geste-as-romance-in-england/84926368EA04292605F559F09504A817.

IMAGE CREDITS

INDEX